The Best American Short Plays
2007-2008

# The Best American Short Plays

## 2007–2008

# The Best American Short Plays

## 2007-2008

edited with an introduction by
Barbara Parisi

**APPLAUSE THEATRE & CINEMA BOOKS**
An Imprint of Hal Leonard Corporation
New York

*The Best American Short Plays 2007–2008*
Edited with an introduction by Barbara Parisi

Copyright © 2009 by Applause Theatre & Cinema Books (an imprint of Hal Leonard Corporation)

Published in 2009 by Applause Theatre & Cinema Books
An Imprint of Hal Leonard Corporation
7777 West Bluemound Road
Milwaukee, WI 53213

Trade Book Division Editorial Offices
19 West 21st Street, New York, NY 10010

Printed in the United States of America
Book composition by UB Communications

ISBN 978-1-55783-750-9 [cloth]
ISBN 978-1-55783-749-3 [paper]
ISSN 0067-6284

www.applausepub.com

To William and Gloria Parisi,
Rochelle Martinsen,
and my husband—
Michael Ronald Pasternack

# contents

# foreword
# all the things
# you are
### by John Guare

I entered a one-act play contest my freshman year in college and won second prize. It was a spoof called *She Conks to Stupor*. Hey, it was a start. It gave me the experience of working with actors and hearing actual live-audience response.

The one-act play as skit.

I kept writing one-act sketches for the yearly musical and one-acts for the contest but kept dreaming of the elusive, grown-up Holy Grail of writing the full-length play.

In 1960, I saw Edward Albee's *The Zoo Story*. I walked around for hours after seeing it, trying to decipher its power. What was this one-act saying to me?

How could a one-act have so much power?

I knew about one-acts like Strindberg's *The Stronger* or Pirandello's *Man with a Flower in His Mouth* or Arrabal's *Picnic on the Battlefield*, even Beckett's *Krapp's Last Tape*, which shared the bill with Albee's, but those plays were European. Part of the terror of *The Zoo Story* for me was it had been written by an American only ten years older than me.

I went to Yale School of Drama to learn how to write the three-act play.

In my second year, I discovered Thornton Wilder's one-act plays. *The Happy Journey from Trenton to Camden* so knocked me out that I wrote my version of it and called it *The Happy Journey from 58th Street and Ninth Avenue to 59th Street and Eighth Avenue*. It was an incident in the life of an old man and woman as he walked her from their tenement in Manhattan to the hospital on the next block. We would realize this would be the last time they would be together. Our professor said I had written a believable relationship with real emotional impact. The Nobel Prize!

I expanded that playlet into a one-act called *Something I'll Tell You Tuesday*, which we performed at Yale to great response. I played one of the parts myself and had the exhilarating experience of walking around within the mechanics of my own play.

When I was twenty-five, I got into the Air Force Reserves, a six-month gig, a few days before being drafted into the Army for two years. Safe! Here I was in Texas, a wise guy New Yorker with a masters from Yale. Everybody else was in their teens from the South and had barely finished high school.

The drill sergeant screamed at me during some exercise: "You! What do you do when you're not taking up my time?"

"I am a playwright, *Sir*!"

"What's that?" he sneered at top volume.

"I write plays. *Sir*!"

"Like what?" He screamed.

I said, proudly, "*Something I'll Tell You Tuesday*."

He screamed, "I want to know *now*!"

I screamed the title back at him.

And it went on.

If he didn't like me before, he really hated me now.

I had to repeat a week of basic training.

The one-act play as suffering for one's art.

I got back to New York. Edward Albee had started a playwrights unit in a theatre on Van Dam Street. I expanded *Something I'll Tell You Tuesday* into a one-act called *To Wally Pantoni, We Leave a Credenza* and presented it there.

The one-act play as workhorse/stopgap until you figure out how to write that full-length play.

*Wally Pantoni* was done on an NBC Sunday afternoon program called *Experiment in Television*.

One act-play as TV drama.

But I ached to write the full-length play. I wrote the first act of *House of Blue Leaves* for the 1966 Eugene O'Neill Theater Center, which went over well. Except that everyone asked where's the second act? I knew what the events should be, but I didn't have the craft to write a second and third act with lots of people onstage. I only had the craft to write that first act.

I kept writing one-acts.

In 1971, I had finally finished my three-act play (act two was in two scenes); *House of Blue Leaves* was in rehearsal.

I realized in previews that Bananas, the female lead, needed a scene in the second act in order to complete the play. What could it be? I remembered a moment in *Wally Pantoni* in which the wife told her husband since she could no longer feel, she needed to be in a place where she could remember feeling. It fit.

The one-act play as safety deposit box for a rainy day.

The years went by. I only wrote one-acts when asked to by groups like the Acting Company to adapt a Chekhov short story, "A Joke," into *The Talking Dog*, a Shakespeare sonnet into *The General of Hot Desire*.

The Signature Theater is a New York theatre that devotes a season to the work of one playwright by presenting two or three revivals of that playwright's work plus one new play.

In 1998–1999, I was the lucky recipient. The last slot would be two parts of a trilogy I had written called *Lydie Breeze* in rotating rep. (I was now writing trilogies!)

A couple of months before opening, the theatre realized it did not have the resources to pull off this adventurous undertaking. Did I have a new play I could substitute?

I had been thinking of *Wally Pantoni* and that old couple on their last day together, and wondering what they were like when they were young and on their first outing?

I wrote a one-act based on painful family lore: the time my mother brought my father to New Hampshire to meet her family. She asked my father one favor: not to give her uncle Martin a drink. My father did and uncle Martin was dead by Sunday. My imagining of that event would be act one. I edited *Wally Pantoni* into its act two.

Young actors would play the couple in act one, old actors in act two.

I called the play *Lake Hollywood*.

We opened in time.

The one-act play as lifesaver.

The Guthrie Theater in Minneapolis then produced *Lake Hollywood*. My exhilaration at having this sudden new play inspired me to do rewrites, allowing the same actors to play the young couple as well as the old. I had a field day.

Dramatists Play Service published that version. In 2008, Amy Wright, a remarkably gifted actress and director who had been in the original Signature production, told me she felt my exuberant Minneapolis rewrites had disfigured my play. The only thing she liked was that the same actors played both the young and old couple. She asked my permission to present the Signature version of *Lake Hollywood* at the HB Studio for a brief run. I said yes. The evening had a real effect. Was she right? Had I disfigured my play?

The one-act play—keeping it simple?

Or did I have two versions of the same play? Take your pick? I still don't know the answer to this question.

I wanted to show you the many faces of a single one-act play and raise a question: What is a one-act? Is the one-act play only a stepchild to the superior adult two-, three-act/full-length play?

Weren't the first Greek plays one-acts? Doesn't a one-act mean one action? How will Oedipus find out who is the cause of the plague? How will Medea revenge herself on her husband who has abandoned her?

The one-act as the original soul of tragedy?

Edward Albee said a full-length play is simply the correct length the play must be to do its job. His play *The Sandbox* takes less then fifteen minutes to achieve its task of being an emotional knockout.

Something has proliferated in the last few decades—the ten-minute play. Beware of that: it can be a form (a form-let?) designed to give producers the illusion they're producing new work. At Yale, where I now teach playwriting, Paula Vogel, head of the playwriting program, encourages the playwrights to write as much material as they can—work only ten minutes in length—to discover what interests them, to generate and amass as much new material for themselves as they can to develop in the future.

The only poison in today's world of the one-act is the model of the sitcom. The playwright writes twenty-two minutes of snappy wisecracks and dialogue and calls that a one-act play.

No.

Go to Thornton Wilder's one-acts and learn from his experimentations in style. Look at one-acts of Tennessee Williams, such as *Lady of Larkspur Lotion*, and see Blanche DuBois struggling to be born. Look at Sophocles.

The one-act play as bottomless well.

**John Guare** was awarded the Gold Medal in Drama by the American Academy of Arts and Letters for his Obie- , New York Drama Critics' Circle- , and Tony Award-winning plays which include *House of Blue Leaves*, *Six Degrees of Separation*, *Landscape of the Body*, *A Few Stout Individuals*, and *Lydie Breeze*. His screenplay for *Atlantic City* received an Oscar nomination. He teaches playwriting at the Yale School of Drama.

# introduction
## by Barbara Parisi

This is my fourth edition as editor of Best American Short Plays, which has been annual since 1937. As in the past, it has been a complex and rewarding journey for me selecting the plays that are part of this edition. Previously in my introductions, I have explored the concept of writing one-act plays and themes and plots of one-act plays. In this edition, I have decided to focus on the importance of characterization and the development of character in the process of creating a one-act play.

What is character? In his textbook *Playwriting in Process*, written in 1997, Michael Wright asks:

> Why should you look at character before plot? Partly because it's my opinion that we're writing weakish characters these days, and partly because character is at the center of theatre. . . . A play without any characters—a piece with vacuum cleaners as characters, for example—is still defined by character because we understand it by measuring the absence of humans.

Characterization is a process that reveals the personality of the character. The book *Playwright's Process—Learning the Craft from Today's Leading Dramatists*, written in 1997 by Buzz McLaughlin, quotes playwright Terrance McNally: "If you're not really interested in those people, then it's a play no one's going to be very interested in."

To create characters that an audience can relate to, you must make sure that each character has a distinct voice, that their speech patterns and language reflect their backgrounds and personalities, that their dialogue sounds natural, and that their behavior reveals thoughts, motivations, and attitudes in refined and subtle ways. An audience does not always recognize realistic characterizations immediately. Audiences relate to characters they can see themselves in and can sympathize with. Characters need to have to have the same problems the rest of us experience. Heroes, heroines, and villains need to have recognizable attitudes. A character's name can mean a lot to telling a strong story. To understand characters you look at their backgrounds, their physical and mental qualities, their dress, hobbies and occupations, and their relationships with other characters.

In the *Playwright's Process*, quoted playwright Edward Albee believes the writer of a play who is developing characters "must invent the life of their characters before the play and after the play, and they should know how a character is going to respond in a situation that will not be in the play." To create characters you must know their past and future lives. As a playwright, you enter the characters' world and make the audience understand it.

In an Internet article written in 1991, entitled "You and Your Characters," James Patrick Kelly states:

> It seems there are all kinds of characters: developing characters, static characters, round characters, flat characters, cardboard characters (oh, are there cardboard characters!), viewpoint characters, sympathetic characters, unsympathetic characters, stock characters, confidantes, foils, spear-carriers, narrators, protagonists, antagonists.

Kelly goes on to say, "A short story is not a play. The playwright can enter the consciousness of his characters only with great difficulty." A playwright must enter the consciousness of their characters.

In *The Playwriting Seminars, 1995–2007*, Internet articles by Richard Toscan explore the playwright's craft in depth. In "Taking Characters Seriously," Toscan states:

If you can't take your characters seriously, you'll end up making fun of them or creating little more than stick-figures. When that happens, subtext (motivation and thoughts underneath the spoken dialogue) vanishes and the forward movement of the play feels like molasses on a cold day.

If you take characterization seriously, you develop complex characters through their spoken language. Richard Toscan believes:

> Most playwrights rely on their characters to tell them who they are through what they say in dialogue on the page. They're willing to risk having to write most of a draft before understanding the backgrounds, secrets and mental baggage of their creations. But when they start over again, they have rich and complex characters who have revealed themselves rather then having been mechanically constructed.

I believe this is the way to develop real characters that audiences will connect to. Characterizations need to be real for an audience to relate.

In the Toscan Internet article "Subtext...What Characters Don't Tell Us," playwright David Mamet is quoted as saying:

> There's nothing there except lines of dialogue. If they're sketched correctly and minimally, they will give the audience the illusion that these are "real people," especially if the lines are spoken by real people—the actors are going to fill a lot in. So a large part of the technique of playwriting is to leave a lot out.

And in his Internet article "Dramatic Conflict," Toscan states that "dramatic conflict draws from a much deeper vein, rooted in the subtext of your central characters driven by opposing desires." Playwright John Guare is quoted as saying: "Is there a good argument going on? It all starts with a fight...a disagreement." Strong characterization always builds dramatic conflict.

A play's point of view is determined by the playwright's primary character. Through one or many characters, your story is revealed. Playwrights know the importance of the development of strong characterizations to tell their theatrical stories.

For the introduction, I asked all the playwrights to express their theme, plot, and inspiration for writing their one-act play. As you can see from this edition, it is the characters who tell the stories in the one-act plays.

## *The Hysterical Misogynist*
### by Murray Schisgal

It was a balmy, star-studded spring evening in East Hampton. My wife… let's call her Esmeralda. Esmeralda and I were at Nick and Tony's restaurant on North Main Street, sitting opposite our oldest and dearest friends. Let's call them Skyler and Angelina. We had ordered dinner and were enjoying our first round of cocktails. I nursed my martini—a regular Bombay, dry, with a single olive, stirred, not shaken—with the punctilious reverence that it justly deserved. I recall having said something humorous when in a rather strain, incomprehensible voice, I heard Angelina say something like: "That's because you're a misogynist." Shocked, stunned, and partially paralyzed, I managed to emit, in the voice of an enfeebled castrato: "I'm sorry. I'm not sure I heard you correctly. Will you please say that again?" And, oddly, this time around, Angelina chose a tone of voice that was both clear and comprehensible: "You are a misogynist. You always were a misogynist and you will always be a misogynist." And with that Angelina clamped her lips shut and tacked her eyes to mine. I'm certain I responded, but the fact is I can't recall what I said. Nor what my wife, Esmeralda, said. She, too, appeared utterly bewildered by Angelina's venomous outburst. I do recall that when my soft-shell crab arrived on a bed of mixed greens, I sent it back, ordered a third martini, and said very little for the rest of the evening. Skyler spoke on my behalf, politely and, I thought, convincingly. He said that in all the years he had known me, he had never, not once, seen me abuse my wife, a waitress, a receptionist, or any of my former girlfriends. I thanked him the following day and he reminded me that I forgot to pick up half the bill.

Was I a misogynist? Me, the unabashed idolater of all things even remotely feminine? Me, a man dedicated since birth to the absolute equality of the sexes? We'll see about that, my dear, malevolent Angelina!

Since the four of us frequently play tennis together, it was easy conjuring time and place.

And hocus-pocus Jiminy crocus, theme, plot, and inspiration fall amiably into place.

## *Elvis of Nazareth*
### by Jay Huling

The theme reflects my feelings to have audiences gain a more personal understanding of Jesus' words when he said, "I desire mercy, not sacrifice." Much of the action in *Elvis of Nazareth* is symbolic of man's relationship with God. Our rebellion is depicted in the absolute zaniness of the characters— Marion thinks Jesus' living water is Gatorade . . . Moses thinks Jesus' middle initial is "H." . . . the Centurion's response to hearing that Jesus fed 5,000 with mere loaves and fishes responds, "You can never get large portions nowadays." And yet, Jesus' response to all of this is, "Thy sins are forgiven thee." None of these characters do anything to earn it. Yet Jesus freely gives. He forgave us; therefore, we should in turn forgive others.

My inspiration for this play came from thinking about the idea of how we've all played the game in our minds of asking ourselves, "If I could go back and do it again, knowing what I know now, what would I do differently?" I wanted to explore that possibility. And I thought by taking the life of Elvis Presley and putting him in that position, I could depict what he might do. Would he really choose to be the king of rock and roll? Or would he—as we all might—choose to do something greater with his life? And what else is greater than getting to know and serve the creator of the universe? (If we only had a second chance.) But I did not want to explore this in a heavy-handed, dogmatic way. I wanted to create a group of crazy characters and put them in a crazy situation and slay a lot of sacred cows. And yet, at the same time, I wanted to preserve the spiritual message. I believe that is exactly what *Elvis of Nazareth* does.

## *A Roz by Any Other Name*
### by B. T. Ryback

My inspiration for *Roz* came as part of an assignment for a playwriting class at UCLA. My interest in writing the piece began with my desire to "toy" with Shakespeare's language. For a while I'd been playing with the idea of telling Rosalind's story—a character that Shakespeare gives hardly any notice to, yet acts as the inciting incident for why Mercutio takes Romeo to the Capulet gala, without which Romeo and Juliet would never have met. As I began to imagine what kind of character could break Romeo's heart, I thought about how anyone could become close to such a person and sort of inadvertently stumbled on an exploration of the friendships between teenage girls. I think Rosalind and Vera's journey as friends is truly the heart and theme of the play.

The lesson they learn from each other is that you have to look beyond what you get on the surface to find the real value that any person has to offer.

The plot finds Romeo's ex-lover, Rosalind, just arriving home from the infamous Capulet gala where Romeo meets his new flame, Juliet. Enraged that she was trumped by a Capulet, Rosalind plots with her best friend Vera to win Romeo back. The unexpected appearance of an innocent young poet named Stefano, who has a great admiration for Rosalind, suddenly creates the opportunity for her to get her revenge. Despite the protestations of Vera and Rosalind's nurse, Cordonna, Rosalind invites the man to her chambers to begin the seduction. In a humorous turn of events, Rosalind finds that the young man is not exactly who she thought he was. She is forced to confront the rash decisions she has made and comes to realize the value of true affection.

# *Weïrd*
## by B. T. Ryback

The plot of *Weïrd* comes from the three Weïrd sisters from Shakespeare's *Macbeth* and takes place on the lam in Denmark. Warned by the "signs," the eldest sister, Torrence, and the youngest sister, Harper, fear that the awful deeds they committed in Scotland have finally caught up with them, and once again they make plans to flee. One thing, however, stands in their way: their middle sister, Linn. Tired of life on the run, she disavows her sisters, pledging to do anything, even turn them in, if it meant they would no longer have to run away from their past. A knock on the door brings a mysterious traveler into their home, and with him the opportunity for Linn to lead a normal life at the cost of leaving her family. Ultimately she must decide between a newfound hope for life and love, and the family who cares for her more than anything else.

My inspiration for *Weïrd* came from wanting to write a companion piece to my play *A Roz by Any Other Name*. The conceit for both pieces is the exploration of a minor Shakespearean character's story. With *Weïrd*, I wanted to explore something deeper and darker about humanity. In the story, Linn tries to rise above her family's status of "witch." And for a moment, she is able to, as Douglas sees her for who she is, and not just what society and circumstance has deemed her. But then, as the truth comes out, his reaction to her forces Linn to become, and indeed embrace, what it was she fought not to be. The poignancy of the theme is the fact that whether we like it or not, we will always belong to the family from which we came.

## *Bricklayers Poet*
### by Joe Maruzzo

I was inspired to write *Bricklayers Poet* in one sitting, and it came out of me without any forethought or structure to write. I was living alone, broke and lonely. It was *New Year's Eve* and I walked to a bar. It was packed with happy people. I was standing at the bar and had this intense feeling inside myself; it said, "*I wish I could turn around here at the bar, and there would be my woman. We'd hold each other and everything would be all right.*" That's what I wished for. Before I new it, I was staying at a friend's apartment that night; he was out of town and I was lying on the floor with pad and pencil and it wrote itself. No structure, rewrites, nothing. It was my first finished play. It won me Best Playwright in the Turnip Short Festival in 2007. My father was a bricklayer, and in retrospect, this is a love letter to my father. The theme of the play is longing for love.

## *Laundry and Lies*
### by Adam Kraar

In a society that has the habit of lying, are we crazy to tell the truth? How can we balance our need to honestly connect with other people with the necessity of navigating an ocean of deception, denial, and downright flakiness? Isn't making things up sometimes dangerous—and sometimes a lot of fun?

In *Laundry and Lies*, a man obsessed with the truth encounters a woman who is unable to tell the bald truth. Patsy doesn't lie out of maliciousness or laziness; she lies in order to overcome the sad circumstances of her existence. George's need to get at the truth so consumes him that it almost drives him crazy. The manic sparring of these two people leads each of them to a better understanding of how to reconcile their obsessions with their need for a hug.

The play was inspired by a series of questions: Why are candor and sincerity so unfashionable? Why do people lie so much? Are there occasions when lying is a virtue? Aren't I, as a playwright, inventing things in order to reveal a deeper truth? *Laundry and Lies* was written in hopes of provoking an audience to laughter and questions.

## Light
### by Jeni Mahoney

Thematically, I hope that the audience will take away some questions: How do I let go of my past without letting go of myself? How do I remember my past without being held captive by it?

As strange as Helena's religion may seem at first, there is something attractive in its ambition to create a whole new person, free of the past and living in a constant state of happiness. But at what cost?

The plot explores a spiritual rebirth, under the guidance of a mysterious, self-proclaimed guru: Helena's motivation for reconnecting with her childhood friend, and recent divorcee, Abby. But the joyous reunion is short-lived when Abby discovers that Helena's new path requires her to forget her past...including Abby.

My inspiration for this play came from a friend who immersed herself in a belief system that I would call cult-like. Although we were not as close as these two characters, I somehow ended up as one of a small circle of folks who tried to keep her connected to the outside world—even as this other group was pulling her more closely into its fold. Although I found the group's belief's alternately ridiculous and troubling, I sometimes envied her happiness, and struggled to find a way to make difficult, mundane reality seem a more attractive choice. All that being said, "giving light" is probably the only part of the play that is based on my actual experience with this person. Eventually she disappeared into the group. I have no idea what happened to her. I hope she is happy.

## *House of the Holy Moment*
### by Cary Pepper

The plot of *House of the Holy Moment* takes place in the town of Appleton, which has no property taxes on houses of worship. So Appleton, which has a population of 3,000, now has 300 churches. Including the Second Coming Car Service, and Messiah Mike's House of Stereo. With the town's tax base eroding, Henry Billings, of the City Assessor's Office, is visiting every church in town to determine that each is a legitimate house of worship. This Sunday, he walks into the House of the Holy Moment, which is run by Butch Haggerty, whose idea of a church is *very different* from what the city fathers had in mind when they enacted the bylaws that brought Butch to Appleton.

But what is a church? What makes a religion?

As Butch tells Henry, "This isn't *your* idea of a church. But it's *exactly* what *I* think a church should be." Minutes after Henry storms out in frustration, in walks Charlie, an Everyman depressed by the shape the world is in. Charlie is going to every church in town, looking for answers. And Butch has 'em. Even if they are unlike any Charlie's heard in any other church. By the time he leaves, Charlie has found religion. Or Butch's version of it, anyway. In the House of the Holy Moment.

Two things inspired me to write this play. The first was my ongoing examination of spirituality. The second was learning about a town that had done what the city fathers of Appleton did—made religion their number-one priority, with unexpected results.

My theme and the message I want audience to take away from my piece is this: what's holy to one person isn't necessarily holy to another. What helps a person spiritually is dependent on his or her inner world and external circumstances. And that's okay. Everyone's entitled to their belief system. No one should be judged or punished for it; no one should try to force their beliefs on others, or hurt anyone in the name of those beliefs. I'll show you mine...you show me yours...and then let's forget about it.

## *The Disruptive, Discursive Delusions of Donald*
### by Michael Roderick

The theme reflects that moments of indecision can breed the wackiest occurrences. The plot finds Donald having a lot of trouble making decisions in his life, but when Bo and Dayna (two middlemen between heaven and hell) step into the picture, he'll have to make quick decisions as he's thrust into a world with a dead lover, time travel, and a dominatrix obsessed with squeaky toys. As time ticks backwards Donald must decide what's most important, or lose it all. My inspiration for the play began when I was asked to write a companion piece for Christopher Durang's *'Dentity Crisis* during my undergrad, and after reading that play, I tried to think of the craziest scenario possible. Having worked in a costume studio for a good portion of my undergrad, I found a lot of my costume knowledge applied to the strange situations I was creating in this play and I had a really good time. Next thing I knew, I had developed this world that was making me laugh, and I hope it does the same for others.

## *The Perfect Relationship*
### by Jill Elaine Hughes

I originally wrote *The Perfect Relationship* as part of Chicago's Boxer Rebellion Theatre's annual Martin de Maat New Works Festival. In this annual festival, playwrights are assigned three actors at random who then "audition" for the playwright to display their range and characterization abilities. The playwrights are then assigned a topic at random to serve as inspiration for writing a script for the three assigned actors. I was assigned three quirky young women performers who all had unique comedic abilities, and was assigned "A Lover Spurned" as my topic. The result was this play, *The Perfect Relationship*, in which three young women gradually discover that they are all romantically involved with the same man. The piece is always a big hit with audiences, since it seems most people today know at least one New Age wacko type (Orchid), as well as are quite familiar the type of young unlucky-at-love urban single woman that both Mary Ann and Christine represent. The comedy becomes more and more outrageous as the women begin to discover that they've all been tricked and deceived—by their mutual love interest, by Orchid's fraudulent New Age "healing," and by each other.

The theme of the piece is that when it comes to love and relationships, things are almost never what they seem on the surface. It's received several productions around the U.S., most recently at Seattle's 2006 Mae West Fest.

## *The Perfect Medium*
### by Eileen Fischer

*The Perfect Medium* presents scenes from the lives of two historical characters: Hester Dowden (1868–1949) and Oscar Wilde (1854–1900). Hester Dowden was an Irish journalist and psychic medium who conducted séances and automatic writing sessions. In *The Perfect Medium*, set in London, 1923, Oscar Wilde sends psychic messages to Hester Dowden. Mysteries abound—especially so since Oscar Wilde died in 1900. Original music for the play has been composed by Charles Porter. *The Perfect Medium* is very loosely based—which is also to say suggested by—Hester Dowden's pamphlet of essays, *Oscar Wilde from Purgatory*.

Interests in spiritualism and theatricality converge here. *The Perfect Medium* invites audiences to consider questions of faith, fame, life after death, and the authenticity of psychic investigations.

## *Outsourced*
### by Laura Shaine

I wrote *Outsourced* as an act of rebellion—against credit card-o-cracy, the evil empire of 29.99% debt. How many of us suffer similar crises because of insane interest rates charged by the major credit cards? I think this causes the new nervous breakdown—inability to deal with unseen electronic possible beings that control our financial lives.

What message? I always heard—if you want to send a message, use Western Union.

The theme is apparent—human beings are heat-seeking and will somehow prevail against this hideous computer and credit card culture that is sapping our souls.

The inspiration for *Outsourced* is a *cri du coeur*, cry of the heart, against the awful way we are forced to live today. I wrote *Outsourced* for us all, as we are pitted against the outsourced bank operatives who may or may not be living, breathing humans on the other side of the world. I wrote the play for everyone who is awake at 3 a.m., and might be watching an infomercial on strengthening "Abs! Abs! Abs!" while struggling with credit cards. I wrote *Outsourced* for love as an antidote to debt.

The plot finds Max, a New York man, suffering a midnight financial crisis—he reaches out to an unseen but possibly gorgeous, potentially warm human being on the subcontinent. Is she Kimberley, an automated voice in South Dakota, the capitol of credit? Or is she Sonali, the yearning temptress in India? He must find out, or die of debt.

## *Dead Trees*
### by Rick Pulos

*Dead Trees* tells the story of a Malawian carpenter turned coffin maker. The idea for the story was inspired by an article that appeared via Reuters in 2004, entitled "Malawi Coffin Makers Cash in on AIDS Pandemic." I became interested in writing a story about the social impact of AIDS without actually including a single character who suffers from the disease. This concept then led me to examine how the business of this disease is lining the pockets of many people, from CEOs at pharmaceutical companies to makers of coffins and headstones. Who are these people that are getting rich from the suffering of others?

Citseko, the main character in *Dead Trees*, was once the designer of items for the living (chairs, tables, beds, etc.). He abandons this work for the more lucrative business of making coffins, much to the chagrin of his son. He feels deeply that by creating a profitable and sustainable business for his son (and his son's future family) that he is providing the love and security required of a father. Unfortunately, his son sees the business as something that has come between them and created a distance too great to overcome.

In exploring these particular ideas and characters, I discovered that a person in pursuit of one thing often inevitably undermines the very reason that they ever sought that thing out in the first place. We seek shelter by building homes, all the while destroying the forest that breathes life into our planet, our only true home in the universe.

## G.C.
### by Theodore Mann

What I wanted to convey in writing *G.C.* was the delight of working in the theatre while you are walking on cracked egg shells to hopefully overcome the numerous obstacles that are presented in a production. The play deals with high tensions that exist in producing a play anywhere, but with even higher tensions when the play is about to open on Broadway with a great, but explosive, leading actor and a beautifully simple but complex Chekhov play entitled *Uncle Vanya*.

Putting on a play, from my point of view as a director and producer, is to present it as truthfully as possible in accordance with what I believe was the author's intention. In this case, since I wrote the play and one of the characters is myself, I had complete insight into every moment of my character's thinking and the playwright's intentions.

This is the first play that I have ever written, and until I was presented with an opportunity to enter a one-act festival in Los Angeles, the idea had never occurred to me. But then the gauntlet had been thrown down, and it rankled in my head. I went to visit my son in France, and on the second night after my arrival, as I was sleeping, the complete play came into my head. The next morning, I got on the phone to New York and dictated the play to my assistant. While I was directing the play, adjustments were made to the script. It was then produced in L.A. in a one-act festival and was received very favorably. Since that time, there have been several other productions across the country.

## *Five Story Walkup*
### compiled and directed by Daniel Gallant

Thematically focused on the idea of home, *Five Story Walkup* is a collection of short plays and monologues about the places we call home. The characters in these works—mismatched lovers, a Webcam provocateur, small-town philosophers, and urban pioneers—are united by a conflicting need to preserve and yet escape from their domestic situations. These works cover wide narrative territory, exploring cityscapes and rural settings, but are tied together by an intimate focus on the bond between identity and home.

In Laura Shaine's *Web Cam Woman*, a cagey exhibitionist explores the ups and downs of online voyeurism. In Daniel Frederick Levin's *A Glorious Evening*, a nervous man rehearses for a momentous first date. Quincy Long's *Aux / Cops* follows an excitable police recruit as he is vetted by a buttoned-down lieutenant. Clay McLeod Chapman's *birdfeeder* details the romantic cause and aftermath of a rural tragedy. In Daniel Gallant's *Tripartite*, two vacationing brothers compete over a woman who has dual personalities. In Neil LaBute's *Love at Twenty*, a resourceful college student grapples with a star-crossed love affair. And in John Guare's *Blue Monologue*, a man reminisces about the dreams that brought him to New York City, as well as the realities of urban life that held him back.

I was very inspired to create *Five Story Walkup*. The works that constitute this piece were contributed by seven different authors; the show was originally conceived and staged as a benefit to save the Thirteenth Street Repertory Theatre. As small theatres and performance spaces around Manhattan closed their doors, the Thirteenth Street Repertory Theatre was engaged in a struggle against real estate developers. With the future of this historic arts organization in danger, the artists featured in *Five Story Walkup* donated their time and effort to benefit the Thirteenth Street Rep's legal fund. It is fitting that a production mounted to save a theatrical home features plays and monologues.

# The Best American Short Plays

## 2007–2008

# The Hysterical Misogynist

## Murray Schisgal

# Murray Schisgal

Murray Schisgal has an extensive career spanning plays, screenplays, fiction anthologies, and as a producer of five feature films. His Broadway plays include *Luv* (Tony nominated), *Jimmy Shine*, *All Over Town* (Drama Desk Award, Outstanding New Play), *The Chinese and Doctor Fish*, *Twice Around the Park*, and *An American Millionaire*. His films include *Tootsie* (Oscar nominated), *The Tiger Makes Out*, and *Luv* (based on play).

Murray's Off-Broadway plays include *The Typists and the Tiger* (Vernon Rice Award, Outer Circle Award, *Saturday Review* Critics Poll Award), *Fragments*, *The Basement*, *The Flatulist*, *Walter*, *The Pushcart Peddlers*, *Sexaholics*, *Extensions*, *Road Show*, *Jealousy*, *Circus Life*, and *Angel Wings* (Off-Off-Broadway Award for Excellence).

Published works include *Days and Nights of a French Horn Player* (novel), *Luv and Other Plays* (collection), The Best American Short Plays (twelve short plays over a number of years; published by Applause Books), and Great American One-Act Plays.

**scene**

The patio of the East Hampton Golf and Tennis Club.

At the rim of the club's outdoor dining area, an isolated, round, white, Formica table with four red-canvassed deck chairs. On the table, a small vase filled with seasonal flowers, a bottle of chardonnay in an iced bucket, a pitcher of water, wine and water glasses, condiments and the half-eaten remains of lunch. Tennis racquets and containers of tennis balls lie about.

**pre-rise sound**

Offstage a main-court match is in progress. We hear a tennis ball being whacked back and forth. The crowd of spectators responds with shouts and applause to a well-played volley.

**sound**

Fades out, gradually, before ...

**at rise**

EMANUEL "MANNY" BROOKS, wearing tennis garb, is slouched in a deck chair, disheartened if not depressed.

**time**

Summer. Mid-day.

• • •

[PHILIP GRANT *enters from offstage, upstage/right, also in tennis garb. He wears a brimmed tennis cap, which he soon removes. MANNY hears PHILIP approaching and he immediately jumps to his feet, energized, a note of urgency in his voice.*]

**MANNY**   Where is she?

**PHILIP**   In the ladies room.

**MANNY**   Is my wife in the ladies room with her?

**PHILIP**   No. Your wife went home.

[PHILIP *sits at table. He fills a glass with chardonnay; drinks.*]

**MANNY**   Did they quarrel?

**PHILIP**   Not to my knowledge.

**MANNY**   How long will she be in the ladies room?

**PHILIP**   Who?

**MANNY**   Your wife!

**PHILIP**   It's anyone's guess.

**MANNY**   Five minutes, ten minutes, an hour? Give me an estimate. I must talk to her. She owes me an apology. I can't wait all afternoon until she gets out of the ladies room!

**PHILIP**   Easier said than done.

**MANNY**   Did she throw up? Does she have cramps?

**PHILIP**   Not to my knowledge. She is upset.

**MANNY**   She's upset? God in heaven, what do you think I am? I have never been subjected to such a vicious, gratuitous assault from anyone! And what is totally incomprehensible to me is that we were in the midst of a pleasant, leisurely lunch of delicious crab cakes and chilled chardonnay, when she, your wife, attacked me at! this! very! table!

[*Bangs fist on table with each exclamatory word.*]

[*Dishes on the table rattle, precariously; a dish or glass smashes to the ground.* PHILIP, *reluctantly, morosely, picks up the shards.*]

**PHILIP**   Manny, I believe I made my position clear to you during the discussion.

**MANNY**   Discussion? You call what went on between your wife and me a discussion?

**PHILIP**   Do you prefer that I call it a quarrel? A confrontation? An imbroglio? Choose whichever you prefer. They're one and the same to me.

**MANNY**   Nay, nay, nay, not to me are they!

**PHILIP**    I speak solely on my own behalf. I did not agree with Ellen. In my opinion she misspoke. But she does have the inalienable right under our Constitution to voice her opinion. You don't have a quarrel with that, do you?

**MANNY**    [*Sits at table.*] Philip, how many years do we know each other?

**PHILIP**    More than I care to count.

**MANNY**    How many years? It's a simple question.

**PHILIP**    Since I could walk.

**MANNY**    And talk.

**PHILIP**    And talk.

**MANNY**    We were?

**PHILIP**    Three years of age. According to our parents.

**MANNY**    Did you ever, in your entire life, have a friend closer to you than I am?

**PHILIP**    No. I haven't.

**MANNY**    Do you love me, Philip?

**PHILIP**    Yes, I do.

**MANNY**    Other than your wife and your sons, is there anyone in the entire world whom you love more than you love me?

**PHILIP**    No one.

**MANNY**    And I love you.

[MANNY *kisses* PHILIP's *hand, twice, with a lip-smacking noise.*]

**PHILIP**    You love your wife and your daughters, too, don't you?

**MANNY**    It's not the same. Britany is my second wife. I've only been married to her for six months. My daughters? Of course I love them; they're priceless.

**PHILIP**    How long were you married to Hannah before she . . . passed on?

**MANNY**    Twenty-three irreplaceable, glorious years. Unfortunately, I knew Britany barely a month before we were married. Living with her has been a radical, difficult adjustment for me. How long have you been married to Ellen? Is it twenty-four years?

**PHILIP**   Twenty-five. I knew her over two years before we were married.

**MANNY**   A lesson to be learned and treasured.

[*A somber tone.*]

Philip, why did Ellen attack me with such vehemence? What drove her to it? Did I speak out of turn? Did I provoke her? Insult her? Goad her into it?

**PHILIP**   No. None of that. As you should know by now, Ellen is a scrupulously honest and forthright woman. What she thinks, she speaks. Apparently, when you asked her at lunch for her thoughts on the reading of your play last night at the John Drew Theatre . . . she had no choice. She was going to answer you honestly and forthrightly.

**MANNY**   The reading went well, didn't it?

**PHILIP**   Incredibly well. You had a full house and the audience loved it.

**MANNY**   And you loved it, didn't you?

**PHILIP**   I did. Without qualification. If it had been staged in a Broadway house, you would have had a smash hit.

**MANNY**   You're too generous. On reflection, conscience compels me to say this to you: regardless of how my quarrel with Ellen resolves itself, I have to admit that she is a very special woman. How she managed to raise your rambunctious sons to maturity and simultaneously continue her employment as a tenured professor of feminist studies is an accomplishment that few of her gender can boast of.

**PHILIP**   She is a very special woman. But as I said, I do not share her opinion, neither on the merits of your play or, regretfully, other, more personal matters.

**MANNY**   You two aren't . . . ?

**PHILIP**   [*Finger to lips requesting silence.*] Speak no evil. I suggest you don't take her accusation to heart. She spoke to you, honestly and forthrightly. Leave it at that.

**MANNY**  Philip...

[*Tormented.*]

She called me a misogynist, a man who hates women! She hurled that hideous M-word straight at me, without fanfare, without even telling me what she thought of the play. I was ready to explode!

[*Incredulously.*]

Me, a misogynist? A man who has been married twice, to women! Me, a misogynist? A man who has two grown daughters, both women! Me, a misogynist? A man who adored his mother, a woman! Me, a misogynist? A man who has worshipped women since puberty, a man who has placed women of every conceivable temperament and disposition on a lofty, golden pedestal. Me, a misogynist? A man who has loved women, the smell of them, the touch of them, the sight of them, all the days and nights of his life? And not only did I have two wives, two daughters and a mother, each and every one of them a woman, but I've had dozens and dozens of girlfriends: social girlfriends, professional girlfriends, sleepover girlfriends, live-in girlfriends, engaged girlfriends, married girlfriends, each and every one of them a woman! A woman whom I treated with respect, dignity and sensitivity! Am I lying? Am I making it up, imagining it? If so, free me from this dark cave of self-deception in which I have imprisoned myself since puberty!

**PHILIP**  No, my friend, you're not making it up. I can vouch for everything you said, including the list of girlfriends you described.

**MANNY**  Conscience compels me to...

**PHILIP**  There's no need to go further.

**MANNY**  Please. Permit me to plead my case. You'd grant that much to a rapist, a pederast, a homophobic. Why not a misogynist, a man who hates women?

**PHILIP**  I won't interrupt you again.

**MANNY**  I have been a working playwright and screenwriter for some
thirty years. I've had success and I've had failure. The awards, the
applause and shouts of "Bravo" I received were a verification of
my achievements and a faint whisper of immortality. The failures
I endured? They were comparable to having a knife thrust and
twisted brutally into the arteries of my heart and along with it a
burning, raging fever of degradation and humiliation. Equally
upsetting is the awareness that, during the course of my career,
there have been actors, directors and producers who have found
working with me an unpleasant ordeal. In my defense, let me say
that I am not one to place congeniality and camaraderie above the
quality of the work that's being done. I am not a pet playwright to
be dismissed with a squeeze and a pat on the ass. The quality of
the work, at any given moment, is what counts, nothing else, not
the company, not the reviews, not the receipts at the box office,
not the specious applause of a fawning audience. No one has ever
accused me of duplicity. I never put word to paper in order to
denigrate and demean a fellow human being or to satisfy a
fashionable prejudice. I write not from imagination, but from
experience. I write, primarily, to find out what makes me tick as a
corporeal being and, yes, to take issue with the sacrosanct
conventions of our morally bankrupt society.

[*Vigorously.*]

To be denounced by your wife as a misogynist, which, nowadays,
is a battle cry to castigate, to ostracize, to persecute the offender,
as the Christian was persecuted during the reign of the Roman
emperor Nero, as the Jew was persecuted during the Spanish
Inquisition, and as the black man has been persecuted for decades
in these United States of America.

[*His voice resonates.*]

I am not . . . nor have I ever been . . . a misogynist . . . a hater of
women. I swear on the souls of the women I loved who have
passed on and on the heads of my two priceless daughters!

**PHILIP**  My friend, my dear friend, you grossly exaggerate the weight of
Ellen's criticism. As your attorney, I can reassure you: had she

known that you would react to her comments with such anguish and abhorrence, she would never have said what she said. Remember, she's your friend, too. For twenty-seven years. She has been and is inordinately fond of you. And, to repeat myself, know that I agree with you. You are not, nor have you ever been, the hideous M-word. I would say the same in a court of law.

[MANNY *kisses* PHILIP's *hand, several times, with lip-smacking noises.*]

**MANNY**  Thank you. Thank you. Thank you.

[*A beat.*]

Philip?

**PHILIP**  Yes?

**MANNY**  Can you imagine the consequences if I, an esteemed playwright and screenwriter, a member of the Dramatists Guild, the Writers Guild, the Actors Studio and the Academy of Motion Picture Arts and Sciences, was publicly accused of being a . . . a . . . a misogynist?

**PHILIP**  It would, doubtlessly, create a nasty uproar.

**MANNY**  Do you think I'd be able to raise money to do a play of mine . . . ? Forget Broadway. Forget Off-Broadway. Would I be able to raise money to do a play of mine . . .

[*Stammering.*]

. . . Off-Off . . . Off-Off . . . Off-Off-Off . . . Off-Off-Off-Off-Off-Off-Broadway?

**PHILIP**  No, I don't. But be reassured: Ellen would never say anything to anyone, publicly or privately, that would threaten your stature or your career.

**MANNY**  Not even to her sister?

[*No response from* PHILIP.]

[*A notch louder.*]

Not even to her sister?

**PHILIP**  Is that the reason for your hysteria, Ellen's sister?

**MANNY**   Since her sister, a woman who I was once engaged to, is now a theatre critic for the *New York Times*, I do not think my...

[*A sob in his throat.*]

...my hysteria is unwarranted!

**PHILIP**   Dismiss it from your mind. I can guarantee you, Ellen hasn't spoken to her sister. What I didn't tell you is that we talked about the reading of your play when we got home last night.

**MANNY**   Of course you did! Why didn't I think of that!

[*Jumps to his feet.*]

What did she say? Did she exercise her Constitutional right? Did she refer to me as the M-word?

**PHILIP**   I don't believe so. At least I have no memory of it.

**MANNY**   What, then? What did she think of my play?

**PHILIP**   Naturally, she had reservations.

**MANNY**   [*Pacing back and forth, hitting fist into palm of hand.*] Aha! I knew it! I knew it! I knew it!

**PHILIP**   Will you stop carrying on? She liked ninety percent of what you wrote. Her only criticism had to do with the character of Margarita Whitbee.

**MANNY**   Margarita Whitbee? What was wrong with Margarita Whitbee?

**PHILIP**   She's a weak, passive, wimpy, indecisive, verbally abused young woman who can't stand on her own two feet and give tit for tat.

**MANNY**   She wanted Margarita Whitbee to give tit for tat?

**PHILIP**   Metaphorically speaking, yes.

**MANNY**   What else did she object to?

**PHILIP**   She asked me to answer this question: "Where, in the entire corpus of Manny's work, is his *Hedda Gabler*, or his *Major Barbara*, or his *Mother Courage*?"

**MANNY**   [*Dumbfounded for a beat.*] How did you answer her?

**PHILIP**   "For all I know," I answered, "Manny may be writing it as we speak."

**MANNY**   My *Hedda Gabler*?

**PHILIP**   Or any of the others.

**MANNY**   *Major Barbara* or *Mother Courage*?

**PHILIP**   Yes.

**MANNY**   All three of them?

**PHILIP**   No, not all three of them! Any one of them!

**MANNY**   Did your answer satisfy her?

**PHILIP**   It did not.

**MANNY**   It did not.

**PHILIP**   No, it did not. She followed that question with this question: "Can you name a play that Manny has written that has as its main character a strong, caring, vital, compassionate, self-confident, independent woman?"

**MANNY**   To which you answered?

**PHILIP**   No.

**MANNY**   You answered no?

**PHILIP**   Yes.

**MANNY**   You didn't know of a play I wrote that has as its main character a strong, caring, vital, compassionate, self-confident, independent woman?

**PHILIP**   No, I did not. I couldn't in good conscience name such a play. Did you write such a play?

**MANNY**   [*Dumbfounded for a beat.*] No, I did not.

**PHILIP**   Which is what Ellen said.

**MANNY**   For cryin' out loud, of course I haven't written such a play for a woman! I haven't written such a play for a man! All my characters, women and men, are corrupted by an absence of character! They can't possibly be strong, vital, caring, yatata, yatata, yatata, yatata! Did you forget? I'm a satirist, a humorist, an ironic commentator on the idiocy of both sexes!

**PHILIP**  Bizarrely enough, I expressed the same thought to Ellen.

**MANNY**  And?

**PHILIP**  She didn't buy it.

**MANNY**  Philip, why is your wife persecuting me? What do I have to do to make certain she won't...inadvertently say something to someone? Don't you see, everything I worked for is in jeopardy! How can I go on living a normal life with the charge of misogyny hanging over my head? All I can see in front of me is a bleak, barren future of bankruptcy and depression, with crowds of people mocking me, poking me, laughing at me, laughing at me as if I were the embodiment of some poor...pitiful...pathetic Pagliacci.

[MANNY *bows his head. Although he sheds no tears, his shoulders quake and he groans and moans, softly, Pagliacci-like.*]

[PHILIP *moves to* MANNY. *In an effort to console him, he massages* MANNY'*s tense neck muscles. He looks, now and then, offstage, upstage/right, to see if his wife is coming.*]

**PHILIP**  You better grab hold of yourself, my friend. You'll be no match for Ellen when she gets here. She can be a formidable adversary. Although she didn't speak to her sister about the reading last night, they are inseparable. It stands to reason that she bears you a grudge for reneging on your engagement. It would be naive of you to...
[*Interrupts himself.*]
What's taking her so long? I'll go get her. I'll only be...a few minutes.

[PHILIP *tries to move off, but* MANNY *jumps to his feet and holds on to him.*]

**MANNY**  No, no, don't leave, not yet! What do I say to her? Should I mention her sister? Should I bring up how unfair her criticisms are, how biased and bigoted they are, or do I wait for her to bring them up? Tell me! You have to tell me!

[*They both return to their chairs.*]

**PHILIP**  I will. It'll be worth the effort. We can't ignore reality. Ellen *is* a tenured professor of feminist studies and her sister *is* a theatre critic for the *New York Times*.

**MANNY**   If I were writing a play inspired by what I'm living through today, I couldn't have found a worse pair of enemies. It occurs to me, the odds are against us, Philip. As womankind ascends to empowerment, mankind descends to irrelevancy. Woe is mankind. Woe, woe, woe is mankind.

**PHILIP**   Your point is well taken. But let me address how you should handle Ellen. To begin with: first, you do not bring up the subject of her criticisms unless she brings them up first. Second, you do not give tit for tat.

**MANNY**   I don't bring up the subject of her criticisms and I don't give tit for tat.

**PHILIP**   Third, you do not, under any circumstances, raise your voice to her; you do not speak when she speaks; you remain silent; only when you are positive that she has finished speaking and she is silent for a count of ten do you speak.

**MANNY**   I do not, under any circumstances, raise my voice to her; I do not speak when she speaks; I remain silent; only when I'm positive that she has finished speaking and she is silent for a count of ten do I speak.

**PHILIP**   Fourth, only then, do you speak, speak politely and casually, neither too fast nor too slow. Is that clear to you?

**MANNY**   Yes.

**PHILIP**   Count to ten.

**MANNY**   1, 2, 3, 4, 5, 6, 7, 8, 9, 10.

**PHILIP**   Don't rush it. Don't run to number 10. 1 … 2 … 3 …

**MANNY/PHILIP**   … 4 … 5 … 6 … 7 … 8 … 9 … 10.

**PHILIP**   That's better. You'll have to prove to her …
[PHILIP *sees* ELLEN GRANT *coming down from the restrooms.*]
Get up, get up, she's here, she's coming. You look like a cadaver. Let me …

[*They're both on their feet.* PHILIP *pulls up* MANNY'*s socks, pulls down on his shirt, etc.*]

**MANNY** [*Desperately.*] I can't stay! I can't deal with this! Not now! I'll call her tonight!

[MANNY *tries to move off, but* PHILIP *holds on to him.*]

**PHILIP** Stop it! She's watching us!

[ELLEN *enters, designer-framed sunglasses covering half her face, wearing skirted tennis garb and carrying a blue cardigan sweater, which she drapes at the back of her chair. She sits at the table, pours herself a chardonnay, continues eating her lunch and drinks her wine. She is, unexpectedly, relaxed and congenial. She will shortly remove her sunglasses.*]

**ELLEN** I ran into Michael Dillon. He just returned from London. He said he couldn't believe how expensive everything was. Its two dollars to the pound. The taxi fare from the airport was over a hundred dollars. Later on when he went to Harrods to buy four pairs of boxer shorts; they were so expensive he bought a pair of swimming trunks, which he rinsed out every night for the following morning.

**PHILIP** He'll do anything to save a pound!

**ELLEN** He cut his stay in London from two weeks to three nights.

[ELLEN *and* PHILIP *share a laugh.* MANNY *pastes a silly grin on his face, turns his head, back and forth, from one speaker to the other.*]

**PHILIP** Is he out for the weekend?

**ELLEN** For the week. He's invited us to dinner Friday.

**PHILIP** We'll go. There are some tax papers he has to sign for me.

**ELLEN** He's at the bar now. Why don't you join him? Manny and I have some business of our own to discuss.

**PHILIP** No sooner said than done. But a request before I leave.
[*A ministerial tone.*]
Be courteous to one another. Don't rush to judgment. Don't desecrate the edifice of friendship, which took us a lifetime to build. Traditionally, the East Hampton Golf and Tennis Club is a sanctuary for sociability. Let's keep it that way. Catch you both later.

[*He moves offstage, upstage/left.*]

**ELLEN**   [*Speaks at a steady clip.*] I see you haven't finished your lunch. I guess you were as upset as I was. Do sit down. We have to pick up where we left off. Bitter thoughts left unsaid tend to be toxic.

[MANNY *sits at table, the silly grin still on his face.*]

Frankly, I can't recall the two of us ever speaking vis-à-vis for more than a few minutes. That is regrettable. Twenty-seven years. I have known you for twenty-seven years. And still, I don't know you. And I don't believe you know me. If you did, you wouldn't have reacted so vehemently when I called you a misogynist. Did you think I was being malicious? Did you think that it was enjoyable for me to confront my husband's best friend and accuse him of being a man who hated women?

[MANNY *dwells a beat before dropping the grin. He nods his head, fervently.*]

How could you think that? Wasn't I a maid of honor at your wedding to Hannah *and* a bride's maid at your wedding to Britany?

[MANNY *nods his head, fervently.*]

Weren't you engaged to my sister for almost a year?

[MANNY *nods his head, fervently.*]

And when you arbitrarily ended the engagement, breaking my sister's heart so that to this day she hasn't married or delivered a child from her loins, did I say one disparaging word to you?

[MANNY *shakes his head, fervently.*]

And even though I thought you had behaved like a sleazy scoundrel toward my sister and deplored the staged reading of your play, did I create a scene at the theatre last night?

[MANNY *shakes his head, fervently.*]

Was I *ever* verbally abusive toward you?

[MANNY *shakes his head, fervently.*]

You can question my judgment, but you cannot change it. You have no respect for nor insight into what constitutes a contemporary woman. In your plays and in your private life you are an irredeemable misogynist. You always have been and presumably you always will be!

[MANNY *jumps to his feet. He can't let this last remark of* ELLEN'*s go unchallenged. And yet, to abide by* PHILIP'*s warning, he feels it's imperative he doesn't speak while she continues to speak. He waves his hand to get her attention. Then he holds up three fingers, determined to prove that* ELLEN *has criticized him unfairly.*]

[*From the start,* ELLEN *participates in this game of charades, eagerly and enthusiastically. It's apparent she's played it in the past with* MANNY.]

[*On her feet; ready to pounce.*]

Three words!

[MANNY *nods. He holds up one finger.*]

First word!

[MANNY *nods. He jabs his finger at his chest.*]

Your chest!

[MANNY *shakes his head, continuing to jab his finger at his chest.*]

Your heart!

[MANNY *shakes his head.*]

Your rib cage!

[MANNY *shakes his head, waving his hand over his entire body.*]

Your body! Your physique! You! You!

[MANNY *shakes his head, holds up one finger.*]

I! It's I! Singular! I! I!

[MANNY *nods, holds up two fingers.*]

Second word!

[MANNY *places his arms around an imaginary woman, tilting her to the side, and kisses her, silently, on her imaginary lips.*]

Kiss!

[MANNY *shakes his head.*]

Smooch!

[MANNY *shakes his head.*]

Embrace!

[MANNY *shakes his head.*]

Hug! Hug!

[MANNY *shakes his head, lowering the imaginary woman closer to the ground in a rather awkward pose.*]

Cuddle!

[MANNY *shakes his head.*]

Lustful! Libidinous! Lust! Lust!

[MANNY *shakes his head, places his hands on his heart, looks skyward with an expression of adoration.*]

Adoration!

[MANNY *shakes his head.*]

Veneration! Worship!

[MANNY *shakes his head, fluttering his eyebrows.*]

Love! It's love! Is it love?

[MANNY *nods.*]

I love...

[MANNY *holds up three fingers.*]

Third word!

[MANNY *nods, thinks a beat, then minces back and forth, hand on hip, hips swiveling from side to side.*]

Prostitutes! I love prostitutes!

[MANNY *shakes his head as he continues his mincing walk.*]

Floozies! Tarts! Tramps! Hos. Hos. I love...!

[MANNY *shakes his head.*]

Chorus girls! Models!

[*Throughout the above,* MANNY *shakes his head, exasperatedly now, continuing his swiveling walk, his hips swinging* wildly *from side to side.*]

Bisexuals! Metrosexuals! Transsexuals! Transgenders! Transvestites! Transportation! Is it transportation?

[*Throughout the above,* MANNY *shakes his head, fiercely, until he explodes into a tantrum, wagging his finger at her, stomping up and down.*]

[*When he regains his senses, he shapes, repeatedly, with his two hands, the silhouette of a curvaceous woman.*]

Woman! Is it woman?

[MANNY *silhouettes several curvaceous women, one next to the other.*]
Women! It's women! Plural! Three words. I love women! I love women! Is it I love women?
[MANNY *nods, breathlessly. With relief, they sit down at the table, mopping their faces with handkerchiefs.*]
Why did we do that?

**MANNY**   Do what?

**ELLEN**   Play charades.

**MANNY**   Would you have preferred that I gave you tit for that?

**ELLEN**   Tit for tat?

**MANNY**   Or counted from one to ten?

**ELLEN**   Why would you do any of that?

**MANNY**   Philip explained to me...

**ELLEN**   Let's not talk about Philip.

**MANNY**   Are you upset with him, too?

**ELLEN**   It'll be known soon enough, so there's no reason not to tell you. Philip and I are separating.

**MANNY**   [*Incredulously.*] No.

**ELLEN**   Yes. After Labor Day. When the boys return to school.

**MANNY**   I...I can't believe it. I would have sworn you and Philip had the most successful marriage of anyone I know. I *must* be losing my mind.

**ELLEN**   Our marriage has dwindled down to a habit. We just go through the motions of a marriage. Separating will be the most exciting adventure we've had together in years.

**MANNY**   I am sorry.

**ELLEN**   We're glad. It was nice learning you love women, Emanuel, even if I...

**MANNY**   Don't call me Emanuel!

**ELLEN**   Thin-skinned, are we?

**MANNY**   Hannah called me Emanuel. I miss her. Immensely.

**ELLEN**   [*Cynically.*] How sweet of you. As I was about to say before you rudely interrupted me, it was nice learning that you love women, even if you weren't terribly convincing.

**MANNY**   May I speak?

**ELLEN**   Your politeness is disarming. It's not like you.

**MANNY**   Not like you would have me be. Say what you will, I do love women. I always have. I love being with them, talking to them, traveling with them, working with them, having sex with them. As I say those words, "having sex with them," I'm inundated with memories of the many beautiful, remarkable women I've had sex with since puberty.

**ELLEN**   Am I supposed to be impressed?

**MANNY**   That's not what I'm getting at. You took it upon yourself to call me the M-word. I am trying my best to convince you otherwise. I've learned this much over the years: there's no respite for a man on this godforsaken planet without a woman. The very act of having sex with her, the titillating foreplay, the pelvic thrust of penetration, the blissful release of orgasm, grants man sufficient purpose to go on with his life, in spite of being "born astride the grave." The truth is, Ellen, I'm ecstatically happy when I'm making love to a woman.

**ELLEN**   You mean, when you're fucking a woman.

**MANNY**   Why do you have to put a negative spin on everything I say? You may fuck a man, if that's your preference, but I...I make love to a woman.

**ELLEN**   But you just told me of the many beautiful, remarkable women you had sex with since puberty. You couldn't possibly have made love to all of them. Making love demands more than a thrust and an effusive orgasm. It requires sharing, tenderness, nurturing, an expression of love that rises above physical love and touches, when you've reached authentic intimacy, the fringes of transcendence. Since you mentioned none of that, there must have been, during the course of your sexual odyssey, one or two you merely fucked . . . so to speak.

**MANNY**   If it gives you pleasure to think of me in that light, go right ahead.

**ELLEN**   It comes down to this: I can't recall being with you and Hannah or Britany or any one of your many beautiful, remarkable girlfriends when you didn't, in one way or another, use and verbally abuse her.

**MANNY**   Hannah? You have the gall to say that I used and verbally abused Hannah?

**ELLEN**   It doesn't require gall for me to reply yes. I know that it strokes your ego to think that you were a saintly husband prior to her death; bringing medicine to her and emptying her bedpan hardly make up for all the years you were preoccupied with your career and completely indifferent to her and your daughters. Oh, that reminds me, did Britany come back here to say good-bye to you?

**MANNY**   Is that supposed to be relevant to what we're discussing?

**ELLEN**   Britany and I were chatting in the restroom about our plans for the rest of the summer when she suddenly broke down and started crying. Do you want me to continue?

**MANNY**   No. I don't.

[*Deflated.*]

It was a mistake. My marriage to Britany was a mistake. From the get-go.

**ELLEN**   You knew her a month before you married her. What was the rush?

**MANNY**   [*A beat after each period.*] Age. Eating alone. Sleeping alone. Fear. Mostly, fear.

**ELLEN**   I am sorry.

**MANNY**    I am, too.

**ELLEN**    Britany is a charming young woman.

**MANNY**    That's the problem. She's young, twenty years too young. I'll tell you a secret. Except for my children, I've come to dislike young people, especially those young people who have too much money, too much attention, too much of everything.

**ELLEN**    We finally have something in common.

**MANNY**    It must be difficult teaching them.

**ELLEN**    In the classroom they're compelled to behave themselves, but elsewhere I refuse to fraternize with them.

**MANNY**    Noisy and obnoxious, huh?

**ELLEN**    Selfish, spoiled and shallow is how I would describe them.

**MANNY**    I couldn't agree with you more. I prefer the company of my peers.

**ELLEN**    Only the company?

**MANNY**    And all that goes with it.
[*Solemnly.*]
Do you believe me?

**ELLEN**    Yes. I do. It takes time to become a decent human being.

**MANNY**    Like good wine, cheese . . .
[*With a grin.*]
. . . and older women.

**ELLEN**    You've come to that conclusion, have you?

**MANNY**    The hard way. I'm invariably more comfortable with older women. I'm attracted to their resourcefulness, their sophistication, their experiential sexuality.

[ELLEN *appears somewhat flustered by* MANNY'*s observation. She takes a beat to reply.*]

**ELLEN**    Are you and Britany separating?

**MANNY**   She asked me to go with her to see a marital shrink. I think it's a waste of time.

**ELLEN**   It's worth a try. Philip and I discussed it, but it's too late for us.

[*She looks down at her clasped hands.*]

**MANNY**   Ellen?

>[*She looks up at* MANNY.]
>
>On rare occasion I have used and verbally abused women. I don't think that, in and of itself, makes me a misogynist.

**ELLEN**   Younger or older women?

**MANNY**   Both. I have, since puberty, lied to them, deceived them, traded my self-esteem to satisfy my... desire or, to put it less delicately, to get my rocks off.

**ELLEN**   I suppose you're no different from the vast majority of men. You all share several common traits that define the word "misogynist." Would you like me to earmark those traits for you?

**MANNY**   I don't have the courage to say no.

**ELLEN**   First, the misogynist is the boss, the control freak, the macho man who lays down the law and executes his numerous do's and don'ts with absolute authority. Second, by your own admission, the misogynist lies and deceives women to get his rocks off. Third, the misogynist is an inveterate investigator of his wife or lover: he observes, collects and records errors of fact, errors of perception and errors of memory. He uses the information he has collected from his investigations to subsequently prove that his wife or lover is either of inferior intellectually or suffering from Alzheimer's disease. Conversely, the misogynist is perfect. Fourth, it's imperative that the misogynist raise his voice and bark like a pit bull on prearranged days of the week. Fifth, he never changes diapers, cooks a meal or turns on the dish-washing machine. Sixth, every evening before he goes to bed, the misogynist scratches his balls to make certain that he still has them.

[*Silence: 1, 2, 3, 4, 5, 6, 7, 8, 9, 10.*]

**MANNY**  [*Slowly rises to his feet; as intoned at AA meetings.*] My name is Emanuel Brooks. My friends call me Manny. I am a misogynist.

**ELLEN**  That wasn't too difficult, was it?

**MANNY**  [*Sits down.*] I feel miserable.

[*Their eyes cling to each other's face.*]

**ELLEN**  As well you should.

**MANNY**  My stupidity always surprises me.

**ELLEN**  That's a beginning.

**MANNY**  I apologize.

**ELLEN**  Change your attitude toward women and your apology is accepted.

**MANNY**  Will you help me change?

**ELLEN**  How?

**MANNY**  Talk to me again, vis-à-vis?

**ELLEN**  I can recommend a shrink.

**MANNY**  Been there, done that.

**ELLEN**  No ulterior motive to talking to me again, vis-à-vis?

**MANNY**  Yes. There is. I enjoy being with people who can teach me something. You're at the top of my list.

[*Their eyes hold: 1, 2, 3, 4, 5, 6, 7, 8, 9, 10.*]

**ELLEN**  Let's take it a step at a time.
  [*A beat.*]
  Please.

**MANNY**  Don't make the steps too many.
  [*A beat.*]
  Please.

[ELLEN *looks offstage, upstage/right.*]

**ELLEN**  Philip's coming.

[*They rise, quickly.*]

[PHILIP *enters, clapping his hands.*]

**PHILIP**    Let's go. Let's go. Britany's back. She's at the bar with Michael. Britany, the Karelsons, the Langners. They're waiting for us.

[*Glances from one to the other.*]

Did you two resolve your "business" problems?

**MANNY**    [*To* ELLEN.] Did we?

**ELLEN**    We have a few problems left to thrash out.

**MANNY**    But we're getting there.

**ELLEN**    Yes, we are getting there.

**PHILIP**    That's encouraging.

[*To* MANNY.]

Why didn't you tell us about Snoopy?

**ELLEN**    Who's Snoopy?

**PHILIP**    They bought a puppy. What is it, a Shih Tzu?

**MANNY**    I think so. I didn't buy it, Britany did.

**PHILIP**    It wears a Burberry dog collar. It's the cutest little thing.

**ELLEN**    Let's join the others.

[PHILIP *and* MANNY *pick up the tennis racquets and containers of tennis balls.* ELLEN *puts on her sweater.*]

**MANNY**    Great idea. Knobby is bartending. He makes the best martini in the Hamptons.

**ELLEN**    I don't approve of dogs living in the city.

**PHILIP**    I couldn't disagree with you more.

**MANNY**    I couldn't agree with you more. That's why Britany didn't ask for my approval. She knew she wouldn't get it.

**PHILIP**    Ellen's been proselytizing against dogs in the city ever since we moved to the West Side.

**MANNY**    I applaud her courage to stand up against the pro-animal brigade. Dogs don't belong in the city. In my building there are tenants who have two, three, four dogs to a family. And I'm not talking about lap-size dogs. I'm talking about Great Danes, Irish wolfhounds, Saint Bernards, dogs that are bigger than horses!

**ELLEN**    We have the same problem. Try getting into an elevator in our building when there's a tenant inside with four Alaskan huskies!

**MANNY**    Been there, don't that.

**ELLEN**    They crawl between your legs...

**MANNY**    Crush you against the wall...

**ELLEN**    Shed hair over your clothes...

**MANNY**    Once an Irish wolfhound farted in my face.

**ELLEN**    No.

**MANNY**    What do you mean no?

**ELLEN**    You're serious?

**MANNY**    I'm serious. I almost fainted.

**PHILIP**    How can you two be so heartless. Ask a blind person or a child or members of the fire department if dogs should be banned from the city. Listen to what they have to tell you!

**MANNY**    [*Builds to an outburst.*] One dog per family with the owner being responsible for picking up and disposing of the dog doo-doo is reasonable. And I'm certain Ellen would agree with me. But for your information, in the borough of Manhattan, which has a human population of one and a half million, there are two hundred and eighty-three thousand dogs! In Manhattan alone, two-hundred and eighty-three thousand dogs! And as we said before there are families that own two, three, four dogs! It's insane! It's barbaric! You can't walk down the street without stepping into a pile of dog doo-doo. From the Battery to the Bronx, the whole borough of Manhattan is one, big, toxic, smelly, slushy pile of dog doo-doo!

[*That puts an end to* PHILIP's *rejoinder. He shakes his head: there's no talking to these people.*]

**ELLEN**   Why don't you run ahead, Philip? I want another word with
      Manny. We'll join you in a minute.

**PHILIP**   Don't be long. I have a brief I have to finish before dinner.

[*And he quickly exits.*]

[MANNY *and* ELLEN's *eyes hold for several beats.*]

**ELLEN**   Sit down.
      [*A beat.*]
      Please.
      [*He sits in chair, staring up at* ELLEN. *She walks slowly up to him, cuddles
      his face between her hands and tongue-kisses him, effusively, for what could
      very well be five minutes.*]
      Thank you.
      [*They have eyes hold for several beats.* MANNY *rises. He clasps her hand or
      twines his arm around her waist as they move offstage, upstage/right.*]

## sound

Reprise PRE-RISE SOUND at the top of the play. Go out on "spectators
respond with shouts and applause..."

## lights and sound

Fade out.

• • •

# Elvis of
# Nazareth

Jay Huling

# Jay Huling

As the creative director for a Florida advertising agency, Jay Huling's radio and television commercials have been honored with national and regional awards—including numerous TELLY®, ADDY®, and Silver Microphone® awards and Best of Category (Public Service) at the International Wildlife Film Festival.

As a playwright, his works have been produced in California, Connecticut, Florida, Indiana, New York, Pennsylvania, Texas, and Washington, D.C. His accomplishments include:

- First Place Winner in the Porter Fleming Literary Competition, sponsored by the Greater Augusta Arts Council in Augusta, Georgia
- First Place Winner in the Premiere Performances International Playwriting Contest—where his play was voted "Judges' Favorite" and "Audience Favorite"
- First Place Winner in the McLaren Memorial Comedy Play Writing Competition
- First Place Winner in the Drury University One-Act Playwriting Competition
- Honorable Mention in the Stage Play Script category of the 73rd Annual *Writer's Digest* Writing Competition—which attracted nearly 18,000 entries
- Finalist in the Elmira College Playwriting Competition
- Finalist in the Mildred and Albert Panowski Playwriting Award
- Winner of the Robert J. Pickering Award for Playwriting Excellence

His plays include *Trilogy for Two*; *The Sing Sing Suite*; *Plumber's Butt*; *Rheumatoid Floyd*; *Hard Luck Sings the Blues*; *Insert Laugh Here*; *Twelve Bar Blues*; *Elvis of Nazareth*; *Two Fives and a Ten*; *The Wily Ray Riley*; *Bonjour Raconteur*; *Bob Juan*; *The Church of Diminishing Marginal Returns*; *Runs, Drips & Errors*, and numerous short plays and comedy sketches.

Jay Huling graduated from Jacksonville University, earning his BFA in theatre arts. He is a member of the Dramatists Guild.

## cast of characters

**THE YOUNG ELVIS**, The most celebrated recording artist of all time

**MARION**, Office manager for Sun Records and the Memphis Recording Service

**MOSES**, Hebrew prophet and law giver

**KING SOLOMON**, King of Israel, the second son of David and Bathsheba

**ROMAN CENTURION**, A commander of a hundred soldiers in the Roman army

**JESUS OF NAZARETH**, The central figure of Christianity

## set

The reception area of Sun Records, the home of the Memphis Recording Service. The set includes an office desk and chair, filing cabinets, soda machine, coffee table and magazines, guest chairs, a couch, and gold record awards hanging on the wall.

## time

The summer of 1953

## at rise

Marion works at her desk as the yet-to-be-discovered Elvis awaits his turn to make a private recording for his mother.

• • •

[THE YOUNG ELVIS, *about as nervous as a man can get, is seated on a long couch in the receptionist area. A sign above his head reads: "Memphis Recording Studio. Make Your Own Personal Records." He fidgets with his guitar.* MARION, *the office manager, sits near him, at her desk, bored, working on a stack of papers. His fidgeting begins to get on her nerves, and she gives him a look. He stops and smiles.*]

**ELVIS**    I'm gonna record a song for my mama.

**MARION** [*Looking away.*] That's nice.

**ELVIS** Kind of a present.

**MARION** That's nice.

[*She tries to continue her work, but* ELVIS *starts fidgeting again. She stares him down.*]

**ELVIS** Sorry…Mr. Phillips is gonna discover me and not give you any of the credit.

**MARION** That's ni—I beg your pardon?

**ELVIS** They're gonna call me the King.

**MARION** Yeah, yeah, what's this about me not getting any credit?

**ELVIS** Do you think I'm doing the right thing?

**MARION** Look, I want credit where credit is due. What am I not getting credit for?

**ELVIS** I'm gonna record a song for my mama. Kind of a present. You're gonna discover me; Mr. Phillips is gonna get the credit, and I'm gonna go on to be the king of roll and rock.

**MARION** Roll and rock?

**ELVIS** It's a little gospel and rhythm and blues thing I put together.

**MARION** Roll and rock doesn't quite "roll" off the tongue. Why don't you call it rock and roll?

**ELVIS** Okay—but you're still not getting any credit. Of course, it all seems so pointless anyway. My grave will become a tourist attraction.

**MARION** That's nice.

[*A buzzer sounds at the door.* MARION *presses a button on the intercom system at her desk.*]

Come in!

[MOSES, *who's come directly from Mount Sinai, circa 1225 BC, enters, staff in hand, and approaches* MARION's *desk.*]

May I help you?

**MOSES**  Let my people go!

**MARION**  Let who go?

**MOSES**  Art thou deaf? Am I not enunciating my consonants? Let my people go!

**MARION**  If you could just have a seat, Mr. Phillips will be with you in a moment.

**MOSES**  So that ye may know that the Lord—the God of Abraham, Isaac, and Jacob—hath sent me, this miraculous sign I now perform...

[MOSES *throws down his staff, and it lands near* MARION's *desk with a thud. There is an awkward silence.*]

**MARION**  That was supposed to turn into a snake, wasn't it?

**MOSES**  Uh-huh.

**MARION**  Do you need a moment?

**MOSES**  'Preciate it.

[*He takes up his staff and has a seat near* ELVIS. MOSES *ponders over the staff, perplexed as to why it didn't work.*]

**ELVIS**  You okay?

**MOSES**  I was told—cast down thy rod and it will become a serpent! Did you see me cast down my rod?

**ELVIS**  Yes.

**MOSES**  Did it become a serpent?

**ELVIS**  No.

**MOSES**  That's what I thought.

**ELVIS**  Pleasure to meet you. My name's Elvis.

**MOSES**  I am Moses, discovered by Pharaoh's daughter hidden in a basket among the reeds near the river's bank. I received my call from the great bush which burned—yet was not consumed. I have come to lead my people out from bondage.

**ELVIS**    I'm gonna record a song for my mama. Kind of a present.

**MOSES**    Honoring thy father and mother. That's good. I should write that down.

**ELVIS**    They're gonna put me on *The Ed Sullivan Show* and shoot me from the waist up. Won't be able to see me wiggle.

**MOSES**    Thou wiggles?

**ELVIS**    I wiggle when I sing.

**MOSES**    Are you taking anything for that?

**ELVIS**    I do it on purpose. It's how I express the song.

**MOSES**    I always wanted to be a singer. Never worked out.

**ELVIS**    Why?

**MOSES**    The material I was given!
[*Quoting.*]
"The horse and his rider hath he thrown into the sea."
[*Then.*]
What can you do with that?

**ELVIS**    I never knew you wanted to be a singer.

**MOSES**    The truth is I just wanted it for the groupies. Break up the monotony.

**ELVIS**    But your life's purpose is so extraordinary.

**MOSES**    I wandered in the desert for forty frickin' years. I was willing to stop and ask for directions—but no!

**ELVIS**    I've always wished for a higher calling.

**MOSES**    It ain't what it's cracked up to be.

**ELVIS**    But you are a true man of God.

**MOSES**    Yeah, right. And just because I hit the rock instead of speaking to it—no Promised Land for me! Who speaks to a damn rock?
[*To* MARION.]
Pardon my French.

**MARION**    Pardon my indifference.

**ELVIS**    You saw the glory of God.

**MOSES**    I saw his back! His back! I wanted to see his face, but then—
[*Mocking.*]
Of course, I'd have TO DIE!
[*Calmly.*]
I was never really given a proper explanation. Trust me, kid, stick to singing and wiggling.

**ELVIS**    You don't understand. Somewhere deep inside me there's an empty space. What's it gonna take to fill that up? I gotta find something. I'm not sure gyratin' like a jackhammer is it.

**MOSES**    Thou must choose. The pleasures of sin for a season, or an eternity of never getting past second base.

**ELVIS**    But I think I hear the voice of—

**MOSES**    No more opportunities to dunk your donut, if you know what I mean.

**ELVIS**    You're not listening to what I'm—

**MOSES**    —To sum it up, the Red Sea might be the only thing you ever part.

**ELVIS**    But what is that compared to a life making disciples for the Kingdom?

**MOSES**    My son, I gotta do what I gotta do. You don't. Thou understandeth?

**ELVIS**    Not really.

**MOSES**    Think about it. Excuse me.
[*Crossing to* MARION.]
Let me let you in on a little secret.

**MARION**    What?

**MOSES**    Frogs.

**MARION**    Frogs?

**MOSES**  Frogs. Big green juicy amphibians. On your bed, down your drawers, in your chicken potpie. Frogs the size of baseball mitts. Everywhere! Unless thou hearken unto me.

**MARION**  And you're telling me this because . . . ?

**MOSES**  Because thus saith the Lord—LET MY PEOPLE GO!—that they may serve me.

**MARION**  Mr. Phillips is the only one who can approve such a request.

**MOSES**  Behold! A sign, a great wonder I perform before your stiff-necked eyes that ye may believe! Put now thine hand to thy bosom.

**MARION**  I beg your pardon?

**MOSES**  Behold! It hath become leprous as snow!

**MARION**  [*Showing him her hand.*] It's the same as usual.

**MOSES**  [*Pointing to something on her hand.*] Has that always been there?

**MARION**  Always.

**MOSES**  [*Disappointed again.*] Can I have another moment to regroup?

**MARION**  Certainly.

[MOSES *returns to his seat.*]

**ELVIS**  You okay?

**MOSES**  To tell you the truth, I knew it wouldn't work. Supposed to turn my arm leprous. Can't do something cool like make fire rain down from heaven. Gotta turn into a leper. Gotta make locusts swarm! Ever seen a swarm of locusts?

**ELVIS**  No, sir.

**MOSES**  Looks like a flying blob of pork and beans coming smack at you.

**ELVIS**  You're just trying to discourage me, aren't you?

**MOSES**  Think not! I am Moses! I brought you into the Promised Land, and I can take you out!
[*Calmly.*]

Now if you will pardon me.

[*Crossing to* MARION.]

My good lady. Hast thou anyplace where I may cover my feet?

**MARION**   Excuse me?

**MOSES**   No, excuse me. Thy servant needs to—as King James put it—ease thyself abroad.

**MARION**   Huh?

**MOSES**   Moses has to take a dump, honey.

**MARION**   Oh!

[*Pointing.*]

In there.

**MOSES**   I thank you.

[MOSES *exits.*]

**ELVIS**   I don't think I can go through with this.

**MARION**   You're not about to chicken out, are you? Mr. Phillips will be with you any moment. Your future is waiting.

**ELVIS**   You don't know what I know. They're gonna have me singing to a dog, man. Then I get drafted. And then come the Beatles.

**MARION**   The who?

**ELVIS**   No, not the Who, the Beatles.

**MARION**   Beetles and locusts. Why don't we just let the people go?

**ELVIS**   No—they're four lads from Liverpool. Lots of mediocre stuff that's hailed as genius.

**MARION**   Will I get any credit for them?

**ELVIS**   I should just go home.

[*The door buzzer sounds again.*]

**MARION**   Come in!

[*The door opens and* KING SOLOMON *enters, in all his splendor. He approaches* MARION.]

May I help you?

**SOLOMON** Behold, thou art fair, my beloved, yea, pleasant: also our bed is green.

**MARION** Come again?

**SOLOMON** Thy two breasts are like two young roes that are twins, which feed among the lilies. Thou art all fair, my love; there is no spot in thee.

**MARION** That's really very sweet of you. But not very office appropriate. Is there something I can help you with?

**SOLOMON** Turn away thine eyes from me, for they have overcome me!

**MARION** If you'll just have a seat, Mr. Phillips will be with you as soon as possible.

**SOLOMON** For you, I will be a young stag upon the mountains of spices.

**MARION** That's nice.

[SOLOMON *turns and sits next to* ELVIS.]

**SOLOMON** Gets 'em every time.

**ELVIS** That was some smooth talking.

**SOLOMON** You ain't seen nothing yet.

**ELVIS** My name's Elvis. It's a pleasure to meet you.

**SOLOMON** I am Solomon, the third and last king of united Israel. The son of David, son of Jesse.

**ELVIS** I had a twin brother named Jesse.

**SOLOMON** I had some seven hundred wives and three hundred concubines.

**ELVIS** I'm gonna marry Priscilla and buy Ann-Margret a bed.

**SOLOMON** I made gold in Jerusalem as common as dirt.

**ELVIS** I'm gonna earn more than a hundred and fifty gold records.

**SOLOMON** Oh, yeah, well, I wrote three thousand proverbs.

**ELVIS**   I'm gonna sell more than a billion records worldwide.

**SOLOMON**   I have written more than one thousand songs. Including Song of Solomon—the greatest love song of all.

**ELVIS**   Did any of them go to number one?

**SOLOMON**   Art thou challenging me?

**ELVIS**   I just asked a question.

**SOLOMON**   We shall see who is asking the questions!

[SOLOMON *takes some sheet music out of his pocket and hands it to* ELVIS.]

Hast thou anything as artful and lovely as this—?

**ELVIS**   [*Reading.*]

"Except the Lord build the house,

They labour in vain that build it:

Except the Lord keep the city,

The watchman waketh but in vain."

**SOLOMON**   Read 'em and weep.

[ELVIS *pulls a piece of paper from his pocket and hands it to* SOLOMON.]

**ELVIS**   Try this on for size. From one of my movies.

**SOLOMON**   [*Reading.*]

"I feel it in my leg,

I feel it in my shoe,

Tell me pretty baby,

If you think you feel it too."

[*Then.*]

How profound.

[*Handing* ELVIS *more lyrics.*]

But surely you are no match for me.

**ELVIS**   [*Reading.*]

"It is vain for you to rise up early,

To sit up late,

To eat the bread of sorrows:
For so he giveth his beloved sleep."
[*Then.*]
Well played.
[*Handing lyrics to* SOLOMON.]
But, as well as this—?

**SOLOMON**    [*Reading.*]
"Some people like to rock,
Some people like to roll,
But movin' and a-groovin',
Gonna satisfy my soul."
[*Then.*]
Satisfaction of soul? Intriguing. Thou art a worthy adversary.

**ELVIS**    They don't call me "the Pelvis" for nothing.

**SOLOMON**    [*Handing* ELVIS *more lyrics.*] What sayest thou of this?

**ELVIS**    [*Reading.*]
"As arrows are in the hand of a mighty man:
So are children of the youth.
Happy is the man that hath his quiver full of them:
They shall not be ashamed,
But they shall speak with the enemies in the gate."
[*Then.*]
That's gold, Solomon, pure gold.
[*Handing* SOLOMON *more lyrics.*]
But this is platinum!

**SOLOMON**    [*Reading.*]
"I've never kissed a bear,
I've never kissed a goon,
But I can shake a chicken,
In the middle of the room."

**ELVIS**   Checkmate.

**SOLOMON**   [*Breaking down.*] Vanity of vanities! All is vanity! I have seen all the works that are done under the sun; and, behold, all is vanity and vexation of spirit. There is no new thing under the sun!
[*Calmly, pointing to* ELVIS.]
Until now.

**ELVIS**   I just kind of stumbled upon it.

**SOLOMON**   Art thou a prophet?

**ELVIS**   No, sir, but I did study to be an electrician.

[SOLOMON *pulls out a small memo pad and pencil from his pocket and kneels down before* ELVIS.]

**SOLOMON**   Wilt thou teach me to be artful in song as thou?

**ELVIS**   Me? Teach you? You have written some of the most beautiful verses of the holy Scriptures.

**SOLOMON**   But I want something different. Hell, I want a pop song!

**ELVIS**   And I want to be wise like you.

**SOLOMON**   Look, if you're talking about that cutting-the-baby-in-half thing—I was bluffing. I can't believe they fell for that baloney!

**ELVIS**   But your life as a man of God is so important.

**SOLOMON**   Ever heard of a King Solomon impersonator? Huh? No one's ever won a karaoke contest doing me.

**ELVIS**   I'm just not so sure it's right for me anymore.

**SOLOMON**   Thou fool. The only thing that is right is to fear God and keep his commandments. Now teach me to rock my fanny off.

[ELVIS *stands up, begins to demonstrate.*]

**ELVIS**   You kinda got to let the rhythm ooze out of you.

**SOLOMON**   Showest thou me this ooze.

**ELVIS**   [*Shaking his leg in rhythm.*] This is ooze. With a beat. Four/four time.

**SOLOMON**    [*Writing something down.*] Time, yes, time. That's good.

**ELVIS**    [*Snapping his fingers.*] Some people snap their fingers.
[*Tapping his toe.*]
Some people tap their toes.
[*Swaying back and forth.*]
And some people sway back and forth. I kinda put 'em all together, I guess. That's how the blues is born.

**SOLOMON**    [*Pleased.*] A time to be born. Yes.

**ELVIS**    Then you just rock till you drop.

**SOLOMON**    [*Writing something down.*] A time to be rocked. And a time to be dropped. I like this. It's almost like there's a time for every season under Heaven.

**ELVIS**    Add a few karate moves, and—

**SOLOMON**    Cease! A handful of quietness, please.
[*Crossing to a chair on the other side of the room.*]
I'm on a roll! And I'm not going to give you any of the credit.

[SOLOMON *begins writing furiously.*]

**MARION**    Isn't there any credit worthiness going on here?

[MOSES *enters. There is a long trailing roll of toilet paper stuck to his sandal.*]

**MOSES**    [*To* MARION.] Thus saith the Lord God of the Hebrews—Let my people go, that they may serve me!

**MARION**    [*Seeing what's attached to his shoe.*] Uh, excuse me, but—

**MOSES**    For if thou refuse to let them go, and wilt hold them still—

**MARION**    I really think you should—

**MOSES**    Behold, the hand of the Lord is upon thy cattle which is in the field, upon the horses, upon the asses—YES!—I said asses! Asses! The hand of the Lord is upon thy asses!

**MARION**    You've got toilet paper stuck to your shoe.

**MOSES**    Holy crap!

[MOSES, *humiliated, sits next to* ELVIS *and starts wrapping up the roll.*]

**ELVIS**  You okay?

**MOSES**  Do you realize how much adultery I could have had? But I gave it all up. For what? That I may have t.p. stuck to the sticky place!

**ELVIS**  Are you at all appreciative of who you are?

**MOSES**  Day after day of burnt sacrifices. Sin offerings. Grain offerings. Peace offerings. Wine offerings. Wave offerings—who's ever heard of a wave offering? All for what? To remove sin? Ha! There's got to be a better way!

[*The door buzzer sounds again.* MARION *presses the intercom button.*]

**MARION**  Come in!

[*The door opens and a* ROMAN CENTURION *enters with his prisoner,* JESUS OF NAZARETH.]

May I help you?

**CENTURION**  Your Excellency, this man claims to be the Christ, the king of the Jews!

**MARION**  [*To* ELVIS.] I thought you said you were the King.

**ELVIS**  No, I'm the king of roll and rock.

**CENTURION**  The people want him crucified.

**MARION**  His singing can't be that bad.

**CENTURION**  Not him!

[*Pushing* JESUS *forward.*]

Him!

**MARION**  [*To* JESUS.] Oh. I'm sorry, what was your name?

[JESUS *is silent.*]

**CENTURION**  He is called Jesus of Nazareth.

**MARION**  And who do you sound like?

[*Again,* JESUS *doesn't answer.*]

**CENTURION**  He doesn't sound like nobody.

**MARION**   Do you sing hillbilly?

[JESUS *remains silent.*]

**CENTURION**   Yea, he sings hillbilly.

**MARION**   Who do you sound like in hillbilly?

[*Silence.*]

**CENTURION**   He doesn't sound like nobody.

**MARION**   Is he always this shy?

**CENTURION**   He didn't say much in the cab on the way over.

**MARION**   Well, have a seat. Mr. Phillips will be with you as soon as possible.

**CENTURION**   I beseech you, say the word to Lord Phillips. For I also am a man set under authority, having under me soldiers, and I say unto one, Go, and he goeth; and to another, Come, and he cometh.

**MARION**   And I say unto you, siteth.

[*The* CENTURION *takes* JESUS *by the arm, and they both sit next to* ELVIS.]

**ELVIS**   [*To* CENTURION.] My name's Elvis. Pleasure to meet you. This here is Moses; that's Marion—

**MARION**   Charmed—

**ELVIS**   And that's Solomon, son of David. I didn't quite catch your name, sir.

**CENTURION**   I really have no desire to make nice with you people.

**ELVIS**   [*To* JESUS.] I'm gonna record a song for my mama. Kind of a present. [JESUS *is silent.*]
Mr. Phillips says if he can find a white man with the Negro sound and feel, he could make a billion dollars.

**CENTURION**   Pontius Pilate says the same thing—the nerve!

**ELVIS**   All I really want to do is sing in a gospel quartet. [*To* JESUS.]
You like gospel?

[JESUS *thinks for a moment; then gives* ELVIS *a "so-so" motion with his hand. The* CENTURION *stands and approaches* MARION.]

**CENTURION**   Woman, when will Lord Phillips prepare himself to meet us?

**MARION**   First of all, I'm not your woman. Second, I wouldn't be your woman if you were the last of the Mohicans. And thirdly—
[*Pointing to* ELVIS.]
the one with the jumpin' beans in his jeans was here before you.

**ELVIS**   Well, that's all right, ma'am.
[*To* JESUS.]
Just doesn't seem proper that I come before you.

**JESUS**   Suffer it to be so for now.

**MARION**   He speaks!

**CENTURION**   And he sayest something stupid! What's wrong with you? Sideburns here says we can go first.

**ELVIS**   Really, it's okay.

**JESUS**   For thus it becometh us to fulfill all righteousness.

**CENTURION**   [*Standing over* JESUS.] What in tarnation is wrong with you!? The boy's letting us cut in line. Don't you know that I have the power to crucify you!

**JESUS**   Thou couldest have no power at all against me, except it were given thee from above.

**CENTURION**   [*Sitting down.*] My bad.

**ELVIS**   Are you really Jesus of Nazareth, the Christ, the king of the Jews?

**JESUS**   Ye say that I am.

**CENTURION**   Wiggles knows that's what he said. What he wants to know is are you the king of the Jews?

**JESUS**   I am.

[ELVIS *is awestruck.*]

**MOSES**  [*To* JESUS.] Jesus Christ. You've always been such a mystery to me. Just exactly what does the "H." stand for?

[*Everyone slowly and simultaneously looks at* MOSES *in disbelief.*]

**MARION**  Would any of you care for anything to drink?

**MOSES**  I could go for a Diet Dr Pepper right now.

**MARION**  I have regular Dr Pepper.

**MOSES**  No thanks.

**MARION**  Anything for the King?

**ELVIS**  Got any decaf?

**MARION**  Not you—him!

**JESUS**  Whosoever drinketh of this water shall thirst again.

**MARION**  I'm sorry. I don't have any Gatorade.

**JESUS**  If any man thirst, let him come unto me, and drink.

**CENTURION**  What are you—running a concession?

**ELVIS**  You're talking about living water, aren't you?

**JESUS**  I am the bread of life.

**MOSES**  You guys are making me hungry.

**CENTURION**  [*To* ELVIS.] Kid, can I have a word with you?

**ELVIS**  Sure.

[CENTURION *takes* ELVIS *aside.*]

**CENTURION**  No fraternizing with the accused on my watch, kapeech?

**ELVIS**  What is he accused of?

**CENTURION**  If he were not a malefactor, I would not have delivered him up.

**ELVIS**  A mal-a-what?

**CENTURION**  This man maketh himself a king, the Son of God.

**ELVIS**  But he is the Son of God.

**CENTURION**  [*Beat.*] Get outta here.

**ELVIS**  It's the truth.

**CENTURION**  What is truth? He is a friend with publicans, tax collectors, and sinners.

**ELVIS**  That's because they are the ones who need him.

**CENTURION**  Thou hast proof?

**ELVIS**  He fed a whole crowd with only five loaves of Wonder bread.

**CENTURION**  You can never get large portions nowadays.

**ELVIS**  He healed the sick, made the blind see, raised the dead.

[CENTURION *looks over at* JESUS, *stares a little bit, then waves.* JESUS *waves back.*]

**CENTURION**  I thought he was just some freaky long-haired weirdo.

**ELVIS**  Hardly.

[*They return to their seats near* JESUS.]

**CENTURION**  Dude, that crown of thorns thing—sorry.

**JESUS**  Man, thy sins are forgiven thee.

**CENTURION**  You're gonna forgive my sins? Lordy, lordy, truly, this man is the Son of God.

**ELVIS**  Lord, is this what I'm really supposed to do? I know you have a plan for my life.

**JESUS**  Whoso eateth my flesh and drinketh my blood hath eternal life.

**MOSES**  How can this man give us his flesh to eat?

**JESUS**  My flesh is meat indeed, and my blood is drink indeed.

[*There is an awkward silence.* MOSES *whistles to himself, self-consciously.*]

**MARION**  Anyone for Chinese?

**MOSES**  Back home I'd make an excellent quail soufflé.

**CENTURION**  My lady—and notice I did not say "woman"—why doth Lord Phillips tarry?

**MARION**   He'll be with you shortly. Please hold your horses.

**CENTURION**   Hold my horses? My horses cannot be held, thank you very much.

[SOLOMON *stands, excited, clutching his latest manuscript.*]

**SOLOMON**   Hearken unto me! I hath made me a great work! I gave my heart to know wisdom, and I hath found it!

**ELVIS**   Found what?

**SOLOMON**   The answer! The answer, my friend. It was blowing in the wind!

**MOSES**   Oh, if only I had lyrics like that!

**ELVIS**   Hang loose, man. Let's hear the words of the preacher.

[*As a spotlight focuses on him,* SOLOMON *clears his throat and begins to read his new manuscript.*]

**SOLOMON**   [*Reading.*] "To every thing there is a season, and a time to every purpose under the heaven. A time to be born, and a time to die. A time to plant, and a time to pluck up that which is planted. A time to kill, and a time to heal; a time to break down, and a time to build up. A time to weep, and a time to laugh; a time to mourn, and a time to dance. A time to cast away stones, and a time to gather stones together; a time to embrace, and a time to refrain from embracing. A time to get, and a time to lose; a time to keep, and a time to cast away. A time to rend, and a time to sew; a time to keep silence, and a time to speak. A time to love, and a time to hate; a time of war, and a time of peace."
[*Then, to* ELVIS.]
How do you like them apples?

**ELVIS**   Now, that's a pop song!

**SOLOMON**   You really think so?

**ELVIS**   I know so. The Byrds will take it to number one.

**MOSES**   Frogs, flies, pestilence, beetles—now birds!—is there no end!?

**SOLOMON**   I owe you a debt of gratitude, my friend with the bump and grind in his loins. Thou art sure you like it?

**ELVIS**   You're really gone, Solomon; you're the most, man.

**SOLOMON**   [*To* MARION.] Et tu?

**MARION**   Pardon?

**SOLOMON**   Even you, daughter of Jerusalem? Thy navel is like a round goblet, which wanteth not liquor: thy belly is like an heap of wheat set about with lilies.

**MARION**   How radiant and ruddy thou art!

**SOLOMON**   Let us take our fill of love!

**MARION**   Oh, gee! I'm yours!

[MARION *and* SOLOMON *are about to embrace when they are interrupted by the buzzer on* MARION'*s phone. She picks up the receiver.*]

[*Into phone.*]

Yes, Mr. Phillips. Yes, I'll send him in right away.

[*Then.*]

Oh, by the way, Mr. Phillips . . . I know this new group I think you should hear. They're called the Beetles . . . Yes, like the insect.

[*Disappointed.*]

Certainly.

[*Hangs up the phone; to* ELVIS.]

Mr. Phillips will see you now.

**ELVIS**   No!

**MARION**   No?

**ELVIS**   No! Lord, I want to follow you wherever you go.

**JESUS**   Foxes have holes, and birds of the air have nests; but the son of man hath not where to lay his head.

**MARION**   Mr. Phillips is waiting. Your whole future is waiting.

**ELVIS**   [*To* JESUS.] What should I do?

**JESUS**    Verily, verily, I say unto thee, except a man be born again, he cannot see the kingdom of God. As Moses lifted up the serpent in the wilderness, even so must the son of man be lifted up.

**MOSES**    So that's what that meant.

**ELVIS**    So, I should leave everything and follow you—right?

**JESUS**    I will have mercy and not sacrifice.

**ELVIS**    I don't understand. They're about to discover me.

**JESUS**    Peace be unto you. As my Father hath sent me, even so send I you.

**ELVIS**    But you're sending me to do what? What is my purpose?
[*To* SOLOMON.]
Solomon, I need wisdom.

**SOLOMON**    Rejoice, O young man, in thy youth; and walk in the ways of thine heart.

**MARION**    I think what they're telling you, E, is—make that record for your mama.

**ELVIS**    [*To* JESUS.] Is that right?

**JESUS**    Thou sayest.

**ELVIS**    [*To* MARION.] Roll and rock?

**MARION**    Anyway you want it.

**ELVIS**    Mo?

**MOSES**    I have set before you life and death, blessing and cursing: therefore choose life.

**ELVIS**    I guess "Love thy neighbor" isn't too far off from "Don't Be Cruel."

**CENTURION**    Go out there, man. There's more than one way to fulfill your purpose.

**SOLOMON**    And let thy garments be always white.

**ELVIS**    Kinda like a "Gi"—huh?

**SOLOMON**   Remembereth thou ooze.

**ELVIS**   I'll remember.

> [ELVIS *takes his guitar, straps it on, and strolls toward center stage. He bows his head for a moment, then looks back at* JESUS.]
>
> And this is what I'm supposed to do? Mistakes and all?

**JESUS**   Lo, I am with you always—even unto the end of the world.

**ELVIS**   That's right. I'll never forget it.

> [ELVIS *prepares himself to do his performance, striking a G chord.*]
>
> [*To* JESUS.]
>
> If you are willing, it would be an honor to have you join me.

**JESUS**   [*Standing.*] I am willing.

**MOSES**   All right, let's rock!

[MARION, MOSES, SOLOMON, CENTURION, *and* JESUS *join* ELVIS *as if background singers.* ELVIS *strums the intro and sings the song "Dear Jesus." (Words and music by Jay Huling.)*]

**ELVIS**   [*Verse One.*]

> Dear Jesus,
> I don't understand,
> Why did you have to go away?
> You were a friend to hoodlums, harlots, and thieves,
> Sinners just like me.
> To the poor and the meek,
> The humble and weak,
> You opened up your loving arms.
> You gave a damn for the damned;
> Every woman and man,
> Sinners just like me.
> [*Chorus.*]
> When all the finger-pointers were pointing at you,
> You said forgive—they know not what they do.

Love your enemies,
And learn to turn the cheek;
Give and it will be given you.
[*Verse Two.*]
Dear Jesus,
I'm afraid I'd a-been,
One of the ones to do you in.
I would have lied and cried,
And three times denied,
Before the mornin' light.
I can see myself now,
Doubting what, when, and how—
Show me the wounds so I can see;
Blessed are the ones who've not seen yet believed,
Sinners just like me.
[*Repeat Chorus.*]
[*Verse Three.*]
Dear Jesus,
I don't understand,
Why did you have to go away?
You were a friend to hoodlums, harlots, and thieves,
Sinners just like me.
You said if we believe like the mustard seed,
We can accomplish any deed;
If the Son sets you free,
You will be free indeed,
Dear Jesus, help my unbelief;
Dear Jesus, help my unbelief.

[*Curtain.*]

• • •

# A Roz by Any
# Other Name
### and **Weïrd**

B. T. Ryback

# B. T. Ryback

B. T. Ryback won the 2007 Tennessee Williams Once-Act Competition for his play *Weird*. His play *A Roz by Any Other Name* was the winner of the 2007 Henrico County Theatre One-Act Competition. He wrote the book for the musical *Darling*, a co-wrote the music and lyrics for *Quit India* (Richard Rodgers Award Finalist). He is a regular composer for Milwaukee's Skylight Opera Theatre's education program, Kidswrites, which pairs the uncorrected writing of inner-city grade school students with professional actors and composers. Mr. Ryback received a BA in music composition from UCLA, where he studied with acclaimed composer Paul Chihara (*Sophisticated Ladies, Shogun*), with whom he has recently begun work on a new musical based on Georg Buchner's *Leonce and Lena*. Mr. Ryback lives in Los Angeles, where he also works as an actor.

## cast of characters

**ROSALIND**, a very beautiful young woman who gets what she wants

**VERA**, her best friend

**CORDONNA**, her no-nonsense nurse

**STEFANO**, a young, simpleminded poet

## time

The early 1600s

## place

Rosalind's bedroom chamber, Verona, Italy

*Note: It is the playwright's intention that this play not be done with any dialect. Though the actors must weave naturally in and out of heightened language, the characters should at all times maintain a modern sensibility.

**Note: This play can be done in rep with *Weïrd*. If so, the doubling is as follows:

**ROSALIND/HARPER**

**VERA/LINN**

**CORDONNA/TORRENCE**

**STEFANO/DOUGLAS**

• • •

[*The curtain rises on a bedroom chamber. There is an archway at left, which acts as a door to the room. The door is framed by various lit candles, which offer the only source of light in the room. In the back of the room are two glass doors that open onto a balcony, beneath which we can see a few trees or shrubs. There is a moment of silence before it is shattered by* ROSALIND *bursting into the room. She is dressed in a princess costume, complete with tiara.*]

**ROSALIND**  [*Screaming.*] That Mule! That stubborn, stupid. . . . *bloodsucking* Mule! I have never been so humiliated in all my life!

**VERA**  [*Rushing in after* ROSALIND.] Roz, stop, please . . .

**ROSALIND**  I just—I mean, who does he think he is? Who does he think I am?

**VERA**  Sit down, you'll feel better.

**ROSALIND**  I have been sitting all night, Vera! I don't think I'll ever need to sit again after tonight. Waiting for that stupid, stubborn—

**VERA**  Blood-sucking?

**ROSALIND**  Blood-sucking Mule! A cloth! A cloth for my head!
[VERA *brings her a cloth*. ROSALIND *dabs herself furiously*.]
I'm sweating, Vera. Look at me sweat. I never sweat. I hate sweating.

**VERA**  We rushed home so quickly.

**ROSALIND**  [*Still dabbing*.] Oh, no, this isn't "rush sweat." This is *anger* sweat.

**VERA**  Careful you don't dab yourself to death.

**ROSALIND**  [*She stops with a cry*.] Oh! And he never asked for one dance. After all I did for him, all the time we shared, he acted like I wasn't even there.

**VERA**  You broke his heart.

**ROSALIND**  He deserves it after tonight!

**VERA**  Rosalind, hush, you don't want to wake anyone up. I'll get the tea and then we can talk. You'll feel better, I promise.

[VERA *exits back down the steps*.]

**ROSALIND**  The nerve he has! Did he think no one would see? Did he think *I* wouldn't see? I sat there all night waiting for him to ask me to dance.

I ought to tell his parents. Ha! His mother would die right on the spot if I marched up to her and said, "Lady Montague, do you know who I saw your Romeo locking lips with all night long? That's right, m'lady, *Juliet Capulet*! CAPULET!" Ha! Oh, she would die on the spot.

[VERA *enters with a tray, two cups, and a teakettle.*]

I've got it! I'll report Romeo to his parents and suggest that Lord Montague demand a pound of Juliet's flesh in restitution for this embarrassment.

**VERA**  [*Rather uninterested.*] What a brilliant idea, Roz. Forgive me if I don't move fast enough.

**ROSALIND**  Ten pounds! And they can take it off her behind!

**VERA**  Pound for pound I'd say it's the worst idea I've ever heard.
[ROSALIND *fumes.*]
I swear, the situations I find myself in with you. How do you handle all this... excitement?

**ROSALIND**  I'd hardly call this exciting. Insulting is more like it.

**VERA**  Oh, come, Roz, he wasn't breaking any rules.

**ROSALIND**  How dare you take his side! Am I not your best-sworn friend? After all we've been through together, you join with him in scorning me! 'Tis not friendly—'tis not maidenly! What allegiance do you owe that Mule?

**VERA**  I'm only trying to help you think rationally. You have always been a challenge, Roz, but I care enough to fight you *because* I am your best-sworn friend. Here, try some tea.

[ROSALIND *reluctantly does.*]

**ROSALIND**  Chamomile. Thank you.
[*A beat.*]
Ugh! Those stupid Montague boys. Put six of them together and you still don't get half a brain.

**VERA**  Was all of this so surprising? *You* found *him*, Roz. That day we were all at the beach. You, me, and Giovanni. You saw this wretched-looking, scrawny little thing walking along the sand and you turned to me with that look. Poor Gianni was so oblivious.
So you waited for him to go into the water, and then you walked up to that stick of a boy and said something typically Rosalind—

**ROSALIND**    He was using a piece of driftwood and I think I said, "You must be a painter or a poet. You handle your stick so well."

**VERA**    [*Laughing.*] I don't know where you come up with those.

**ROSALIND**    Practice.

**VERA**    And you came back over to me and looked at me and said, "A Montague. Not bad." Poor Gianni never figured out what happened.

**ROSALIND**    It wasn't Romeo that happened, Vera. You needn't tear a dead leaf from a tree; the right gust of wind will do the job on its own.

**VERA**    And Rosalind had her wind. [*A beat.*] He was very handsome and strong, but oh, how that boy cried. Like a poet he cried.

**ROSALIND**    You sound just like him.

**VERA**    I said he cried is all. You forget, Roz, that the best friend must often serve two masters.

**ROSALIND**    Well, rest assured you won't need to be holding Romeo's hand. He found some whore to do it for you. I just…I don't understand. A Capulet! I mean, it's one thing to see manure on the street, but to actually pick it up and take it home with you? But then what can one expect from a Mule? But honestly, a Capulet! To go from a Constantini to a Capulet. Even alphabetically it's backwards.

**VERA**    The Capulets aren't as undistinguished as they once were. Why do you think there has been a resurrection in the fights between the two houses? You should consider it a blessing to be out of that mess.

**ROSALIND**    [*Blood rising.*] A blessing! Is gold blessed to have been exchanged for silver? I couldn't be more humiliated if he ran off with a Putori, the trashiest family in Verona!

**VERA**    Maybe he saw something more in her.

**ROSALIND**    More than what? Than me?

**VERA**   It isn't impossible.

**ROSALIND**   I dare you to continue that thought.

**VERA**   Believe it or not, Rosalind, there are other women in the world besides you. A little competition never hurt anyone.

**ROSALIND**   I don't recall Helen of Troy having any competition!

**VERA**   And I don't recall Helen of Troy losing any men!

**ROSALIND**   Well, thank you, Vera, for the wonderful history lesson!

[*This last outburst is the loudest. We hear a door slam, and heavy feet, exasperatingly making their way up the stairs.*]

**VERA**   I told you, you would wake someone up!

**ROSALIND**   Not that wretched woman, please!

[*Appearing at the door is* CORDONNA. *She has just been woken up and is obviously not pleased about it.*]

**CORDONNA**   Rosalind Constantini, if you don't shut your godforsaken mouth, I'll have the smith drive a nail through your lips that'll have you sipping soup through a straw for the rest of your life.

**ROSALIND**   Well, it'd be nice to find that *some* of the help does work around here.

**CORDONNA**   [*Shaking her head.*] Ungrateful brat.

**ROSALIND**   [*Meeting her.*] Vicious horse.

**CORDONNA**   [*Mildly.*] Evening, Vera. I can only imagine what this one has roped you in to doing here at all hours of the night.

**VERA**   We just returned from a costume party, ma'am.

**CORDONNA**   Oh, dear, you can call me Cordonna.

**ROSALIND**   She also answers to "Dinner is served."

**CORDONNA**   You know, I'd say you were raised by wolves if it wasn't such an insult to wolves.

**ROSALIND**   Given *your* family history, I'd say I was raised by wolves, too.

**CORDONNA**   Putori trash!

**ROSALIND**   Careful, Vera, I think she's going to rear.

**CORDONNA**   And what are you supposed to be? A prostitute?

**ROSALIND**   I'm a princess.

**CORDONNA**   [*She laughs.*] Yeah. And I'm the Pope. What are you two doing making all that noise up here?

**VERA**   Rosalind had bitter luck tonight.

**CORDONNA**   No one's replaced poor Romeo?

**VERA**   Someone's replaced poor Rosalind.

[ROSALIND *turns, shocked at what* VERA *just said.*]

**CORDONNA**   My, my, my, how the mighty do fall. So who was it?

**ROSALIND**   I don't believe this has anything to do with my *laundry*, so perhaps you should keep your little hooves out!

**CORDONNA**   Give her another day. She'll find someone new to build up, lead on, and then dump like yesterday's bread.

**ROSALIND**   [*Breaking slightly.*] Cordonna, please.

**CORDONNA**   [*She considers.*] Well, if you do happen to find some tears in there, be sure to let them out quietly. Some of us sleep at night. Good night, Vera.

**VERA**   Good night, Cordonna.

[CORDONNA *exits.*]

**ROSALIND**   That is exactly what I'm afraid of. The minute people find out that Rosalind Constantini has been trumped by a Capulet, I'm ruined. My reputation, my dignity, my pride—all gone. I must do something to get Romeo back. I need a plan...

**VERA**   [*Becoming excited.*] Like what?

**ROSALIND**   I'm not sure. But whatever it is, it must be brilliantly clever.

**VERA**   What if you simply apologized and asked to have him back?

**ROSALIND**  Too easy. He'd never fall for it. I've got it! Perhaps I will dress as a boy, befriend Romeo, and then convince him to take back his true love, the lustrous Rosalind!

[VERA *laughs.*]

I'm serious!

**VERA**  You dress as a boy? That is for some other Rosalind. Get some rest, Roz.

[VERA *goes to open the large glass doors. As she does, we see* STEFANO *appear at ground level. Unbeknownst, he has been waiting, anxiously for these very doors to open. Excitedly, he hides just below the balcony.*]

The night air will calm you. Sunrise must be only a few hours away.

[*At this moment, in an effort to get their attention,* STEFANO *hoots like an owl.*]

**STEFANO**  Who!

**ROSALIND**  [*Walking out to the balcony.*] Vera, it cannot nearly be sunrise soon. The night-owl still sings.

[STEFANO *hoots again.*]

**STEFANO**  Who!

**ROSALIND**  I wonder what he's doing now.

**VERA**  Who?

**ROSALIND**  Romeo! [*She sighs.*] Oh, Romeo. Wherefore art thou such a stupid idiot?

**STEFANO**  Who?

**ROSALIND**  What do you mean 'who'? I just told you.

**VERA**  I didn't say anything.

**ROSALIND**  Um, yes, you did, I just heard you. I said "Romeo, Oh, Romeo, wherefore art thou such a moron," and you said, "Who?" just like that stupid night-owl.

[*A beat. She sees* STEFANO, *gasps, and rushes back into the room.*]

There's someone outside my window!

**VERA** [*Teasing.*] Who?

**ROSALIND** Oh, would you stop already! There's a man prowling outside my window! Just below the balcony. He was staring at me all wide-eyed. He must be insane! Of course! Romeo has sent an insane murderer to slay me while I sleep! Oh, I am undone!

**VERA** Stop. He cannot get to us in here.

**ROSALIND** Right. Because no one's ever *climbed* the balcony before!

[STEFANO, *confused at what has taken place, hoots again.*]

**STEFANO** Who!

**VERA** He calls.

**ROSALIND** Summoning some devil no doubt! Romeo seeks to destroy me with witchcraft.
[*She steps defiantly toward the window.*]
How now, spirit! Speak your purposes or else retreat to the depths from whence you came.

**STEFANO** [*Timidly.*] Please, m'lady, I mean no mal-intent.

**ROSALIND** What's that? I couldn't hear you over the growl of my two hungry Rottweilers. Who sent you?

**STEFANO** I come of my own accord, I swear!

**VERA** He sounds harmless.

**ROSALIND** No man is harmless around a woman. He's always poised to draw his weapon.

[VERA *sneaks forward onto the balcony to take a look.*]

**VERA** I recognize him. He was at the party!

**ROSALIND** Was he?

**VERA** What's your name, scoundrel?

**STEFANO** Stefano, your grace.

**ROSALIND** [*Aside.*] Stefano Capulet? Can that be right?

**VERA** State your purpose.

**STEFANO**    I have followed your graces from the masquerade, where I first laid eyes on such beauty.

**ROSALIND**    [*To* VERA.] Followed our graces? Chased our skirts is more likely.

**STEFANO**    Your companion was in such an upset state, that it didn't seem appropriate to approach you at the time. When I saw you run into the house, I thought for sure I had lost you, until the light from yonder window broke upon the dew-kissed grass, betraying your secret counsel, leading me to the fair maiden of the house!

**ROSALIND**    [*To* VERA.] A likely story! Romeo must have put him up to this.

**VERA**    Sir, as the light doth betray our counsel, so doth the wind betray your words, mis-delivering your compliments to the wrong ears. I am not the maiden of this house.

**STEFANO**    Not you, miss. Your friend. The lustrous Rosalind.

[*At this,* ROSALIND*'s ears perk up. She inches forward.*]

**ROSALIND**    Who was it, again, that did catch your eye?

**STEFANO**    Rosalind was her name. Or so I was told. But if it is not, then lend me some parchment that I may write it down and tear it to bits, so that the name never resounds on my lips again.

**ROSALIND**    No need for the parchment. My name is Rosalind.

**STEFANO**    Can it truly be that I am beholding such beauty in my presence? That on yonder balcony, becrouched and hidden, lies the true object of my eyes' fancy.

**VERA**    He's awful.

**ROSALIND**    Shh. Let him finish.

**STEFANO**    Oh, happy night that has brought me through forest, meadow, and a few really wet areas that I'm not too sure about to your window's edge.

[STEFANO *pauses for a beat, and then lets out a shout of joy.*]

**VERA**   What was that?

**ROSALIND**   Excitement, I think.

**VERA**   Or a war cry. We should probably step away from the window.

**ROSALIND**   Nonsense. He's harmless.

**VERA**   He could be signaling other Capulets! They're a very close pack, you know. I hear they tell one another everything.

**ROSALIND**   They tell one another everything?

[*There is a stirring by the stairs.* CORDONNA *has once again awakened and begun making her way up the stairs.*]

**CORDONNA**   [*A hoarse whisper from the stairwell.*] Rosalind!!

**VERA**   I hear some noise within!

**ROSALIND**   Anon, Nurse!
      [*To* STEFANO.]
      Stay there.

[CORDONNA *has appeared at the top of the stairs.*]

**CORDONNA**   Don't you "anon" me! Get your butt away from that window. I told you to button it so that decent people could get some sleep.

**ROSALIND**   Excuse me, but I have a visitor. Mother and Father allow me to have visitors whenever I please.

**CORDONNA**   It isn't that same pipsqueak that's been hooting outside all the windows, is it? I thought I told that pervert to get lost!

**ROSALIND**   You leave him alone. He's of the Capulet house, and I personally invited him over here.

**CORDONNA**   What are *you* doing with a Capulet?

**ROSALIND**   That is absolutely none of your business. Now go and let my friend in the house.

**VERA and CORDONNA**   What!?

**ROSALIND**   Go on.

**CORDONNA**  I'd rather throw you over that balcony. You tell me right now what you're up to.

[ROSALIND *stays silent.*]

Don't think I won't figure you out. I'll let you have your secret, but mark me, child, if that boy isn't gone by sunrise, I will roast the both of you.

[CORDONNA *exits down the stairs.*]

**VERA**  Rosalind, what are you up to?

**ROSALIND**  Shh! I have a plan.

[ROSALIND *steps out onto the balcony.*]

Stefano, you have been so bold in pursuing me; my audience is the least I can offer you. Therefore, I graciously invite you up to my chambers.

**STEFANO**  [*Still in hiding.*] I graciously accept your gracious invitation, your gracious . . . -ness.

**ROSALIND**  Why do you still hide yourself?

**STEFANO**  I'm afraid of your dogs.

**ROSALIND**  My dogs?

[*A beat.*]

Oh, yes! My Rottweilers! Don't worry, I have put them away, and I have sent my page to bring you up.

**STEFANO**  The woman who yelled at me before from her window?

**ROSALIND**  Yes, her. Why?

[STEFANO *considers for a moment.*]

**STEFANO**  Perhaps you could send your dogs instead?

[STEFANO *exits as* ROSALIND *steps back into her room.*]

**VERA**  Rosalind, you're making me nervous.

**ROSALIND**  If Romeo can have his fun, then so can Rosalind. And once he finds out that a Constantini has dumped him for a Capulet, he'll be sure to come crawling back to my arms.

**VERA**  But how will he find that out?

**ROSALIND**  Stefano *Capulet*. Juliet *Capulet*.
[VERA *puts it together.*]
A certain slip of the tongue should do the trick!

**VERA**  Somehow I feel like this isn't a good idea. If I were you, I would reconsider the whole thing.

**ROSALIND**  Well, you're not me, Vera.

**VERA**  Did you ever think that maybe Romeo is satisfied with his Juliet?

**ROSALIND**  She's not *his* Juliet! Romeo never knew what was best for him. He needs me, and I don't care what I have to do to get him to see that. But soft, the fish approaches his hook.

[STEFANO *appears at the door, followed by* CORDONNA. *Awestruck at the room, he carefully crosses the threshold with noticeably controlled excitement. He surveys the entire room as the three women look on. Finally, he stops, takes in* ROSALIND *and exclaims.*]

**STEFANO**  It's so clean!

[*A beat.*]

**ROSALIND**  I beg your pardon.

**STEFANO**  This place looked so beautiful from the outside, but who'd have imagined...
[*Off the women's stare.*]
I've never been in a lady's chamber before. I mean, except for my mum's. But she makes me stand at the door and do my alphabet and my numbers before I she allows me to enter. I mean—she *made* me, when I was in my youth. Now I just have to do my numbers.

**ROSALIND**  Your numbers?

**STEFANO**  Of course. Three times two is six. Three times three is nine. Three times four is twelve. Three times five is fifteen.

**ROSALIND**  Right! Your numbers!

**STEFANO**    No, wait, I'm not done. Three times six is eighteen. Three times seven is twenty-one. Three times eight is...um...three times eight...

[*He stops to count.*]

**ROSALIND**    [*Trying to help.*] Tweeeeentyyy...

**STEFANO**    Twenty...

**ROSALIND**    Ffffff—...

**STEFANO**    Ffffffiiii—

**ROSALIND**    Ooooohhh—...

**STEFANO**    Ffffooooooohhh—

**ROSALIND**    Rrrrrr.

**STEFANO**    Twenty-four!

**ROSALIND**    Whew! Almost didn't make it in!

**STEFANO**    [*Sheepishly.*] The eights always trip me up.

**CORDONNA**    So we see.

**STEFANO**    [*Seeing* ROSALIND*'s costume.*] Are you a princess!?

[*A beat.*]

**ROSALIND**    Yes. Yes, I am.

**STEFANO**    A real live princess! I can't believe it! I am most honored to stand in your royal presence.

[CORDONNA *bursts out laughing.*]

**ROSALIND**    Ahem! You are excused, madam.

**CORDONNA**    And thank God for that. Good luck...your highness.

[CORDONNA *exits.*]

**STEFANO**    She's not very pleasant. She mumbled to herself all the way up the stairs. And it was dark and she did not offer any candlelight. People are so unwilling to help these days.
    [*He notices* VERA.]

Hello.

**ROSALIND**  Oh, my! Where are my manners? Stefano, you must meet my dearest friend, Vera—*Lady* Vera!

**VERA**  Delighted.

**STEFANO**  My dearest lady, to be the best friend of her highness is to be the air that surrounds the earth, the stars that bejewel the moon, and the rays that enrobe the glorious sun. She is made all the more wondrous and beautiful by your mere presence.

**VERA**  Why, thank you, sir. Your words do become me very prettily.

**ROSALIND**  Yes, yes, well enough about you, Vera. Sit, Stefano. I simply must know more about you.

[ROSALIND *motions for* STEFANO *to sit next to her on the bed.*]

**STEFANO**  Oh, no. I couldn't possibly share a bed with a princess.

**ROSALIND**  The night is young!

**STEFANO**  It is truly a gift to be sitting next to such radiance.

**ROSALIND**  It is truly a gift to have been tracked down so boldly. One wonders what encounter led you to believe so strongly in my beauty.

**VERA**  Do tell us the story.

**STEFANO**  As I am but a fool in your highness's presence, it is only fitting that I shall entertain your grace with the tale of how, with gentle wickedness, you stole my fancy.

The peak hour of the festival had long passed. The whole night was filled with disappointment, right down to the embarrassing fact that no one had informed me it was a costume party. I sat down to rest my throbbing feet when—Lo! Across the room from me: a maiden, also at rest. Her hair was as strong as its mahogany color, but soft as its gentle glow. Her eyes, fierce and adventurous, her lips, tender and full, her bosom . . . oh, her bosom. She had beauty fit to drown Helen and turn Narcissus away from his reflection. But beyond all that strength, beyond all that fire and adventure, there was sadness. Very small, very brief, but I saw it in the heaviness of her breath; and all my disappointment, all the night's boredom and embarrassment felt so inconsequential in the face of such pure...sadness. My heart broke. And as I wiped the tears away from my eyes, I turned and saw she had gone. So I ran out and followed whichever carriage I guessed to be hers, never knowing that I would soon be sitting in royal chambers, on a royal bed, next to royal blood.

[*There is a silence as both* ROSALIND *and* VERA *take in his story.*]

**VERA**   That was very beautiful, Stefano.

**ROSALIND**   Yes. I hope you don't think that I'm depressed or anything! How unattractive. Surely, you caught me in some ponderous moment, wherein I remembered some tragic detail of my vast responsibilities as a princess.

**STEFANO**   I could only think that I wanted to relight your glorious fire.

**ROSALIND**   Well! The night is young.

**VERA**   You have such an interesting way with words.

**STEFANO**   I'm a poet.

**ROSALIND**   Of course you are.

**STEFANO**   At least, I want to be. I'm not very good, I know.

**VERA**   Nonsense. Everyone must start somewhere.

**ROSALIND**   And if your first poem isn't good enough, you toss it out and write a new one.

**VERA**   Or perhaps you should work with the old one and try and help it to become better.

**ROSALIND**   Certain poems just don't belong in the world, however.

**VERA**   Yes, but certain poets will never end up writing anything at all if they don't give one poem a chance.

**ROSALIND**   Certain poets give every poem a chance! Not every poem lives up to expectations.

**VERA**   Well, perhaps certain poets should change their expectations!

**STEFANO**   Wow, you ladies must really like poetry.

**ROSALIND**   It's sort of a thing with royalty.

**VERA**   You know what I think, my dear Stefano?

**STEFANO**   What?

**VERA**   I think that you just need to find your muse. Once a poet finds his muse, he can write anything he wants.

**ROSALIND**   Of course! Your muse!

**STEFANO**   I don't understand.

**VERA**   Your muse is someone to whom you turn for inspiration.

**ROSALIND**   Perhaps it is someone who you admire.

**VERA**   Or someone who admires you.

**ROSALIND**   Someone who possesses great beauty.

**VERA**   Who is honest.

**ROSALIND**   Who has great depth of emotion.

**VERA**   Someone trustworthy.

**ROSALIND**   Someone who raises your pulse with her voluminous bosom.

**STEFANO**   But who is that person? Who do I know who possesses great beauty and who is honest, yet holds back floods of emotion with her voluminous bosom?

[*He stops to think for a long beat.*]

**ROSALIND**   [*Finally, as though shocked that he would consider her.*] Me!?

**VERA**   You?

**STEFANO**   You?

**ROSALIND**   Me! Oh, I couldn't possibly accept. I mean, I'm honored, really, but a muse! Gee! A princess has her own responsibilities, I just don't know...I mean...I guess I'm free *Tuesdays*...

**STEFANO**   Is it possible that the fates have turned in my favor? That I have found my muse and my love in one night?

**VERA**   Well...

**ROSALIND**   Of course it's possible!

**STEFANO**   Then so be it! Lady Rosalind, if you will so have me as your humble tool, then, inspired by your radiant beauty, I shall write the best sonnets, songs, and odes in all of fair Verona.

**ROSALIND**   Oh, Stefano, of course you can be my tool.

**VERA**   Surely, one cannot simply step into muse-dom as easily as that. It's much like being canonized if I remember correctly.

**ROSALIND**   How's that, Vera?

**VERA**   Well, in order for a person to become a saint, they must perform some sort of miraculous act.

**ROSALIND**   When did you become such an expert on saints?

**VERA**   Some of us *pray* when we're on our knees. I do believe, my dear Stefano, that a poem must be inspired first.

**STEFANO**   Of course. I have reacted much too quickly. How can I assume that you will suffice as my muse until you've actually inspired me? I am a fool! Do forgive me, your highness, for trespassing so unkindly on your night.

[STEFANO *begins to leave.*]

**ROSALIND**   Wait! Why do you give up so easily? If Vera speaks the truth, that I must first inspire a poem, then give me a chance! Did Odysseus arrive at Ithaca in one night? Did Dante pass through heaven and hell in an hour? Clearly I have more faith in myself than you do.

**VERA**   Clearly.

**ROSALIND**   A poem! I will inspire you to write a poem right now.

**STEFANO**   Now?

**ROSALIND**   I don't see why not.

**VERA**   Inspiration cannot be forced, Roz.

**ROSALIND**   It can when you're a muse, *Ver*!

**VERA**   I don't think you should.

**ROSALIND**   Vera, may I talk to you in private for a moment? It will only take a moment, Stefano, I promise.
>   [*The two huddle together away from* STEFANO.]
>   What are you doing?

**VERA**   Did you listen to his story, Roz? This boy likes you a lot! He is very sensitive and very fragile.

**ROSALIND**   I know. It's almost too perfect! He'll write a poem about me and then I'll get him to read it aloud to Romeo and Juliet. It's bound to get Romeo's blood boiling!

**VERA**   Rosalind, you're not listening! He doesn't deserve this.

**ROSALIND**   And I didn't deserve what Romeo did to me! We don't always get what we want, Vera. Now play along or leave!

[*Before* VERA *can speak,* ROSALIND *turns back to* STEFANO, *who has been attempting to write his first lines.*]

**STEFANO**   I think I have something.

**ROSALIND**   Already! There must be a record for how quickly a muse has inspired her subject's thoughts.

**VERA**   I do believe Rosalind holds many records for speed.

**ROSALIND**   Let's hear it!

**STEFANO**   It's a sonnet.
>   [*He clears his throat.*]
>   Tell me, Love, by what name art thou known?
>   Art thou called Aurora by the dawn?
>   For blinding bright your beauty now is shown.
>   A camel and a squid will never spawn.
>   [*He looks up at them.*]
>   I'm still working on that line.

[*Back to the poem.*]
By midday you are called Eurus's child,
Who blows about me warmly as the breeze,
And shields me from getting much too mild...
[*A beat.*]
What rhymes with "breeze"?

**ROSALIND**   Oh. Um... trees.

**VERA**   Stees.

**ROSALIND**   Bees. Freeze.

**VERA**   Prees.

**ROSALIND**   Squeeze.

**VERA**   Crees. Drees.

**ROSALIND**   [*To* VERA.] Crees? Drees? Those aren't words.

**VERA**   Sorry.

**STEFANO**   I've got it!
Who blows about me warmly as the breeze,
And shields me from getting much too mild,
By feeding me a large amount of cheese.

**ROSALIND**   We'll iron that one out in the rewrites. Let's keep plowing ahead. How about:
At night have you some other Roman name?
Are you known as Luna or Selini?
[*She thinks.*]
Are you known as Luna or Selini...

[*They all think a moment. Finally,* STEFANO *turns to* ROSALIND.]

**STEFANO**   My muse! Of course!
At night have you some other Roman name?
Are you known as Luna or Selini?
In faith, I shall put all of them to shame,
And call thee the beautiful Ros'lind Constantini.

[ROSALIND *is slightly taken back, but does her best not to show it.*]

**ROSALIND**   We are but two lines away, and I have just the pairing.
And still the name above means nothing yet.
Till coupled with Stef'no Capulet.

**STEFANO**   Well done, my grace!

**ROSALIND**   I have inspired a true work of art! And our names are so
entwined in the writing they will be but married in the ear of
anyone who beholds them! You must be very proud.

**STEFANO**   Yes!

**ROSALIND**   You must read this to everyone you know. Your father, your
mother, brothers, sisters, cousins…yes, especially your cousins.

**STEFANO**   Indeed, I shall. Who is Stefano Capulet?

[ROSALIND *stops cold.*]

**ROSALIND**   I beg your pardon?

**STEFANO**   The fellow in the poem I just wrote, who has the same first
name as I, but not the same last name…who is he?

**ROSALIND**   Why don't be silly! It's *your* name.

**STEFANO**   Oh! It's *my* name! I get it.

**ROSALIND**   Yes!

**STEFANO**   It's like a pen name.

**ROSALIND**   Let me get this straight. Your name is—

**STEFANO**   Stefano.

**ROSALIND**   But not Stefano *Capulet*?

**STEFANO**   That's correct.

**VERA**   What *is* your full name?

**STEFANO**   Of course. It's Stefano Giovanni Francesco Putori.

**ROSALIND**   Putori. Stefano Putori.

**STEFANO**   That's right.

**ROSALIND**  So you're not cousins with Juliet Capulet.

**STEFANO**  Uh-uh.

**ROSALIND**  You're not even *related* to the Capulets, are you?

**STEFANO**  Uh-uh. Who are they?

**VERA**  The party. Tonight. It was the Capulets' party. How did you get in?

**ROSALIND**  You weren't even wearing a costume!

**STEFANO**  Well, my father was given an open invitation. He's a mason. He must have done business with them.

**ROSALIND**  Oh, my. I'm afraid I've made a terrible mistake. I thought... You aren't...

**STEFANO**  I hope I didn't lead you astray at all, my grace. It would shame me greatly to know that I have done wrong by you.

**ROSALIND**  Yes, well, perhaps you should have thought of that before you chose not to reveal your whole identity to me. This changes everything.

[STEFANO *is obviously crushed.*]

**STEFANO**  Please...I beg your forgiveness...I...please...

**VERA**  [*Gently.*] Stefano, would you be so kind as to bring us some tea? The fire should still be on.
[*Helplessly,* STEFANO *exits.*]
You ought to be ashamed of yourself.

**ROSALIND**  Me!? You were the one who said he was a Capulet in the first place.

**VERA**  I never said that. I said I recognized him from the party, but like always you invented something else in your head. You built him up to be something he wasn't, and when you finally realized that he's not, you dumped him just like everyone else.

**ROSALIND**  How dare you accuse me of such shallowness? How was I to know who he was?

**VERA**   You never stopped to think about him in the first place! If you had listened to me before—

**ROSALIND**   Me, me, me! That's all you care about. What good has listening to you ever done?

**VERA**   Perhaps you should try and find out.

**ROSALIND**   You're supposed to support me.

**VERA**   You can't treat people like this, Rosalind. It isn't right. People aren't puppets that you can use at your disposal. I say this as your friend.

**ROSALIND**   What would you know about friendship? You have been against me all night. You think I'm out to break every heart I can. If I had *known* that Stefano was some stupid country bumpkin from a trashy family, if I had *known* he couldn't help me get Romeo back, I never would have invited him up here in the first place!

**VERA**   Just because you wear a stupid princess costume, you think you can boss everyone around, don't you! I ought to tear it to shreds!

[VERA *goes after* ROSALIND's *dress.* ROSALIND *turns to run away and the two stop abruptly to see* STEFANO *standing at the door silently. He has heard enough.*]

**STEFANO**   [*Quietly.*] It's a costume?

**ROSALIND**   . . . the party. . .

[ROSALIND *looks as though she about to say more.*]

**STEFANO**   No, no. I can see myself out. There is no need for wasted words. You gave me something so wonderful, I should have known that it did not belong to me.

[*He is about to turn to go, but stops to take one last look at the room.*]

This place really looked so beautiful from the outside.

[STEFANO *exits.* ROSALIND *and* VERA *are left looking at each other. There is a moment of silence. Then.*]

**ROSALIND**   This is all your fault!

**VERA**  My fault!?

**ROSALIND**  You had to go and open your stupid mouth! You are such an ignorant pig!

**VERA**  You're just upset that for the second time tonight someone has left you because they found out what kind of a monster you really are!

[*At this* ROSALIND *winds up and slaps* VERA *directly across the face. After a moment of shock for the both of them,* VERA *turns slowly towards* ROSALIND.]

All these years I pitied the wrong people.

[VERA *quietly grabs her things and walks to the door.*]

No man to bore you, no friend to get in the way: Rosalind Constantini finally has what she wants. She's alone.

[VERA *exits.* ROSALIND *is indignant at first. She takes her tiara from her head and snaps it. She turns quickly and throws it at the door. She takes* STEFANO's *poem and starts tearing it to shreds. As she does, she is suddenly overcome with tears and collapses on the ground, weeping. A few moments later,* CORDONNA *appears at the door.*]

**CORDONNA**  It's going to be all right.

[ROSALIND *turns, surprised. She tries to hide her tears.*]

**ROSALIND**  I'm fine. Please leave.

[CORDONNA *ignores her and walks closer.*]

**CORDONNA**  You sit atop mountains and every now and then you're bound to fall down a little.

**ROSALIND**  I said, I don't need your...

[*She cries.*]

**CORDONNA**  Fine, fine. I'll go.

**ROSALIND**  No. Wait! I'm sorry! Oh, God, I'm so sorry!

[CORDONNA *rushes to hold* ROSALIND.]

**CORDONNA**  Hush, child. It's not that bad. You're going to be all right.

**ROSALIND**   He was right. I'm so hideous inside. All I ever wanted was what I couldn't have. And now all I want is something I don't deserve.

**CORDONNA**   Now, now, there's only one thing anyone your age truly deserves and that's a second chance. What you decide to do with it is what makes you worthy of anything else.

**ROSALIND**   But Vera is right. I'm alone.

**CORDONNA**   As long as Rosalind Constantini keeps waking up her battered nurse in the middle of the night, she'll never be alone.

[ROSALIND *laughs.* CORDONNA *smiles and then picks up a piece of the torn poem from the floor.*]

What's this? Look, here is writ "the beautiful Ros'lind Constantini."

**ROSALIND**   Such a name I do not deserve.

**CORDONNA**   And yet someone believed that you did.

**ROSALIND**   A poor, naive boy who knew nothing of who I am.

[ROSALIND *considers this.*]

He knew nothing about me, and even so he wrote such pretty poetry. Oh, hateful hands, to tear such loving words! Injurious wasps, to feed on such sweet honey, and kill the bees that yield it with your stings! How can I mend this, Cordonna?

**CORDONNA**   I think we have some paste in the cupboard.

**ROSALIND**   I had something beautiful and I tore it up. I will never learn.

**VERA**   You will if you just try.

[ROSALIND *and* CORDONNA *turn to find* VERA *standing in the doorway.*]

**ROSALIND**   You've come back!

**VERA**   Yes, I've come back.

**ROSALIND**   I can't imagine why you would.

**VERA**   [*A beat.*] Neither can I.

**ROSALIND**   You were right to leave. I'm sorry. I was . . . I was wrong. I don't know why I keep making the same mistakes.

**VERA**   It happens. A lot. To you.

**ROSALIND**   I know.

**VERA**   But I stood by you, Roz.

**ROSALIND**   I know.

**VERA**   Every single time.

**ROSALIND**   I know, I know!

**VERA**   For years I envied you. You were beautiful, you were popular, you had anything you asked for, and I hated you for it. But tonight I realized—you aren't perfect at all. You're just Rosalind. And that's what makes me your friend.

**ROSALIND**   Truly?

**VERA**   Truly. But I am not going to watch you hurt those boys any longer. Or yourself!

**ROSALIND**   I suppose I don't know my own strength.

**VERA**   Perhaps you might keep an eye on your weaknesses, too.

**ROSALIND**   I will try, Vera. I promise.
   [*The girls hug.*]
   I hope you'll forgive me.

**VERA**   I came back, didn't I? That seems a good enough start to me.

**ROSALIND**   Me too. But quickly, now, we must grab our things.

**VERA**   Why? Where are we going?

**ROSALIND**   I have to get him back!

**VERA**   Wait, Rosalind, no! What are you doing? You have to stop! You have to LET ROMEO GO!

**ROSALIND**   Romeo? No, silly! Stefano Putori! A poet needs his muse.

[VERA *smiles at her.*]

**VERA**  And Rosalind needs her poet.

**ROSALIND**  Come on! The night is young!

**VERA**  You go. I will hear about it when you return. I've had enough excitement for a while.

**ROSALIND**  Are you sure?

**VERA**  Completely.

[ROSALIND *smiles and runs out of the room.* CORDONNA *follows her to the door and turns to* VERA.]

**CORDONNA**  You are a good friend.

**VERA**  And you, a good nurse.

**CORDONNA**  Perhaps between the two of us she'll become some sort of decent person.

**VERA**  [*She laughs.*] The night is young!

[VERA *follows* CORDONNA *to the door, stopping to blow out the few candles as they exit. The stage goes dark as . . .*]

[*The curtain falls.*]

• • •

## cast of characters

**TORRENCE WEÏRD**, the eldest sister
**HARPER WEÏRD**, the youngest, fearful sister
**LINN WEÏRD**, the middle sister, who is nothing like the other two
**DOUGLAS**, a genuine, benign traveler

## time

The early 1600s

## place

The cottage of the three Weïrd sisters. A wood in Denmark.

*Note: It is the playwright's intention that this play not be done with any dialect. Though the actors must weave naturally in and out of heightened language, the characters should at all times maintain a modern sensibility.

**Note: This play can be done in rep with *A Roz by Any Other Name*. If so, the doubling is as follows:

**TORRENCE/CORDONNA**
**HARPER/ROSALIND**
**LINN/VERA**
**DOUGLAS/STEFANO**

• • •

[*The curtain rises in darkness. There is a sudden crash of lightning and thunder, which reveals a figure alone on stage, her back to us. She is crouched around a cauldron located upstage right, pouring potions in and mixing the brew. A great gust of wind fills the stage and we hear a deep, other-worldly voice speaking indecipherably. Above the din of wind and voice, HARPER WEÏRD cries.*]

**HARPER**    How now! Spirit cry and spirit sing!
        Tell me of the gruesome news you bring.

[*The wind rises as an unworldly voice declares.*]

**VOICE** [*Somewhat muffled.*] With the wind that blows in from the east
Comes to ye a dark and dangerous beast.

**HARPER** Spirit that doth neither die nor live,
Please repeat this warning that you give.

[*Again, the wind rises.*]

**VOICE** [*Clearer now.*] With the wind that blows in from the east
Comes to ye a dark and dangerous beast.

**HARPER** Won't you tell me how or tell me when ... ?

[*Lightning and thunder crash, leaving the stage in silence and darkness for a moment. Suddenly, all the candles light themselves in rapid succession. At this moment,* HARPER *quickly turns out.*]

I don't think I'll use that recipe again!

[*The lights reveal stairs leading upstage to a platform in front of a door, and then continuing up to an upstairs platform that ends offstage right. At the top of the first landing is a large window, which shows a menacing night sky. Below the upstairs platform is a counter connected to a small row of shelves upon which sit various bottles of different-colored elixirs. In front of these shelves is a small fire-pit, upon which sits the large black cauldron. There is a big knock on the door.* HARPER *jumps.*]

Who's there?

[*Another knock.*]

[*Aside.*]

Ay me! A knock at the door with such foreboding as though death himself were desperately seeking shelter from the approaching storm.

**TORRENCE** [*From behind the door.*] Open the door!

**HARPER** [*Aside.*] It speaks! Dare I submit to its commands? My scar doth burn with fear. If only my sister Torrence were here to advise me. I am not one to make such decisions. I must wait.

**TORRENCE** [*Pounding on the door.*] Hurry! Hurry! Open the door! Now!

**HARPER** [*She lets out a small shriek.*] How can I wait when it bids me "Hurry! Hurry!"? I must do something, and yet I know not what to do! Which sin is greater? Action or inaction? Perhaps if I stay quiet—

**TORRENCE**   Harper, you dim beast, I can hear you talking to yourself! 'Tis me, Torrence! Open the door!

**HARPER**   True, the voice doth sound familiar. Do I dare trust...

[TORRENCE *pounds furiously on the door.*]

[*She shrieks.*] Okay, okay! Anon!

[HARPER *opens the door and* TORRENCE WEÏRD *rushes in and shuts the door behind her, making sure that it is properly locked.*]

**TORRENCE**   Quickly, pack your things. We must make haste.

**HARPER**   Make haste?

**TORRENCE**   There is something rotten in the state of Denmark.

**HARPER**   I don't understand.

**TORRENCE**   The signs! They are warning us, Harper. We must take leave at once!

**HARPER**   What signs? What are you saying, Sister?

**TORRENCE**   We have run for so long from our treacherous past, and now it has finally caught up with us. What unspeakable horror is coming our way, I know not, but I can only guess that it will bring with it certain doom.

**HARPER**   Oh no! Pray tell, what you have seen?

**TORRENCE**   'Tis like a fresh nightmare, so vividly does it play still in my mind's eye. In the wood, on my way home from the town, I was thrice passed by a black cat.

**HARPER**   Thrice?

**TORRENCE**   You know as well as I that if she passes once, 'tis good luck.

**HARPER**   Aye.

**TORRENCE**   If twice, 'tis good health.

**HARPER**   Aye.

**TORRENCE**   But thrice! 'Tis . . . good God!

**HARPER**   Ay-yi-yi!

**TORRENCE**   At first, I thought nothing of it. Though very odd, 'tis not impossible that a cat should pass my way three times. But then— horror of horrors!

**HARPER**   What!

**TORRENCE**   A bird!

**HARPER**   A bird?

**TORRENCE**   Vomited upon me!

**HARPER**   No!

**TORRENCE**   Yes!

**HARPER**   Well, that explains it!

**TORRENCE**   Explains what?

**HARPER**   The smell coming from your cloak. Let me take it.

[HARPER *takes the cloak and sets it on the back counter by the cauldron.*]

**TORRENCE**   Harper! It's a sign! The natural world is warning us that something is coming, and that this something is going to . . . you know . . .

**HARPER**   Vomit upon us?

**TORRENCE**   Kill us! I know I have oft let worry carry me down the senseless rapids of my fearful imagination, but this time I am most certain that the current hath quickened and the waterfall approacheth! I mean, I would have thought nothing of it if it were not for the third sign.

**HARPER**   The third sign?

**TORRENCE**   Aye. It began to grow dark as storm clouds blew in from the east. I was not too far from our cottage, contemplating the meaning of the previous two events, when I saw a figure, alone in the wood. It was a dark, foreboding figure, moving slowly through the trees. I tried to make it out, but the dimming daylight obscured its true identity.

**HARPER**   Was it a beast?

**TORRENCE**   Perhaps, but it was like no beast I'd ever seen.

**HARPER**   Oh no! Torrence, the soup! It too gave me a sign.

**TORRENCE**   The soup gave you a sign?

**HARPER**   Yes. You see, I was making soup for our dinner, and, well, at first I thought it was the spices that I used because they were a few weeks old, but I didn't think it would make too much of a difference, so I put them in anyway, and just as I did . . . the soup! It started talking to me.

**TORRENCE**   It talked to you?

**HARPER**   Yes! It foretold the coming of a dark and dangerous beast with the blowing of the wind from the east.

**TORRENCE**   The wind from the east?

**HARPER**   The storm!

**TORRENCE**   And the figure!

**HARPER**   The scar on my face began to burn, as it often does when something dangerous is about to occur, but immediately after it happened you knocked on the door, and I didn't have a moment to think of it until just now!

**TORRENCE**   You are certain it wasn't just your eczema?

**HARPER**   Yes! Your fears prove true! Something is after us!

**TORRENCE**   But what?

**HARPER**   But who?

**TORRENCE**   We dare not stop to think about what it might be.

**HARPER**   How could it have found us? No one knows that we have been hiding in this place.

**TORRENCE**   Only you.

**HARPER**  And you.

**TORRENCE and HARPER**  And...

[*Thunder crashes and the candles all flicker. When they come back to normal,* LINN WEÏRD *appears at the top of the first landing, peering out the window.*]

**LINN**  A storm approaches.

**TORRENCE and HARPER**  Linn!

**LINN**  You two look affright, like conspirators caught whilst plotting murder. Doth the weather suddenly make you nervous?

**TORRENCE**  Linn, what are you about?

**LINN**  I am going to go outside to tend to my garden before the storm becomes too rough. I have newly planted herbs that will uproot in these strong winds lest I bolster them.

**HARPER**  You mustn't go outside! 'Tis dangerous!

**LINN**  I appreciate your concern, child, but the storm has barely just touched ground. There is no need to worry.

[LINN *goes to get* TORRENCE's *cloak to wear it outside.*]

**TORRENCE**  You misunderstand her, Linn. There is more danger out there than that storm. Your sister and I have both been warned by the signs.

**LINN**  [*Putting on the cloak.*] Torrence, your cloak has a funny odor.

**HARPER**  Linn! You are not listening! A bird vomited on Torrence!

**LINN**  [*Taking off the cloak.*] That explains the odor.

[LINN *goes to walk upstairs to get her own cloak.*]

**TORRENCE**  You must pack your things at once. We are leaving tonight.

**LINN**  [*Making her way back up the stairs.*] You and your silly fears. Might I suggest, dear sisters, that you take up some other hobby than wallowing in worrisome nonsense?

**HARPER**  It is not nonsense, Linn! And I *do* have a hobby! I cook.

**LINN**   Aye, just our luck.

**TORRENCE**   Pack your things, Linn. I am not in a good humor.

**LINN**   I am going outside.

**TORRENCE**   Linn, you'll do no such thing.

**LINN**   I refuse to go anywhere until I see my garden will stay planted.

**TORRENCE**   You'll do nothing till you see the same of this family. What care you for cheap seedlings when our lives could be blown away with the right gust of wind?

**LINN**   How quickly the reaper doth forget what she herself hath sown! Oft uprooted plants will nary withstand the familiar elements. I am not the one tearing this family apart, Torrence. We barely settle somewhere before you decide it's no longer safe and we must run away to some other distant land. How far have we come from Scotland and yet still we cannot escape our past?

**HARPER**   My face doth burn! I am afraid!

**LINN**   Oh, you and your stupid eczema! Always prompting and promoting her fears. I cannot stand your constant superstition. "The signs! The signs! My face doth burn!" Did it ever occur to you that you are seeing only what your fearful hearts wish to see?

**TORRENCE**   You know very well that I am only doing what I feel is best for this family.

**LINN**   Aye, I do know. But look at you—we have finally found a place where we have felt safe. You are comfortable with our distance from the town, Harper is able to catch small beasts for our dinner, and I have been able to plant a garden. Let us wait until sunrise, where dawn's light will better illuminate this situation.

[*The soup bubbles as though disturbed.*]

**HARPER**   The soup!

**TORRENCE**   Linn, I apologize for this lifestyle but there is nothing I can do. You will pack your things at once. We are leaving.

**LINN**   Not before I tend to my garden.

**TORRENCE**   Yes, before.

**LINN**   This is ridiculous! All I want is a home that I don't have to run away from! I can't stand living on the run.

**HARPER**   Well, that is the life of a witch, Linn, and you are a witch!

**LINN**   No, it is *your* fault that I am running in the first place!

**HARPER**   My fault!?

**LINN**   Everything was perfectly fine until that night that we ran into Macbeth.

**TORRENCE**   Linn!

       [HARPER *and* TORRENCE *turn in a circle, then spit.*]

       Don't say that name.

**HARPER**   As I recall, you were just as much a part of it as I was.

**LINN**   I was just joking around.

**HARPER**   We were all just joking around, *pretending* to have predicted that he was to become the thane of Cawdor, when really we had just overheard it in the woods. Don't blame me.

**LINN**   Excuse me, but that's not all there was to it.

**TORRENCE**   You two, this is no time for arguing.

**LINN**   All I'm saying is that for the past two years I've been running from a mistake that *she* made!

**HARPER**   That is a lie!

**TORRENCE**   All right, Linn, blame us for all your problems. Can we please drop this now?

**HARPER**   You just can't accept that you're no different from Torrence or me. You were pretending, too, Linn! [*Mocking* LINN.] "All hail Macbeth, thane of Glamis; all hail Macbeth, thane of Cawdor." La la la la la.

**LINN**   But then you turned into Lady Mac-I-Can't-Keep-My-Mouth-Shut and decided to put in your two cents.

**TORRENCE**  Why do you always do this?

**LINN**  "All hail Macbeth, that shall be king hereafter!"

**HARPER**  It was a *joke*!

**LINN**  Yes, a joke that brought about the death of nearly two kingdoms. All that wickedness spurred on by the fear of what Macbeth might do if he found out you had lied. You two are the witches.

**TORRENCE**  Linn!

**LINN**  I will never, ever be as wicked as the two of you!

**TORRENCE**  Do not speak to your sisters that way!

**LINN**  I am exhausted by your telling me what to do! It has solved nothing.

**TORRENCE**  There is nothing I can do!

**LINN**  You could stop making us run.

**HARPER**  Then we'd be found out!

**LINN**  So be it!

**TORRENCE**  Linn!

**LINN**  I would turn us all in in a heartbeat if it meant we would at least get to stay in one place long enough to taste the damn soup!

[*In a fit of anger,* LINN *throws two bottles of potion from the back shelf into the soup, causing it to bubble and steam.*]

**HARPER**  No! You lame preacher's wife! You have ruined my soup!

**LINN**  O, stop crying, it is still fine.

[*She is about to taste it.*]

**HARPER**  No, don't! Those potions have turned it to poison!

**LINN**  Well, it isn't as though we were going to eat it anyway.

**TORRENCE**  Look what your anger has done now, Linn.

**HARPER**  You always ruin things, you ruiner!

**LINN**  Well, the two of you are always teaming up against me!

**HARPER**   We would be happy if it weren't for you! I wish you had never been born!

[HARPER *casts her hands toward the cauldron and the flames from underneath burst up around the pot.*]

**LINN**   I hate you! And I would give anything to see you burn, you *witches*!

[*A loud, ominous knock at the door leaves the room in a cold silence.*]

**HARPER**   A knock! There was a knock!

**LINN**   Yes, Harper, we know.

**HARPER**   But who knows we're out here?

**TORRENCE**   'Tis probably just the wind.

> [*Two more knocks.*]

> A very, very strong wind.

**LINN**   [*Moving toward the door.*] Well, someone should answer it.

**TORRENCE**   No! Don't! They may not know we're here. We have to hide.

**LINN**   Hide?

**HARPER**   Should I blow out the candles?

**TORRENCE**   Yes.

[HARPER *runs up to the first landing and is about to blow out the candles.*]

**LINN**   Hide from what?

**TORRENCE**   No! Wait, leave them lit.

**HARPER**   Are you sure?

[*Thunder and lightning crash.* HARPER *is standing directly in front of the window.*]

**TORRENCE**   Harper! The window!

[HARPER *hits the floor.*]

**TORRENCE**   Make your way upstairs. We have to start packing.

**HARPER**   [*As she slinks up to the next landing.*] My face doth burn! Something terrible approaches!

**LINN**   Will someone please tell me what is going on here?

**TORRENCE**   Yes, Linn, we are getting our stuff and leaving. Now come!

[*She walks up to the first landing just as there are more knocks.* TORRENCE *freezes directly in front of the window and turns to the door.*]

**HARPER**   Torrence! The window!

[TORRENCE *hits the floor.*]

**LINN**   This is absolutely ludicrous! I am done putting up with this ridiculousness.

[LINN *begins to unlatch the lock.*]

**HARPER**   No! Don't! Now the beast knows that someone is in here!

**LINN**   What beast talk you of?

**HARPER**   The soup! It foretold the coming of a beast!

**LINN**   Oh, right, of course. The soup told you.

**TORRENCE**   Maybe if she answers the door, she can buy us time to pack.

**HARPER**   But what if it wants to get us?

**LINN**   It is not going to get you.

**HARPER**   Right! It'll get you first! Good point!

**TORRENCE**   We'll pack you a bag as well. Then we'll all three leave as a family.

**HARPER**   Wait! Torrence, your cloak!

**TORRENCE**   What about it?

**HARPER**   You left it down by the cauldron. What if someone smells the bird vomit? They'll think someone else is here.

**LINN**   Or they'll think I smell like bird vomit.

**TORRENCE**   I think I can maybe reach it.

[*She tries to reach it from the top ledge, but it is not close enough.*]

**HARPER**   I'll go get it.

[*She gets up to walk back downstairs.*]

**TORRENCE**  [*Following* HARPER.] No, no, I'll get it.

[*More knocks on the door stop them cold. Thunder and lightning crash. The two back up against the window.*]

**LINN**  The window!
[TORRENCE *and* HARPER *hit the floor, much to* LINN's *amusement.*]
[LINN *Grabs the cloak and walks it over to them.*]
Here. Now get thee to the bedroom.

**TORRENCE**  Please be careful, Linn.

**HARPER**  Tell them you're alone.

**LINN**  I'd be lying if I said any differently.

**TORRENCE**  We will be ready to leave together in no time. I promise.

[TORRENCE *and* HARPER *exit.* LINN *walks to the door. She reaches for the handle and stops. She steadies herself, takes a breath.*]

**LINN**  Who is there?

**DOUGLAS**  [*From behind the door.*] Please let me in!

**LINN**  [*Aside.*] A man's voice! Of all the creatures in the universe I'd never have expected a man. [*To the door.*] On what business do you come?

**DOUGLAS**  No business, ma'am. Just looking for shelter from the storm. The clouds have burst!

[LINN *reluctantly opens the door to reveal* DOUGLAS. *He rushes in, bundled up and wet.*]

**DOUGLAS**  Thank you, madam. It is wet in the state of Denmark and I am cold at heart.

**LINN**  I see 'tis wet.

**DOUGLAS**  I did not mean to startle you, miss, but like a masterful thief this storm has crept up upon me, robbing me of dry passage. The pathway to your house was too narrow for my horse, so I am afraid some mud has followed me in. May I sit?

[*He does not wait for a reply.*]

**LINN**   Is there something I can help you with?

**DOUGLAS**   Yes! My cloak. Here. [*He removes it.*] It doth hang heavily with the deadweight of rain water.

[*She takes it over by the cauldron.*]

Have you nothing to eat? Some soup perhaps?

**LINN**   Well, yes, I have soup, but I . . . oh, no . . . Actually you can't have any of the soup.

**DOUGLAS**   But it smells so enticing, and I am starving.

**LINN**   You don't understand, it's actually been . . . well, it isn't ready just yet. Perhaps you'd like some ale to warm your spirit?

**DOUGLAS**   And some bread, too? If you have it. I am completely empty.

**LINN**   I'm sure we could manage some bread.

**DOUGLAS**   Thank you, thank you. A truly righteous wench you are.

[*He removes his muddy boots and places them on the table.* LINN *walks to him with bread and ale, sees the boots, sighs, and carries them over toward the door.*]

**DOUGLAS**   Mmm. This ale is fresh, but the bread is a bit stale. Have you any meat that might go with it?

**LINN**   Now you want meat?

**DOUGLAS**   Only if you have it. I really don't mean to intrude.

**LINN**   I have little to spare.

**DOUGLAS**   I understand. [*A beat.*] I don't need much. A little is fine.

**LINN**   I have *very* little.

**DOUGLAS**   I'll take whatever you can offer.

[*She gives in.*]

Your generosity is duly noted.

**LINN**   I would I knew the name of the man who duly notes it.

**DOUGLAS.**   Douglas, madam.

**LINN**   And what, pray tell, brings you to these woods in the midst of this storm, Douglas?

**DOUGLAS**   Why, my horse, madam.

**LINN**   Yes, I know your horse brought you here, but I mean, for what purpose?

**DOUGLAS**   No, you misunderstand me. My horse has a poor sense of direction. I am lost. I have been traveling for quite some time, far from a home that I barely remember.

**LINN**   I see. I too am far from my home, and I don't think I shall ever see it again.

**DOUGLAS**   'Tis the way of the world, I suppose, to take us far from the places we trust.

**LINN**   And where is this home that you barely remember?

**DOUGLAS**   Scotland.

**LINN**   [*She stops.*] Scotland?

**DOUGLAS**   Have you been?

**LINN**   I don't think so.

**DOUGLAS**   Aye. Denmark *is* a fair length away.

**LINN**   That was the idea.

**DOUGLAS**   But Scotland is a beautiful land, so I hear.

**LINN**   So you hear?

**DOUGLAS**   I have never been.

**LINN**   But you just said . . .

**DOUGLAS**   'Tis a home I never really knew. I was conceived there, and quickly exiled—the illegitimate heir to a throne.

**LINN**   A throne! Then you are a prince?

**DOUGLAS**   Someday, yes, I will be a prince. My brief time in Scotland ended after my mother's brief affair with a man who would briefly become a king of Scotland. How brevity doth seem to haunt me.

**LINN**  And who was this man that would become king?

**DOUGLAS**  My father. Macbeth.

[*Thunder and lightning crash.*]

**LINN**  Macbeth!?

**DOUGLAS**  Aye, madam!

**LINN**  He had a son!?

**DOUGLAS**  The man before ye.

**LINN**  I don't understand.

**DOUGLAS**  My mother was a wretched woman, whom my father vowed he would never marry. I was born a bastard and my mother was shamed into leaving. As I grew older, I was told stories of my father, a warrior, who had married some strong, spiteful woman, and I would imagine what it would be like to truly be his son. Then came the news that he had, through a series of unforeseeable events, ascended to the throne of Scotland, only to be quickly undone by the likes of three witches, who had deceived him through their black magic.

**LINN**  You don't say.

**DOUGLAS**  I thought if only I could bring these three hags to justice, I might gain enough honor to claim the throne of my father and legitimize my name! So I set out to find them, journeying across many lands, following the reports of certain witnesses, until, ultimately, I lost my way and ended up in this back wood of Denmark, caught in this horrible storm.

**LINN**  Fascinating.

**DOUGLAS**  And I have vowed to seek out these witches and see them burn for the awful deeds they have done to my family. I swear that I will not rest until that fateful day when we shall finally...you know...

**LINN**  [*Offering him a plate.*] Meat?

**DOUGLAS**  Exactly.

**LINN**   I am truly intrigued at what seems to be a very harrowing tale of heroic vengeance.

**DOUGLAS**   How brave a woman you must be to not tremble at the mention of witches.

**LINN**   Oh, I do tremble.

**DOUGLAS**   Is the soup ready yet?

**LINN**   I doubt it.

**DOUGLAS**   I am still very hungry. I do hope to have some before retiring tonight.

**LINN**   Yes, yes ... um ... pray tell, how exactly to you intend to find these "witches"?

**DOUGLAS**   My, you are truly interested, aren't you?

**LINN**   A silly fascination, I suppose.

**DOUGLAS**   Well, make no mistake, miss. I shall know them the second I see them.

**LINN**   [*Quickly hiding her face.*] Really?

**DOUGLAS**   I have been told by many people of their very unique traits, which make them thus unmistakably identifiable.

[LINN *paces frantically behind him, unsure of what to do.*]

**LINN**   Uh-huh? And they are?

**DOUGLAS**   Well, most importantly, they are three, inseparable sisters. You would, in fact, never meet one without the others. It is quite impossible.

[LINN *stops, realizing what he has just said.*]

**LINN**   Yes?

**DOUGLAS**   They are withered and wild in their attire, like animals, bred from the most vicious demons in the deep ovens of hell. They look not like inhabitants of the earth, though they are on it. Age doth hang from them like bark from a dead tree, cracking here, and rotting there.

**LINN**   Yes?

**DOUGLAS**   They should be women, though their beards forbid one to interpret that they are so.

**LINN**   Their beards?

**DOUGLAS**   Aye, like the wiry hair of a warthog doth their beard grow forth upon their wretched faces. And here, here is the most identifiable marking of all.

**LINN**   What is it?

**DOUGLAS**   There is one, the youngest I am told, though their infinite ages are indecipherable to man's finite eyes, who wears close to her face a bright red *scarf*.

**LINN**   I beg your pardon?

**DOUGLAS**   A bright red scarf that doth seem to burn like the embers of a fire whenever evil deeds are afoot.

**LINN**   A scarf?

**DOUGLAS**   Aye.

> [LINN *laughs.*]

> You are mocking me!

**LINN**   No! No.

**DOUGLAS**   Just as everyone does. I think I shall just eat your food and then leave, thank you.

**LINN**   No, no, please, Douglas, please do not leave. I apologize. I do not mean to laugh mindlessly at the tragic misfortunes befalling your family, nor the horrifying descriptions of these ghastly, bearded women. I am just...so taken with the thought of your quest— journeying beyond odds, to find three wicked women, so as to claim the right to a throne, in a beautiful country you call home. Truly, 'tis a noble life to live.

**DOUGLAS**   I have never heard my tale relived through such beautiful words. What is your name, miss?

**LINN**   Linn.

**DOUGLAS**   Linn, you are truly a virtuous woman.

**LINN**   [*She laughs.*] I have been clothed in many names, but never virtuous. How strange this new fabric feels, and yet how comfortably it doth fit.

**DOUGLAS**   Anyone who would dress you otherwise had never seen the naked truth of your kindness.

[LINN *blushes and laughs self-consciously.*]

[*Laughing nervously.*] Forgive my frankness. I did not mean to embarrass you.

**LINN**   [*Still laughing.*] No, it's fine.

**DOUGLAS**   You must think I am a fool, and you would not be so wrong.

**LINN**   No, Douglas...

**DOUGLAS**   I suppose you have a husband who will be home soon, or something like that.

**LINN**   [*She laughs again.*] No, no, no. I am not married.

**DOUGLAS**   Of course not! A strong woman like you! How provincial of me to think you would need a man.

**LINN**   Douglas, stop, really, you are too funny.

**DOUGLAS**   And you are too beautiful. And brave! To live alone in this wood!

**LINN**   What is there to fear?

**DOUGLAS**   Animals, I suppose. Men must hunt many dangerous animals in these parts.

**LINN**   I'd sooner fear the hunter.

**DOUGLAS**   So sayeth the animal! I suppose the peace and solitude cannot be matched.

**LINN**   Aye, it suits me well. I love this place because for however long it may last, it is my home. How wonderful it would be to have the freedom to travel as you do, unafraid of whatever dangers lay before me or behind me, so long as I have a place to call my own home.

[*A beat. Then, suddenly.*]

**DOUGLAS**   Come with me, Linn.

**LINN**   What?

**DOUGLAS**   Together we can find these women and I will take you back to Scotland with me.

**LINN**   I don't know if that's a good idea.

**DOUGLAS**   Or wherever you are from, or wherever you would like to go. I seek more than just a throne. I seek something that makes me legitimate. Any man can be a king in his own, rightful home.

**LINN**   The thought is very tempting, but…

**DOUGLAS**   Don't even think. I can give you the freedom you wish for.

**LINN**   Douglas…

**DOUGLAS**   And I can bring you home.

**LINN**   [*A beat.*] Okay.

**DOUGLAS**   Okay?

**LINN**   Aye! We shall leave together. But at once.

**DOUGLAS**   At once?

**LINN**   Yes, I am afraid I will back down on my decision.

**DOUGLAS**   But we cannot leave in this storm.

**LINN**   We must face the night.

**DOUGLAS**   Have you any ties to sever? Any family to tell?

**LINN**   None. I have nothing holding me back.

[*At this point there is quite a racket at the offstage edge of the upstairs platform. TORRENCE and HARPER emerge disguised in various cloaks and hats. They talk and move without glancing at LINN or DOUGLAS, making a streamline for the door.*]

**HARPER**   I dare say, good *auntie*, that I had a romping good stay at this *inn*.

**TORRENCE**   Indeed, good *niece*, I haven't slept so divinely in years.

**HARPER**   We must be good enough to thank that sweet *innkeeper* the next time we return from our villa, which is very, very, *very* far away from here!

**TORRENCE**   Huzzah!

[*They exit out the door. There is a crash of thunder and lightning. They emerge a beat later from outside, very wet. They make the same streamline back the way they came.*]

**HARPER**   My, good auntie, the weather has picked up considerably since we arrived.

**TORRENCE**   Indeed, good niece, it shall be good to return to our villa far, far away, where it is always sunny.

**HARPER**   I'm sure that sweet innkeeper will allow us to remain one more night *undisturbed* by any visitors!

**TORRENCE**   Huzzah!

[*They exit.*]

**LINN**   Except them.

**DOUGLAS**   Who are they?

**LINN**   Let's find out.
    [*She walks to the first landing.*]
    Torrence! Harper! Come out here. We must talk!
    [*Nothing.*]
    Don't worry…he's gone!

[*At this the two emerge and begin taking off the various added garments.*]

**HARPER**   Oh, thank Hecuba!

**TORRENCE**   Are you hurt? What did he say?

**HARPER**   We heard laughter, and so of course we assumed he was torturing you!

**TORRENCE**   Well, at least you are all right. I worried unnaturally!

**LINN**   Harper, Torrence, meet Douglas.

[*The two turn to see him sitting at the table. They stare in shock.*]

**DOUGLAS**  Huzzah!

**TORRENCE**  Oh, dear.

**DOUGLAS**  Linn, I had no idea you ran an inn!

**LINN**  Nor I.

**DOUGLAS**  How is it that you all know each other?

**TORRENCE**  How do we know each other? Well...um...you see...

**LINN**  Douglas—you are a very sweet and gentle spirit, and I'm afraid I haven't been entirely honest with you. There is something going on here, and I feel as though I can trust you.

**TORRENCE**  Linn! What are you doing?

**LINN**  I should have said this earlier. You see, Douglas...Harper and Torrence are—rich.

[*A beat.*]

TORRENCE, HARPER, and DOUGLAS  Rich?

**LINN**  Wickedly rich. And they so despise the attention their wealthy lives bring that they often travel incognito to different lands, to escape the dreariness of their rich lives. You must forgive their shyness. If they were seen in public, their admirers would practically burn them with praise and adoration, the fire and fervor of their passion scorching these women with a blaze of horrible, horrible love.

**DOUGLAS**  [*To* TORRENCE.] Is that so?

**TORRENCE**  You could say that, yes.

**DOUGLAS**  From whence do you come?

**TORRENCE**  Oh...you know...

**TORRENCE / HARPER**  Egypt / France.
    [*A beat.*]
    France / Egypt.
    [*A beat.*]
    Egypt, France / France, Egypt.

**LINN**  They're from all over, really. And I often allow visitors, like yourself, to stay at my cottage for periods of time. I take care of them, and I cook.

**HARPER**  *You* cook?

**LINN**  Torrence and Harper have oft found themselves in need of a place to stay in their many travels across the land and so I have met them on many occasions. They cannot go near Denmark without stopping by for a good night's rest, and a delicious cup of my soup.

**HARPER**  *Your* soup!?

**LINN**  Pay the little one no mind. She hasn't any to pay you back.

**TORRENCE**  Harper, darling, perhaps you should go get our luggage so that we can soon be on our way. Linn, tell me about your... um...guest.

**DOUGLAS**  I am a traveler, like yourself, madam. I was traveling in the wood when I found myself at the mercy of this storm and at the foot of Linn's door.

**LINN**  He is in search of three witches, who are to blame for the untimely death of his father, the king of Scotland. Macbeth.

[*Thunder and lightning.*]

**TORRENCE**  Macbeth!? [*She turns in a circle, then spits.*]

**DOUGLAS**  Aye, madam.

**TORRENCE**  He had a son!? Linn, what is going on, here?

**LINN**  Oh, don't worry, Torrence. You see, he has told me of how he plans to identify these witches, and he has assured me that he has not found them anywhere near these parts.

**DOUGLAS**  'Tis true. Like a sailor in unfamiliar seas, I have followed one star, only to have realized, shipwrecked, that it was the wrong one.

**TORRENCE**  I see.

**DOUGLAS**  Yet Aeolus and Aphrodite have combined to give me new wind for my journey, and so I plan to sail this very night.

**TORRENCE**  New wind?

**LINN**  Yes. Douglas and I were actually just leaving, Torrence.

**TORRENCE**  Leaving!?

**LINN**  Yes, leaving. Together. I have offered to help him find what he seeks.

**TORRENCE**  [*Mortified.*] You wouldn't dare!

**LINN**  You mustn't worry, Torrence. We will search in lands very far from here. And if we never find these women, we shall settle in a home, satisfied enough to have found each other.

**DOUGLAS**  Your innkeeper has quite a charm about her.

**TORRENCE**  Believe me, she knows more charms than she will admit.

**LINN**  I have decided to leave this inn to you. You will be completely safe, and anonymous, here.

**TORRENCE**  [*Somewhat aside to* LINN.] But what if another man seeks these same witches here?

**LINN**  You don't understand, these *three* witches are completely inseparable.

**DOUGLAS**  And any man with eyes will know that such kindly beauty could not possibly become such wicked women.

**LINN**  You see? There is nothing left to fear. You can stay as long as you like.

**TORRENCE**  And you?

**LINN**  I will find my home.

**TORRENCE**  Then we are undone?

**LINN**  It is for the best.

[TORRENCE *considers for a moment.*]

**TORRENCE**  There is a packed bag next to my bed. I'm sure many of the clothes will suit you just fine.

**LINN**  Thank you, Torrence.

[*They hug. As* LINN *goes offstage, she passes* HARPER *entering with large sacks of material belongings.*]

**HARPER**   Our things, dear... rich... *auntie.*

**TORRENCE**   Good, good. It turns out that we will be staying here after all.

**DOUGLAS**   Please, ma'am, have a seat. This is your house now, I suppose.

[DOUGLAS *rises and* TORRENCE *walks by him nervously.*]

**TORRENCE**   Thank you, Douglas.

**HARPER**   I don't understand.

**TORRENCE**   I will tell you about it later. It seems Douglas is the son of a king of Scotland. Macbeth.

[*Thunder and lightning.*]

**HARPER**   Macbeth!? [*She turns in a circle, then spits.*]

**DOUGLAS**   Aye, madam!

**HARPER**   He had a son!?

**DOUGLAS**   'Tis an often untold story, apparently.

**HARPER**   We don't get out much.

**DOUGLAS**   Yet you travel?

**HARPER**   Aye, but whenever we travel, we stay indoors.

**DOUGLAS**   Miss! Your cheek!

**HARPER**   What of it?

**DOUGLAS**   You wear a large scar on your face.

**HARPER**   Oh, that. It's just a mild case of eczema.

**DOUGLAS**   Does it hurt?

**HARPER**   No, it is something that has marked me since birth.

**DOUGLAS**   [*Slowly realizing, mid-sentence.*] 'Tis a bright red scar that doth seem to burn like the embers of a fire.

**HARPER**   You needn't make me feel self-conscious.

**DOUGLAS**   [*Aside.*] A *scar*!

**HARPER**   So, whence travel ye this night?

**DOUGLAS**   Pardon?

**HARPER**   You and Linn? You plan to travel in this storm?

**DOUGLAS**   Yes! Um. Yes, yes. I must be leaving right away.

[DOUGLAS *goes to the door and begins to put on his boots.*]

**TORRENCE**   What?

**DOUGLAS**   It was very nice to meet you.

**TORRENCE**   But what about Linn?

**DOUGLAS**   [*Having trouble.*] Damn these boots.

[LINN *enters on his line.*]

**LINN**   Douglas? What's wrong?

**DOUGLAS**   Nothing. Um. My horse is . . . I'm afraid I must leave.

**LINN**   Douglas, I don't understand. What of our plans?

**DOUGLAS**   Yes, well . . . I will come for you. I shall return very soon. You mustn't leave this place. I must know where to find you.

**LINN**   Douglas, your look doth frighten me.

**DOUGLAS**   I am sorry, Linn.

**LINN**   [*She crosses to* TORRENCE *and* HARPER.] Torrence . . . ?

**DOUGLAS**   I will leave the three of you alone together. I must go at once.

**LINN**   [*She crosses to him.*] Please tell me what is going on!

[*He opens the door to go. Wind and rain blow in. Thunder and lightning crash.*]

**DOUGLAS**   My cloak! Where did you put my cloak?

**LINN**   By the soup.

[*He crosses to find his cloak.*]

**HARPER**   Linn, I am scared.

**LINN**   Harper, your scar! How brightly it doth—

> [*She stops, realizing what has just happened.* DOUGLAS *stops, too, and looks at them. He makes his way to the door, when it suddenly slams shut of its own accord, leaving the room in a moment of tense silence.*]

> [*Quietly.*] You cannot leave, Douglas.

**DOUGLAS**   What?

**LINN**   You cannot leave in this storm.

**DOUGLAS**   I must face the night.

**LINN**   You will starve.

**DOUGLAS**   I had some ale.

**LINN**   I believe the soup is ready to be served.

**DOUGLAS**   Linn...

**LINN**   You gave me such hope in the world. Let me hold on to it for one moment longer.

[*A long, tense moment. Finally,* DOUGLAS *sits.* HARPER *pours a bowl of soup and hands it to* LINN.]

**LINN**   This will warm your spirit.

**DOUGLAS**   Aye. 'Tis awfully cold in the state of Denmark.

[*As* DOUGLAS *eats the soup, the sisters hold tight behind him. The lights dim as the curtain falls.*]

• • •

# Bricklayers Poet

## Joe Maruzzo

# Joe Maruzzo

Joe Maruzzo has written two full-length plays. One is called *Red Roses*, a love story during a rehearsal process. Another is called *Leftovers*, about a writer with writer's block. A one-act called *Actor* is about an actor who holds a casting agent hostage. He is currently working on four other plays and a screenplay.

• • •

[*Lights slowly come up on a* WOMAN *sitting at the bar in the Algonquin Hotel in Manhattan. She sips a red wine, a manuscript sits next to her on the bar, along with a pencil, her purse, and a menu. She dials her cell phone, waits; it's the voice mail. She listens, then hangs up. A* MAN *enters, checks the place out. The* BARTENDER *approaches the woman.*]

**BARTENDER**   Have you decided . . . ?

**LUNA**   I'll have the pate please.

[*He takes the menu and heads to the kitchen. The* MAN *moseys his way towards the corner of the bar.*]

*MIKEY*   Mind if I sit here . . . ?

[*She motions a quick "no" over her shoulder. He scoots forward, checks her out, drops his keys on the bar. The bartender approaches.*]

**MIKEY**   Heineken?

[*The* BARTENDER *grabs a glass, sets it down, cracks open a cold one and pours. The* MAN *throws down a twenty. The* BARTENDER *makes change and heads to the kitchen. A beat.*]

**MIKEY**   You see, this is when I feel like a cigarette.

[LUNA *glances towards him.*]

**MIKEY**   I'm tryin' to quit. I hardly inhale. I'm down to a couple of cigarettes a night, usually if I'm at a bar, or a party or somethin', you know, the "ambuance" influences me.

**LUNA**   The what?

**MIKEY**   The "ambuance"! The lights, the people, the excitement.

[*She turns back to her world.*]

**MIKEY**   Do I know you from somewhere . . . ?

**LUNA**   I don't think so.

**MIKEY**   Oh, because I thought I recognized you from somewhere, you look like we talked before. You come here often . . . ?

**LUNA**   No.

**MIKEY**   This is my first time. It's suppose to be famous.

> [*He looks around.*]
>
> Don't look so famous to me. Slow in here. But I kinda like it slow. Yeah, I was just down in the Village. All those kids running around from the college there, not to mention all the out of towners comin' in from all over the place for the holidays, it's like one big gigantic parade down there, you know…!?

[*The* BARTENDER *steps forward with her pate.*]

**LUNA**   Would you mind If I moved to a table…?

**BARTENDER**   Not at all.

[*She grabs her things as the* BARTENDER *leads her to a table downstage. He places her wine and pate down, lights a candle.*]

**BARTENDER**   Enjoy.

**LUNA**   Thank you.

[*He goes to the bar.*]

[MIKEY *looks over at the* WOMAN *from the bar, then looks away. He sits a beat. He reaches for her pencil she left behind, stands and heads towards her.*]

**MIKEY**   You left this.

[*He reaches his arm out holding the pencil, then drops it on the table.*]

**LUNA**   Thanks.

**MIKEY**   How 'bout you? You from around here?

**LUNA**   No.

**MIKEY**   Where you from?

**LUNA**   …Chicago.

**MIKEY**   Chicago, huh? What, you mean you live in Chicago…?

**LUNA**   I live in D.C.

**MIKEY**   What are you doin' in the city…? By the way, my name's Mikey. And yours is…?

**LUNA**   Luna.

**MIKEY**   Luna!? That's "moon" in Italian. You Italian?

**LUNA**   Half.

**MIKEY**   Really? What's the other half...?

**LUNA**   Irish.

**MIKEY**   Really!!? Half Italian, half Irish, that's really something.

**LUNA**   Why?

**MIKEY**   Half Italian, half Irish, my God, the passion, the spirit, the Irish fire with the Italian passionate soul, whew, that's a lot of stuff, you must be on fire...!

**LUNA**   I wouldn't quite put it that way.

**MIKEY**   That was a little too broad, but you know what I mean.

**LUNA**   I get the idea, yeah.

**MIKEY**   Now that you tell me your half Italian, half Irish, I can see it in the eyes, the, greenish brown-yellow, I can see it in the face too, very nice, very beautiful.

**LUNA**   Thank you.

**MIKEY**   Don't mention it.

[*He heads back towards the bar as the* BARTENDER *comes to her table again.*]

**BARTENDER**   How is everything...?

**LUNA**   Just fine.

**BARTENDER**   Would you like another glass of wine?

**MIKEY**   [*From bar.*] I'd like to get the lady a drink!
[*To* LUNA.]
If that's okay with you...?

**LUNA**   No thank you.

**MIKEY**   It would be my pleasure!

**LUNA**   Thanks, but no thanks.

**MIKEY**  For the holidays!?

**LUNA**  Really, no, I'm...

**MIKEY**  You don't even have to drink it.

**LUNA**  Ah...

**MIKEY**  A friendly gesture! A simple toast!

[*Beat.*]

**LUNA**  Sure.

**MIKEY**  The lady'll have a glass of the ah...

**BARTENDER**  Merlot.

**MIKEY**  Yeah, the Merlot. And let me have a Kahlúa and milk, in a straight small glass, with one ice cube.

[*He looks at her and heads her way.*]

They give you these tulip-shaped long-stemmed glasses, I don't know what to do with 'em, I get dizzy lookin' at 'em, the *times*, you know!?

[*He stands there. An awkward moment, then sits.*]

So, what are you doin in the city...?

**LUNA**  I'm here on business.

**MIKEY**  Business, that's interesting. What kind of business you here for, if you don't mind me askin'...?

**LUNA**  To see about a job with the *New York Times*.

**MIKEY**  The newspaper...?

**LUNA**  Yeah.

**MIKEY**  How'd it go for ya?

**LUNA**  I got the job.

**MIKEY**  Hey! Really!? Congratulations! What kind of work will ya be doin'?

**LUNA**  Editing columns.

**MIKEY**  Oh yeah?

**LUNA**  I'd like to get my own column someday, but that could take some time.

**MIKEY**  Hey, you never know. Anything's possible these days. You could own the *Times* in a couple of years!

[*The* BARTENDER *steps in and puts down the drinks.* MIKEY *hands him a twenty.*]

[*To* BARTENDER.]

Keep the change.

**BARTENDER**  Thank you.

[*He exits.* MIKEY *holds his glass up to* LUNA.]

**MIKEY**  Cheers...!

[*She lifts her glass and they clink! He motions to the manuscript.*]

Is that have to do with your work...?

**LUNA**  It's a story I'm writing. A novel.

**MIKEY**  You wrote it?

**LUNA**  Emm-hmm.

**MIKEY**  What's it about...?

**LUNA**  It's kind of hard to explain.

**MIKEY**  Try me.

**LUNA**  In simple terms, it's about the unmasking of our social roles, in order to discover the true self.

**MIKEY**  That sounds interesting. Yeah, well, you know, I write.

**LUNA**  Oh, what do you write?

**MIKEY**  Oh, I play around with like songs and poems, little like sayings and stuff, you know, nothing serious. Hey, who knows, I could be sittin' next to the next Ernest Hemingway over here...!

[*A beat.*]

Well, you know who's a famous woman writer?

**LUNA**  Anais Nin.

**MIKEY**  Yeah. I could be sittin' next to...

[*He's stuck.*]

LUNA   Anais Nin.

MIKEY   Whatever her name is. No, that's great, to be able to write. That's like a private way to express yourself, that's like when you can really be true with yourself, you know, just you, and the paper, and your thoughts. I wish I could do it, but I can only write for like a minute or something, then I gotta get up and walk around, I gotta move, it's weird. Hey, what do you say we have a real celebration, huh...? Can I offer you a glass of champagne, some of NY's finest, to celebrate your future fortune and your good health here...!?

LUNA   I don't think that's...

MIKEY   A little bubbly to bring in the holidays and a new job!

[*He motions to the* BARTENDER.]

MIKEY   Bartender, two glasses of your finest champagne...!
   [*She looks at her cell phone for a message.*]
   I'm not holdin' you up or anything...?

LUNA   No. I have some time.

MIKEY   You gotta go somewhere...?

LUNA   I have a phone call to make.

MIKEY   Oh. Because I don't wanna hold you up or anything like that.

LUNA   It's okay.

[*They sit there.*]

LUNA   So, what do you do...?

MIKEY   Me? I'm a bricklayer. I lay brick, block, stone, walks, patios, anything you want, I'll lay it! Well, you know what I mean.

LUNA   I get the idea, yeah...

[*The* BARTENDER *brings over two glasses of champagne, places them down.*]

MIKEY   Could you run a tab?

**BARTENDER**  Of course.

[*He heads to the bar. MIKEY puts his glass of Kahlúa off on another table, lifts his champagne to her.*]

**MIKEY**  To you!

[*They clink!*]

**LUNA**  Where do you work . . . ?

**MIKEY**  In Brooklyn mostly. But if the job's worth it, I'll go upstate NY, Jersey, Alaska, Texas . . . ! You try all over for work. But you know the story, the little guy can't get the jobs anymore. It's all big company jobs. It's all who you know, and are you willing to work for some bullshit union and lay straight courses all day long, straight courses. You wind up going out of your mind. I worked fifteen years on a union job, every day, twelve-, fourteen-hour days, laying block, one after the other after the other! There's all these gigantic towers going up! There's no style, no curves. Everything's flat, with like, no heart. Yeah, it's like there ain't no heart out there no more. So I quit, and started my own little business. I put this add in the paper and with word of mouth I get by. So that's what I do. I lay brick.

**LUNA**  That's amazing.

**MIKEY**  Amazing . . . ?

**LUNA**  Do you know the history of the Freemasons?

**MIKEY**  Ah . . .

**LUNA**  When I was in college, we had to write a paper for this research class about something we knew absolutely nothing about. One day I was coming out of the dance building, and these guys were working on the steps to the library, placing stone down, and it hit me! The Freemasons! Free, in that there weren't any unions, if you were good, you worked. But the respect the people had for the builder, the awe. He was held in a kind of reverence, by the kings, the pharaohs, the clergy. They worked with and through their bodies, like a painter, a sculptor, a writer. Do you know that Michelangelo was a Freemason . . . ?

**MIKEY**  Oh yeah…!?

**LUNA**  Just think of the buildings throughout our history, all over the world. Churches, homes, museums, libraries, schools, bridges, cathedrals, without the builder, we wouldn't be sitting here talking right now, literally. I learned so much from doing that paper, and I have great respect for what you do.

[*A beat.*]

**MIKEY**  What are you doing later on tonight…?

**LUNA**  Why?

**MIKEY**  You wanna get married…? No, I mean, you speak well. No wonder you're a writer.

**LUNA**  But do you know what I mean by the history of it, and in being proud of what you do?

**MIKEY**  Yeah. No. I'm proud of what I do, it's just, it gets kind of hard, day in day out, doing the same ole thing, mixing mortar, putting up scaffold, taking down scaffold, so forth and so on. But, this last job, can I tell you something…?

**LUNA**  Sure.

**MIKEY**  Don't think I'm crazy or nothin', you see, I'm a very practical kind of guy, black and white, right side of the brain and all that, but this last fireplace I did, I'm doin' this fireplace for the Corsos, sweet old people from Brooklyn, Sal and Bunny Corso, I know them all my life. Sal's in his 80s and he's dying of cancer, rest his soul, so Bunny calls me and she wants him to have a fireplace before he goes, something he always wanted. But at the time I was going through some stuff in my life, and the last thing I wanted to do in the middle of August was a fireplace. It was like 120 degrees in there! I'm doin the job for practically nothin', I charged them just for the material, and I'm like a day into it. And I realize the walls on a slant, it's crooked. I had to do all this special chipping and slanting the stone, the Corsos are sittin right in back of me watchin' my every move, not out of thinking I was gonna screw them or anything, but that they where happy watchin' there fireplace go up! So there I am, the sweats pourin' out of me, my mind is racin' about my life, my father, and I'm lifting this eighty-pound stone towards the wall, but it wont take, it wont stick. And I feel this pain in my heart, like a stake runnin' through me, and I can't move, I'm as stiff as a board, and all of a sudden my body starts to come up out of me! I swear to God! My body is leaving me!

And its goin' up through the ceiling, into the sky, but I can still see myself down there, I could see the Corsos, but I'm goin' higher and higher with all these puffy white clouds, and I hear this humming, this humming of something holy, like kids singin' this sweet sound, and I feel a tickle on my ear, and I turn and there's this angel with the wings and this beautiful little baby face, it's floatin' there and it whispers into my ear, "Love, Mikey, don't forget love." And all of a sudden I was back on the ground, holding the stone like I never left, but I'm cryin', I'm cryin' like a friggin' baby, so I run to the bathroom 'cause I don't want the Corsos to think I was cracking up, and everything got peaceful, and I hear that voice again sayin', "Love, Mikey, don't forget love." I walked out, went back to my fireplace, and it was the most beautiful fireplace I ever laid. I got a picture of it, you wanna see it?

**LUNA**   Sure.

[*He takes it out. Shows her.*]

**MIKEY**   That's me. That's Sal and Bunny. That's the fireplace.

**LUNA**   It's lovely.

**MIKEY**   You're the first person I told about this. That's all I gotta do is talk to the guys in the neighborhood, they'd think I was nuts. I usually don't talk to them about private things.

**LUNA**   Who do you talk to about private things?

**MIKEY**   No one really. My father, he died.

**LUNA**   I'm sorry.

**MIKEY**   Hey, life goes on. That voice, it was my father. He was tellin' me it's gonna be all right. He was tellin' me to love.

**LUNA**   What did he do...?

**MIKEY**   He was a bricklayer. Taught me everything I know. Talk about hands. He had a pair of hands so gentle, he'd hold a brick like it was a piece of cake, so smooth, you couldn't even tell he was layin' brick, like cream. He'd take a brick, you know, he'd chip it because there'd be a problem with the fireplace, so he'd chip the brick and the whole thing would go straight up. He was a craftsman. And clean! When he got through, you think he hired a cleaning lady. They don't make 'em like that no more. He was a little guy, short and stocky, green eyes, light brown hair, and whenever you were in trouble, he was there! If you needed a buck or two, his hand was in his pocket, if a guy needed a day's work, he'd hire him for the week, even if he took the loss. Anyway, it's a funny thing we're talkin' about these things and all, but lately, I feel like I need to talk to somebody, like I gotta share things, inside me, with them. Maybe it's my age or something, but I feel it's time.

**LUNA**   For what?

**MIKEY**   To settle down. Maybe not marriage and all but to live with at least. I'll tell ya, I look around and I see a lot of lonely people. I think if they made a study or somethin', they'd find out there are more people alone in the world now than ever before.
Well, at least in this city. I don't mean to make you scared, or sound stupid or nothing...

**LUNA**   No.

**MIKEY**   It's just the way I been seeing things lately. How 'bout you? You live in Washington, huh...?

**LUNA**   Yeah. D.C.

**MIKEY**   ...You like it there...?

**LUNA**   Sort of like how you described those buildings. Flat. Straight.

**MIKEY**   Lot of politicians running around over there, huh...?

**LUNA**   Oh yeah.

**MIKEY** I don't trust 'em. I always see 'em on TV sayin' this and promising that, but nothin' ever gets done.

**LUNA** I live with one.

**MIKEY** Oh yeah?

**LUNA** He's a lawyer. He's running for office.

**MIKEY** How long you been together...?

**LUNA** Almost nine years. I think it's ending.

**MIKEY** Why?

**LUNA** He's a hard man. It's just not right anymore.

**MIKEY** You love him?

**LUNA** Our lives have changed. Our love has changed.

[*She begins to break down.*]

**MIKEY** Hey...

**LUNA** No.

**MIKEY** You okay?

**LUNA** Really, I'm fine, it's just, everything we've been talking about, this being the holidays and all, gets me thinking of my family.

**MIKEY** You see your family?

**LUNA** I lost both my parents.

**MIKEY** I'm sorry.

**LUNA** Like you said, life goes on.

**MIKEY** What were their names?

**LUNA** Katherine and Michael.

**MIKEY** Hey, Michael?! I'm honored. What did they do?

**LUNA** My father was a history professor and my mother worked for a disability program with kids with cerebral palsy. She was amazing.

**MIKEY** Yeah.

LUNA    She loved those kids. They'd come to the house every Monday. I'd come home from school and they'd be pulling up the driveway in that yellow van-bus. We'd roll them out on their wheelchairs, they'd fall over on the lawn, we'd laugh so hard. And we'd make ham and cheese sandwiches, with potato chips, lots of potato chips and Hawaiian punch. They'd have these Hawaiian punch mouths. You should have seen her when she was taking care of those kids.

MIKEY    Yeah...?

LUNA    She'd glow. Her eyes would shine with this energy. She was filled with this abundant energy of giving. She was radiant. I've been thinking about them a lot lately. Just the other day, I was in the grocery store and I felt her presence so strong. I turned to see if she was there. I called her name. The woman on line thought I was nuts. And today, I was coming out of my meeting in Times Square, I turned the corner and there was my dad standing across the street, our eyes met, he turned and walked away.

I ran across the street but he was gone, I called his name. I know it was him, I know he was there.

MIKEY    They are. They're always with us.

[*She breaks down.*]

It's okay.

LUNA    I'm sorry.

MIKEY    I understand.

LUNA    I've been really vulnerable lately.

MIKEY    It's okay to lose it every now and then.

LUNA    Yeah?

MIKEY    A person doesn't lose it every now and then, I don't trust that person. "There's just as many tears as there is laughter." It's a poem I wrote. You wanna hear it?

LUNA    Sure.

**MIKEY**  "There's just as many tears as there is laughter, there's just as many clouds as there are clear skies. There's just as much joy as there is sadness. And I'm glad I have you." Well, it's not really a poem.

**LUNA**  I like it.

**MIKEY**  It's what I feel.

**LUNA**  It's sweet.

**MIKEY**  That's why I say, if you're happy, well, then you're happy, if you're sad, well, then tough shit, what are you suppose to do, lie about it!!!? That's what I'm saying, you gotta be able to feel the things you're feeling, and they gotta be alright these things, they gotta be... Luna, moon, moon, Luna. I love that name Luna...! What do you say we get out of here. I don't know, we take a walk. We look up at the moon. You hungry? You like Chinese...? How about Italian? I know this great little pasta place in Little Italy, Luna, stay with me forever...!

[*They are there. She gets up, gathers her things.*]

**LUNA**  I can't. I have that phone call to make.

[*She leans into him and kisses him on the cheek. She turns and walks off.* MIKEY *stands there as the lights fade on him.*]

• • •

# Laundry and Lies

Adam Kraar

# Adam Kraar

Adam Kraar's plays include *New World Rhapsody* (Manhattan Theatre Club commission); *The Spirit House* (premiered at Performance Network of Ann Arbor); *The Abandoned El* (premiered at Illinois Theatre Center); *Storm in the Iron Box* (National Play Award runner-up), and *Freedom High* (Queens Theatre in the Park). His work has been produced and developed by Primary Stages, N.Y., Stage and Film, N.Y., Shakespeare Festival, Ensemble Studio, Theatreworks U.S.A., Queens Theatre in the Park, Urban Stages, H. B. Playwrights Theatre, Geva Theatre, Ryan Repertory Theatre, Inge Center for the Arts, and others. Awards: Sewanee Writers' Conference, Bloomington Playwrights Project, Virtual Theatre Project, Southeastern Theatre Conference, New River Dramatists Fellowship, Byrdcliffe's Handel Fellowship, and the Millay Colony. Plays published by: Dramatic Publishing, Smith & Kraus, Sundance Publishers, and Applause Books. Adam grew up in India, Thailand, Singapore, and the U.S., earned an M.F.A. from Columbia University, and lives in Brooklyn with his wife, Karen.

**persons**

PATSY

GEORGE

(Also, briefly, a man's voice, offstage)

**place**

A basement laundry room in an apartment building

**time**

The present

• • •

[*At rise, a large pool of light on a table in a basement laundry room. On the table are a few pieces of women's underwear and a box of poker chips. The rest of the laundry room, including the machines, is in the shadows upstage, unseen.*]

[*Enter PATSY from upstage, with her arms full of white laundry, which she has taken out of a dryer. PATSY wears a man's shirt and very torn jeans. She dumps the pile of laundry on the table.*]

PATSY    Deliver me. . . . Deliver me from Egypt, Manhattan, men.

[*Beat.*]

Why don't you just hack off one of my feet? Or take some thigh—eat, eat; eat my thigh, God, I don't care if it hurts. Only give me a fucking break. A fucking break is all I ask. A break from fucking Rick.

[*Suddenly shifting gears.*]

You'd rather play cards with lawyers than spend the evening breaking up with me?! Fine! We're through! We're all played out!

[*She picks up the box of poker chips and throws them offstage. Beat.*]

Oh God. Its not like I'm asking You to part these walls and deliver me to the Promised Land. I'm only asking for what is mine. For what You lead me to believe—well, Daddy led me to believe.

[*Pause. Then, suddenly shifting gears.*]

One day King David will come, in a white Land Rover, and drive me, through the walls, through the sea, to the Promised Land. There, I will helplessly pour my suffering Jewish soul onto page after page of immortal prose. All day I will write and they will yank the sweat-covered pages from my desk and beg for more; all evening I will make love to King David, with temple maidens and soccer players longingly looking on; all night I will sleep imbibing dreams of honey and organic halva. I will never need to eat!... I will be thin.

[*Beat.*]

Mad. Seriously... mad.

[PATSY's *eyes start to tear. She looks at the pile of laundry, takes a handkerchief, wipes her eyes with it, then puts it into her pocket. Then she picks up the women's underwear from the table and crosses upstage to the dryer, out of the light. Pause.*]

[*Enter* GEORGE, *dressed in polyester pants and a short-sleeve white shirt, carrying some hangers. He is surprised to see the pile of white laundry on the table. He looks at his watch. He goes to the table and quickly sorts through the pile of laundry. Then, calling upstage.*]

**GEORGE**   Excuse me.

[PATSY *enters from upstage.*]

**PATSY**   Oh, hello.

[PATSY *buttons a button on her shirt.*]

**GEORGE**   Did you, uh—?

**PATSY**   Only one dryer's working.

**GEORGE**   I know that.

**PATSY**   Ridiculous, isn't it? Six washers and only one dryer that works. No hot water, no exterminator, no paint job in years. At least my walls match my cockroaches. What do you say we band together and demand our rights from the landlord, and if we don't get 'em, organize a rent strike!

**GEORGE**   Did you take my laundry out of the dryer?

**PATSY**  [*Playfully.*] I have the right to an attorney.

**GEORGE**  I had ten minutes left on my cycle.

**PATSY**  I would've said you had a good ten years left. If you don't let the stress get you.

[PATSY *sits on the table, takes a carrot out of her pocket and eats it.*]

**GEORGE**  Look—Did you take—?

**PATSY**  Oh, so that's how it is. Yes, I took your laundry out of the dryer. It was sitting there idle, and I had a bundle of hogwash, I mean, hand-wash. Do you expect me to sit around here accumulating mildew, waiting for you to come?

**GEORGE**  How could it be sitting idle? Idly. I put in three quarters at quarter to six. It is now six-twenty.

**PATSY**  Why do you wear panties?

**GEORGE**  I da-da-don't wear panties!

**PATSY**  What do you call these?

**GEORGE**  I call those briefs, and, speaking of mildew, they are still soaking wet!

[*Pause as* PATSY *finishes her carrot.*]

**GEORGE**  Would you mind if I were to throw my briefs into—?

**PATSY**  Sorry, I don't know you. Those panties could be positive.

[*Slight pause.*]

**GEORGE**  Another hold-up. Another…
[*He is so furious he cannot speak.*]
…Fine!

[GEORGE *starts putting his shirts, all white, on hangers.*]

**PATSY**  What do you mean another hold-up?
[GEORGE *doesn't answer.*]
Huh? What do you mean another hold-up? Hello? You really think I'd cheat you for twelve and a half cents?

**GEORGE**  You mean, when you came down here the dryer was...?

**PATSY**  [*Lying.*] Yes.

[GEORGE *and* PATSY *look at each other.*]

**PATSY**  Do you have change for a dollar?

**GEORGE**  Sure. Sorry about...

**PATSY**  You don't have to apologize.

**GEORGE**  I shouldn't have leapt to the conclusion that... But everywhere one turns, it's—

**PATSY**  You're telling me. There are people around here who would steal the letters in your name for alphabet soup.

[GEORGE, *who has taken out four quarters, gives them to* PATSY.]

**PATSY**  Thanks.

[*Pause.*]

**GEORGE**  Isn't there a second part to that transaction?

**PATSY**  Oh, your dollar!
[*She laughs.*]
I'll have to pay you back later. I ran down here without any mon—extra quarters.

**GEORGE**  I see.

**PATSY**  Oh, please, let's not start that again. Are you Jewish?

**GEORGE**  Why do you ask?

**PATSY**  You're Jewish. Otherwise you would just say "no."

**GEORGE**  I'm not—

**PATSY**  Don't lie about it.
[*As a stereotypical Nazi.*]
Ve have vays of dealing mit circumcised liars.
[*As herself.*]
...Hey, just kidding. I'm a JAP, a Zionist, and very nosy, that's all.

**GEORGE**   To a Nazi, maybe I'm Jewish—

**PATSY**   Don't wanna get caught with matzoh on your face, do you?

**GEORGE**   I'm just not...religious.

**PATSY**   You're a Jew. A real Jew. Jew. Jew. Jew...I love that word, don't you?

> [*Silence. She takes out a cookie.*]

Would you like a sugarless fortune cookie?

**GEORGE**   No thanks.

**PATSY**   It's kosher....Oh well. This will be your fortune.

[PATSY *opens the cookie as* GEORGE *finishes hanging up his shirts.*]

**PATSY**   [*Reads the fortune.*] Oh my God. You know what your fortune says?...."You are fireball of righteous fury trapped inside ice-cube of fear."

**GEORGE**   Let me see that.

**PATSY**   Ah-hah. I knew it.

**GEORGE**   I am not in the mood to be trifled with.

**PATSY**   Are you ever?

[GEORGE *turns his attention to his laundry, sorting through it. After two seconds.*]

**GEORGE**   My handkerchief.

**PATSY**   *Othello.* Except didn't Othello call it a "napkin"? I always get this image of a big black guy running around hysterical about a missing sanitary napkin.

**GEORGE**   Did you see a handkerchief?

**PATSY**   No.

[GEORGE *walks around the room to see if the handkerchief fell on the floor.*]

**PATSY**   Are you sure there was a handkerchief?

**GEORGE**   Yes! Are you sure you didn't leave it in the dryer? Do you mind if I look?

**PATSY**  Yes, I do mind. I've got my privates in there.

**GEORGE**  I won't look at your... Maybe, could you, could you look? *Please.*

**PATSY**  Alright.

[PATSY *goes upstage.* GEORGE *starts to follow her, but* PATSY *turns around.*]

**PATSY**  If I find it, I'll tell you.

[PATSY *exits into the shadows upstage.*]

**GEORGE**  I need that handkerchief. It's my only one.... I want my handkerchief back right now!

[PATSY *comes back downstage.*]

**PATSY**  What, now I stole your handkerchief?

**GEORGE**  Did you?

[PATSY *shakes her head in disbelief.*]

**PATSY**  What's one handkerchief? A dollar?

**GEORGE**  You don't understand. I have a very important interview tomorrow.

**PATSY**  For fifty cents, you can get one of those little packages of Kleenex.

**GEORGE**  I can't use Kleenex! My nose will break out in a rash!

**PATSY**  On this interview, are you expecting to cry?

**GEORGE**  I might.

**PATSY**  Why?

**GEORGE**  We've got to find it.

**PATSY**  I think we should get to the root of this. Was this handkerchief given to you by your mother?

**GEORGE**  No, it was—What difference does it make?

**PATSY**  It makes all the difference in the world. Was it from your lover?

**GEORGE**  My ex—... fiancée. Now are you happy?

**PATSY**   I don't know what happiness is. Are you happy?

**GEORGE**   No!

**PATSY**   Your ex-fiancée. Oh my God! Did she...die?

**GEORGE**   [*Sullenly.*] No.

**PATSY**   So you're good friends with her?

[*Pause.*]

**GEORGE**   How long are you going to be using the dryer?

**PATSY**   If you didn't act that way, I might allow you to throw your panties in with my privates.

**GEORGE**   They're not—! May I?

**PATSY**   First you have to answer my questions.

**GEORGE**   Why?

**PATSY**   Because you want to.

**GEORGE**   No, I don't.

**PATSY**   Did your ex-wife-to-be run away with another man?
      [*Beat.*]
      By the way my name is Shandalayah Meir. My hand is clean. Do you want to take my hand or stand there like limp celery?

**GEORGE**   I don't know. You scare me.

**PATSY**   Little ol' me?? *Why?*

**GEORGE**   Everyone scares me. Okay? You can't trust anyone, not even yourself.

**PATSY**   You're right.
      [*Slight pause.*]
      You wanna put your laundry in the...?

**GEORGE**   Yes. But I don't want to answer your questions.

**PATSY**   Alright, use my dryer; you don't have to talk to me.

**GEORGE**   That's not what I meant, and you know it.

**PATSY**  Just put your goddamn laundry in the machine.

**GEORGE**  I really appreciate it.

> [*Then he extends his hand.*]
> My name is George.

**PATSY**  George...?

**GEORGE**  George Rubin.

[*They shake hands. Then* GEORGE *takes his laundry upstage.* PATSY *unbuttons a button on her shirt.*]

**PATSY**  You mind putting another quarter in?

[GEORGE *comes back into the light, and holds out his hand.*]

**PATSY**  I mean, I think you should put in a quarter because...

**GEORGE**  You forget: you owe me a dollar.

**PATSY**  Here.

> [PATSY *reaches into her pocket and takes out a quarter.*]
> What are you looking at?

**GEORGE**  Nothing.

**PATSY**  I don't always dress like this if that's what you're looking at.

**GEORGE**  No. I'll just—

**PATSY**  Please don't lie to me. What were you looking at?

**GEORGE**  I couldn't help noticing.

**PATSY**  What?

**GEORGE**  You're not wearing any, uh, uh, underwear, are you?

**PATSY**  Why do you ask?

**GEORGE**  It just slipped out. I mean, the words slipped out.... Would you please button your shirt?!

**PATSY**  Do you find me attractive? Or would you peek at any woman whose shirt happened to be loose?

**GEORGE**  I'll leave.

**PATSY**   Just talk to me.

**GEORGE**   I'm trying to talk to you. What are you trying to do to me? Why must you expose yourself? Can't we have a simple, polite, honest conversation—that isn't nakedly honest?

**PATSY**   I don't know.

[*Pause.* PATSY *gives* GEORGE *the quarter.* GEORGE *goes upstage into the shadows.*]

**PATSY**   What's this job you're going for?

**GEORGE**   Electrocardiogram technician.

**PATSY**   Oh, you're a medical techie?

[GEORGE *comes back downstage.*]

**GEORGE**   Well, up until last month, I installed and repaired lie detectors.

**PATSY**   Really!? That's fascinating!

**GEORGE**   I've come to seriously doubt the efficacy of the lie detector. The best liars can easily fool them, and the most honest people are usually the most nervous—so the lie detector says they're lying.

**PATSY**   I'd love to take a lie-detector test! "Did you murder John Doe on the night of August 12th?" "John Doe? I've never heard of John Doe." "You're lying!" "I mean, I've heard of John Doe, just not the one that was murdered!"

**GEORGE**   What do you do?

**PATSY**   Me? That's the funny thing.

[*She laughs.*]

**GEORGE**   What?

**PATSY**   I administer penile plethysmograph tests.

**GEORGE**   No! You've got to be putting me on!

**PATSY**   Nope.

**GEORGE**   You mean, you administer that test which measures...?

**PATSY**  Male sexual response. That's right. We strap a band around your pee-pee and show dirty movies. It's an incredible coincidence. After all, the plethysmograph is country cousin to the polygraph.

**GEORGE**  What kind of resistors do you use?

**PATSY**  You think I'm lying, don't you?

**GEORGE**  Well, yes.

**PATSY**  Maybe I am. Or, maybe I'm an expert in male sexual response. Maybe your eagerness to think I'm lying is a symptom of your dysfunction. After all, I pronounced plethysmograph correctly, didn't I? Maybe your measured, mild, gentlemanly manner masks a barely controllable desire to tie me down and lash me with your—

**GEORGE**  That's enough, Shandalayah.

**PATSY**  [*Coyly.*] You wicked, wicked man.

**GEORGE**  What do you want?

**PATSY**  I want to help you. And the only way I can help you is if you articulate these hidden desires.

**GEORGE**  I think you might be the one needing help.

**PATSY**  You see? Why don't you say, "You're crazy! You're nuts! You talk like a manic-repressive nymphomaniac!" Instead of folding your paws together and gently venturing, "I think you might be the one needing help."

**GEORGE**  You want me to play cat and mouse with you, and then when I pounce, *I* land in the trap.

**PATSY**  A little paranoid, aren't we?

**GEORGE**  No.

**PATSY**  What, one woman plays Benedict Arnold and so now we're all guilty until proven innocent?

[GEORGE *says nothing.*]

Is that it? Is that why you have to punish us? 'Cause Mommy wouldn't let you stay in your womb?

[*Slight pause.*]

Alright, I'll shut up. We'll just wait till your laundry's done and then you can retreat to your hundred years of electronic solitude. No wonder she left you. You don't let anyone in for a second. I guess you can't.

[PATSY *sits down on the table, and rests her chin in her hand. Silence.*]

**GEORGE**  The thing of it is...

**PATSY**  Forget it.

**GEORGE**  My best friend, my high school buddy, practically my brother...

**PATSY**  Betrayed you with your ex-fiancée? That's okay, I don't need to hear about it. You want a carrot?

**GEORGE**  When she told me there was someone else—someone I supposedly didn't know, my buddy let me cry and carry on and patted me on the back. Commiserated about the treachery of women! What wind was it that blew into this town and made everyone, everyone a liar?

**PATSY**  Some of us... believe in the truth.

**GEORGE**  Oh, we all believe in the truth, as long as it's convenient! Not a day goes by that I am not lied to, either for gain, for amusement, or else out of sheer laziness. That's right, there are people who simply forget what the truth is!

**PATSY**  [*Telling the truth.*] It's a terrible thing.

**GEORGE**  And I'm the fool who's cursed with a photographic memory. My buddy said something, something intimate, that he only could have heard from...

**PATSY**  What did he say?

**GEORGE**  It doesn't matter *what* he said. It's the fact that he knew this phrase that Francine only used with... I thought—me.

**PATSY**  Was it like sex talk? A special word for her nonny?

**GEORGE**  I said that's not the point.

**PATSY**   Oh, please tell me!

**GEORGE**   Don't you understand, I'm exposing my. . . inner pain and you want to sprinkle salt on it.

**PATSY**   Sorry. You're right. . . . Was it "honey pot"? . . . Sorry. Go on.

**GEORGE**   He used the word that only Francine used. And when I confronted him, he still lied up and down. So I went to Francine, who is now married, to a lawyer. She corroborated my suspicions beyond a reasonable doubt. The whole thing amused and titillated her! I had dropped out of med school and developed addictive behaviors, to forget, and they blithely carried on with their lives, as if nothing had happened! After Francine admitted she and Parker had betrayed me, she asked, "Would you like a cup of tea?" A cup of tea!
[GEORGE *turns away from* PATSY.]
. . . The word—the private word we used to use—was "love cup."
[GEORGE *cries.* PATSY *laughs, at first quietly, but she quickly loses control and, in spite of herself, laughs out loud.*]
You're laughing!

**PATSY**   [*Laughing.*] I'm not! Not intentionally!

**GEORGE**   You have a lot of nerve!

**PATSY**   I mean, "love cup"!

[*Laughs.*]

**GEORGE**   Go ahead, laugh along with Francine! Laugh at George Rubin, the rube who blurts the truth while everyone screws and lies behind his back!

**PATSY**   [*Reaching out to him.*] George, I'm sorry.

**GEORGE**   You—you—*liar*! Is that the only way you can get your—jollies? You set me up, you knock me down, you set me up, knock me down! I'm your bouncing ball, aren't I?
[*Perhaps by now he's shaking her.*]
Bounce bounce bounce bounce! Fun, isn't it?!

**PATSY**   No!

**GEORGE**   Liar! You're all liars! Goddamn liars!

**PATSY**   I can't help it!

**GEORGE**   Oh, you can help it, you love lying! Don't you??

**PATSY**   No!

**GEORGE**   Don't you dare lie to me. Admit it: you love to lie—

**PATSY**   No! I try to tell the truth but no one listens!

**GEORGE**   What?!

**PATSY**   The truth is so disgusting! I hate it!

**GEORGE**   No—you—you can't hate the truth.

**PATSY**   I do.

[GEORGE *moves away from* PATSY, *who is very upset and perhaps crying.*]

**GEORGE**   Shandalayah, I'm so sorry.... I'll just—go.

**PATSY**   Please don't.

>  [*Pause.*]

>  Please say something or do something. I'm starting to feel very embarrassed.

**GEORGE**   Well, I, uh . . . Is it alright if I—? . . . Hold you.

**PATSY**   [*Kindly.*] Shut up.

[*He holds her.*]

**PATSY**   George?

**GEORGE**   Yes?

**PATSY**   I hate your pants.

[GEORGE *moves out of the embrace.*]

**GEORGE**   I was saving my good pair for the interview.

**PATSY**   Here.

[PATSY *takes out* GEORGE'*s handkerchief and gives it to him. A moment in which* GEORGE *realizes it's his handkerchief, and looks at* PATSY. *Then.*]

**GEORGE**   Thank you.

[*Beat.*]

Uh, would you like to—?

**PATSY**   That's okay; I've got my sleeve. . . . What is it about that handkerchief?

**GEORGE**   It's broken in. You know how a new handkerchief has a stiffness? I have a very sensitive nose. At this point, a new handkerchief would wreak havoc.

**PATSY**   That one won't last forever.

**GEORGE**   No. But if it gets me through tomorrow, maybe I'll get this job and be able to leave the city.

**PATSY**   You think it's different, outside the city?

**GEORGE**   [*Ominously.*] If it isn't . . .

**PATSY**   What?

**GEORGE**   It's got to be different.

**PATSY**   You know what your problem is? You've never learned the art of lying. Want me to teach you?

**GEORGE**   [*Firmly.*] No.

[*Pause. Then we hear a* MAN's *voice offstage.*]

**MAN**   [*Calling.*] Patsy? Patsy?

**PATSY**   Come on: we gotta hide.

**GEORGE**   Why?

**MAN**   [*Off; closer.*] Patsy, are you down here? I want my poker chips, Patsy.

**GEORGE**   Are you Patsy? You said—

**PATSY**   Yes, to some I'm Patsy.

**MAN**   [*Off.*] Patsy? I have reached my limit! If I have to come down these stairs to get my chips . . .

**GEORGE**   Do you have his chips?

**MAN**   [*Off.*] Is someone down there with you?

**PATSY**   [*To* MAN.] No.

**MAN**   [*Off.*] Patsy, I heard his voice.

**PATSY**   Rick, it's George. My lover.

**MAN**   [*Off.*] What?

**PATSY**   The whole time I've lived with you, I've been seeing George.

**MAN**   [*Off.*] You expect me to believe this utter crap?

[*Pause.* PATSY *doesn't know what to say.*]

**GEORGE**   It's true!

**MAN**   [*Off.*] I'm sick and tired of your fucking games!

[*We hear the* MAN *coming down the stairs.*]

**PATSY**   Come on, we'll use the fire exit!

[*She offers her hand.*]

**GEORGE**   I don't think I should—

**PATSY**   Trust me.... Trust me!

[*Beat.* GEORGE *lets* PATSY *lead him off upstage, as the lights fade to black.*]

• • •

# Light

Jeni Mahoney

# Jeni Mahoney

Jeni Mahoney is a playwright, teacher, and producer. Her plays, including *The Feast of the Flying Cow...and Other Stories of War*, *The Martyrdom of Washington Booth*, *Mercy Falls*, and *Light* have been presented at the National Playwrights Conference at the O'Neill Center, InterAct Theater (Philadelphia), Greenwich Playhouse/Grey Light Productions (London), And Toto Too (Denver), L.A. Theater Center, Mid-West New Play Festival (Chicago), Lark Theater's Playwrights Week, Rattlestick Productions, NYU's hotINK Festival, Village Rep, and Chicago Women's Theater Alliance, among others. *Throw of the Moon* (written with Ben Sahl) and *American Eyes*, commissioned and produced by Gorilla Rep, can be found in *Plays and Playwrights 2001* (NY Theatre Experience). Excerpts from her plays can be found in numerous monologue and scene books. Jeni teaches playwriting at Playwrights Horizons Theater School, a studio school of New York University's Tisch School of the Arts. She is the co-artistic director of id Theatre Company and artistic director of Seven Devils Playwrights Conference in McCall, Idaho, which has developed more than 60 new plays since its inception in 2001. Jeni is a member of the Dramatists Guild of America.

• • •

[*At rise: Two women sit facing each other. One is "giving light" to the other. HELENA (giving light) is intensely involved; eyes closed and hands poised, palms out. ABBY (getting light) stares strangely at HELENA, not sure what to make of it. They sit this way for about fifteen seconds. There is an open beer can near each woman, and four full beers remain in the plastic rings. A stack of booklets sits near HELENA's feet. They aren't drunk, but are enjoying a slight buzz.*]

**ABBY**  Is it working?

**HELENA**  Shhhhh…

[*Ten more seconds of silent light-giving.*]

**ABBY**  I don't feel anything…

**HELENA**  Shhhhhh!

**ABBY**  Helena—

[HELENA *drops her hand in disgust.*]

**HELENA**  Geez! Of course you can't feel it. You're thinking about it too much. You're blocking the light with your negative, doubting attitude.

**ABBY**  I was just checking in.

**HELENA**  You don't need to check in.

**ABBY**  I mean, I was sitting there for a good five…six minutes and I was just wondering if everything was okay. I mean, maybe you could feel if it wasn't going right.

**HELENA**  I can only give the light. I can't tell if you're receiving it.

**ABBY**  Oh. [ABBY *considers this.*] How do I know if I'm getting the light?

**HELENA**  You have to be ready for the light to penetrate you. Otherwise it just bounces right off you—

**ABBY**  Uh-huh.

**HELENA**  In fact, I probably shouldn't even be giving you light. It can be dangerous if you're not ready for it. That's what happens when someone spontaneously combusts.

**ABBY**  [*Amused.*] Spontaneously combusts?

**HELENA**  It happens more than you think.

**ABBY**  Spontaneous combustion?

**HELENA**  Sure. They try to explain everything like it's something else—like it's all so easy. Like it's science. There are forces—in the government and politics and stuff—that want to take away all the mysteries of the world. Like in Sunday school they tell you to "dwell on the mystery," but at the same time they try to explain it all with logic and rationalizations. They present evidence as if evidence creates truth. But evidence—empirical evidence—is a trap. Like Dac says: a demon in sheep's clothing.

**ABBY**  Oh.

**HELENA**  I know it sounds weird, and I don't say it too well yet, but when I'm there and Dac is talking—it all makes sense. When you hear him talking, it's all so common-sense it makes you feel stupid that you never thought of it before.

**ABBY**  Hel, you know I support you in whatever you do...

**HELENA**  I know, I know—[*Indicating the beers.*]—Do you want another?

**ABBY**  Sure—

  [*They don't miss a beat as they open their beers.*]

  And I know you've been searching...

**HELENA**  Everyone is searching.

**ABBY**  Yeah, but some more than others.

**HELENA**  It's the best thing in my life.

**ABBY**  [*Cautiously.*] It's the only thing in your life...

**HELENA**  Dac says that when you commit to God it's all or nothing. Like marriage. You give everything—your heart, your soul, your emotions, your labor and the fruit of your labor—or it's worthless. It's hard, but it's supposed to be hard. If it were easy, then everybody would do it. You have to give up something—sacrifice something—in order to be chosen.

**ABBY**  Yeah, but who decides when you're chosen?

**HELENA**  God.

**ABBY**  But then how do you know...? When you're chosen, I mean...

**HELENA**  You just do—Dac says it's like re-emerging from the womb. You have to breathe a whole new way. Everything is different, but it's also suddenly the most natural thing in the world.

**ABBY**  Dac. What is that? Is that a name? It sounds like an e-mail address, or a Pez candy or something.

**HELENA**  They're initials. Dac says the Judeo-Christian names that we use are tying us to worn-out mythology—superstitions that we no longer need—that are holding us back and imposing these fascist personae on us—and we put that out into the universe without even knowing it. Like Abby...Abigail. Like *The Scarlet Letter*.

**ABBY**  What?

**HELENA**  A marked woman, Abby, an adulteress...and now it's forced its agenda on your life.

**ABBY**  You didn't even read *The Scarlet Letter*—

**HELENA**  But I don't *have* to—that's the point. We all know what happens in the story. And I know what happened with you and Jake—

**ABBY**  The situations are so totally different—

**HELENA**  I'm not judging you. I'm just saying that when your identity is controlled by your name, then you're fucked by destiny.

**ABBY**  I'm sure there are plenty of women named Mary who get divorced and—I don't know—people named for saints—they screw up too you know...

**HELENA**  Oh, sure. Lots of Biblical characters fucked around. Check it out. I'm not making it up.

**ABBY**  I'm sure you're not, but with all due respect—which is probably more respect than it deserves—I don't buy it. I'm not being controlled by a very boring work of fiction.

**HELENA**   It's as real as anything else, you know, by association. It's a cultural myth—it's all fiction really and we collectively—not you Abigail the smart individual—control that. It's like a wave—you know—you can't outrun it.

**ABBY**   I can't believe we're even having this conversation.

**HELENA**   I'm just trying to answer your question.

**ABBY**   Really? Geez, I don't even remember what the question was.

**HELENA**   The name thing. Dac. He encourages us to create new identities that express our new lives—free from "oppressive cultural fictions"—open to change, rebirth, divine intervention. Dac means everything and no-thing. Whatever you can create: Delicate...Angelic...Creator.

**ABBY**   Deadly...Amoral...Con-Artist...

**HELENA**   Dreamlike, Alternative, Captain...

**ABBY**   Deceitful. Arrogant. Cash-man.

**HELENA**   Divine, Alien, Communicator...

**ABBY**   Divine Alien Communicator?

**HELENA**   Just an example.

**ABBY**   And who are you?

**HELENA**   I'm Hep.

**ABBY**   Hep?

**HELENA**   I took it from my initials—Helena Elaine Preston.

**ABBY**   Who the heck is Preston?

**HELENA**   It's my grandmother's maiden name. I was named for her and Dac believes that I may be partially reincarnated from her because usually we are our own relatives. Which makes sense, if you think about it—the whole thing about the family dynamic and the working out of these repeating patterns. Besides, Dac thought "P" was better than "S:" the serpent's letter. The P offers more...possibilities. Peace, progress, prophetess...

**ABBY**    [*Under her breath.*] Painfully Preyed upon . . . Perishing . . .

**HELENA**    [*Somewhat hurt.*] Whatever . . . you're just not giving this a chance, and that's fine. One thing Dac warned us about was preaching to our friends . . . I just thought you'd be more open-minded.

**ABBY**    Come on, Hel, we used to laugh at shit like this! Remember those weirdos from science class—cutting themselves and baying at the moon—

**HELENA**    They were Satin worshippers, Abby!

[ABBY *shrugs as if it's all the same.*]

Dac is about freedom, about joy—about letting go of all the shit that is weighing us down and sucking the happiness right out of us. It's killing us. It's killing you—look at you.

**ABBY**    What about me?

**HELENA**    You know in the Bible people lived to be 120! Shit. I can't believe you're even comparing this to a Satanic cult . . . it's called giving *light*, not giving *dark* . . . geez Louise.

**ABBY**    Okay, okay—let's try it again. You can light me up until I catch fire. I won't say anything. Promise.

[ABBY *offers herself again to get the light.*]

**HELENA**    Forget it.

**ABBY**    Why?

**HELENA**    Forget about it. You aren't taking this seriously. You're fucking with me.

[ABBY *briefly considers arguing, but she's been caught.*]

**ABBY**    I'm sorry, you're right. [*Silence.*] Sorry. Okay.

**HELENA**    It's just that I've found something so good and meaningful and right and I want to share it. Is that okay?

**ABBY**    Of course it's okay.

**HELENA**    You can't imagine how wonderful it is for me there. I've never felt so wanted and like I belong and full of spirit. Really full. Like they told us it would be but it never was. It's like I'm Mary every day. The woman of God, His beloved. The beloved of God. And I can feel it inside me...more than...more than sex is inside. Not like sex, but sensual. A buzzing. A caress. Inside caress, all buzzy warm and pulsing. Like a wave of love and breathlessness. Like a new love all over again every time and every day it gets stronger. [*Pause.*] I know you think I'm out of my mind. You think it's in my mind. That he's in my mind: Dac. But He...the big He... is the one. Inside me. Inside. Be still and He is. Inside me...

[*They sit in awkwardly for a bit.* ABBY *cannot find a response.*]

**ABBY**   It sounds nice. It does. So...they let you...drink beer?

**HELENA**   Yeah, sure. They aren't Nazis, you know. Dac drinks whiskey, says it's more pure, but he doesn't mind beer. He'll have a beer chaser sometimes. [*Another awkward silence.*] Abby...?

**ABBY**   Yeah.

**HELENA**   Do you ever think of me?

**ABBY**   Yeah, sure. If I didn't think about you, then I wouldn't have recognized you when you called, right?

**HELENA**   That's just remembering me, not really thinking about me.

**ABBY**   I guess. I don't know. Why?

**HELENA**   Just curious...

**ABBY**   Yeah?

**HELENA**   It's funny, you know, the past is a dream to me now. Like my whole life up until now happened to another person.

**ABBY**   I know what you mean. It's like remembering in black and white.

**HELENA**   Dac says that the more we break free of our past personae, the more we forget the world of our past.

**ABBY**   You mean, like, you'd forget me?

**HELENA**   ...And that's kind of okay...'cause there's lots of stuff that I want to forget, right? But to let go of everything—even the good—and it was good, don't you think?

**ABBY**  It was more ... simple.

**HELENA**  Safe.

**ABBY**  So that's what this is all about?

**HELENA**  What?

**ABBY**  It's like a good-bye. Am I right?

**HELENA**  Not so much a good-bye as a stroll down memory lane ...

**ABBY**  Before the memory of me disappears completely. Great. That's just great. You know—ten years—nothing. No phone call. Nothing. Then at my darkest moment here's my bestest, oldest friend and I think—great, a sign. Life goes on. But no, it's all just another big *hasta la vista*, Abby.

**HELENA**  The phone works both ways, you know.

**ABBY**  [*Lamely joking.*] Maybe my dialing finger was broken.

**HELENA**  Maybe my entire hand was crushed in a freak circus accident.

**ABBY**  I was deaf.

**HELENA**  I was dumb.

**ABBY**  Oh yeah? Well, I was in a sucky, controlling mind-fuck marriage.

**HELENA**  Okay. You win.

**ABBY**  Yes! [*A pause.*] Stay, Hel. You can stay with me.

**HELENA**  Abby—

**ABBY**  Don't decide—just think about it. It's an option.

**HELENA**  You don't understand, Abbs. With Dac, I'm divine ...

**ABBY**  Yeah, but are you happy?

**HELENA**  Don't I seem happy?

**ABBY**  I don't know, kind of ... but an unreal happy ...

**HELENA**  Jealous?

**ABBY**  Yeah, right.

**HELENA**  Are you?

**ABBY**  Jealous?

**HELENA**  Happy.

**ABBY**  Hel—

**HELENA**  Are—you—happy?

**ABBY**  No. Okay. Life's a roller coaster. You go up, you go down—maybe you learn something and then maybe you're not such a screaming asshole the next time.

[HELENA *shrugs. It may be so.*]

So maybe I have no business grilling you about being happy— heaven knows I haven't got all the answers. But I have been happy, I will be happy. And I'm not willing to give up everything—forget everyone—everything that came before. That doesn't even make sense. I mean, what is left? Right? If you don't have . . . remembering. Remembering is as close to happy as I can get some days.

**HELENA**  But what if it were all like this—like it is right now—? Perfect moments—and the world wouldn't crash in tomorrow morning and screw it all up. What if every asshole thing you'd done—or was done to you—was just gone. Blip. Clean slate. What if that's the trade-off. An eternity of perfect moments, instead of suffering over shit that's so far gone you can't even touch the memory of it.

**ABBY**  But the world's not like that, Hel . . .

**HELENA**  But what if it is? What if it is and we're just not playing it that way? Why shouldn't it be like this?

**ABBY**  You know, I really am going to miss you, Hel. Just knowing that I could call you—you know—even though I never did.

**HELENA**  Yeah. I'll miss you. Miss this.

**ABBY**  No you won't. You'll forget . . . remember?

**HELENA**  True.

**ABBY**  Not even the pleasure of remembering you forgot. You'll wake up one morning and the memory of me will gone—but I'll miss the good ol' days for both of us, okay?

**HELENA**  You don't have to, Abbs. It's a choice.

**ABBY**  I know.

> [*They sit for a moment and take in the evening.*]

> Let's try it again: the light thing.

**HELENA**  I don't know...

**ABBY**  Look, I may never touch the divine—but honestly, I could sure use some light in my life, so if you've got some to spare...and you're willing to give it, with the understanding of course that I don't believe a word of it...

[HELENA *smiles, takes a sip of her beer and puts it down. She positions her hand in front of* ABBY's *head and focuses with her eyes closed.* ABBY *looks at* HELENA *intently.*]

**HELENA**  [*Eyes still closed.*] Are you feeling something this time?

[ABBY *studies* HELENA's *face, with a mix of love, some sorrow—under it all is perhaps even some jealousy in spite of her disbelief. She reaches up as if to touch* HELENA's *hand, but does not. She caresses the air around her: an invisible touch.*]

**ABBY**  Yeah...something...

[*They sit for some time giving/receiving light...*]

[*Fade to black.*]

• • •

# House of the
# Holy Moment

Cary Pepper

# Cary Pepper

Cary Pepper has had work presented throughout the United States and in Europe. *The Walrus Said* won the Religious Arts Guild Playwriting Competition; *Small Things* won the Robert R. Lehan Playwriting Award and the Tennessee Williams/ New Orleans Literary Festival 2006 One-Act Play Contest, and was selected for inclusion in *Best American Short Plays 2005–2006*. His work has also been included in *Audition Monologues for Student Actors II* (Meriwether Publishing), and *Scenes and Monologs from the Best New International Plays* (Meriwether Publishing). Cary is a member of the Dramatists Guild, and a founding member of the San Francisco Bay Area playwrights group ThroughLine.

**BUTCH HAGGERTY**, 40s–50s. He's been around and it shows. If there's a hustle, he'll find it and use it. And he's open to suggestions.

**HENRY BILLINGS**, 30s–40s. Always on the straight and narrow. A bureaucrat. Very neat and orderly.

**CHARLIE**, 30s–50s. A regular Joe weighed down by the mess the world is in.

• • •

[*Sunday morning.*]

[*A big empty space previously occupied by a large store that's moved out. Near the top of the back wall is a faded sign: EVERYDAY LOW PRICES. It's immediately clear that the space is being lived in—by someone extremely unconcerned about housekeeping. It's a comfortable mess, a cross between a college dorm room and a chaotic bachelor pad. Scattered about are pizza boxes, liquor bottles, take-out cartons, paper cups, etc. At first glance it looks like there has recently been a big party. There was . . . But this is how it always looks.*]

[*BUTCH enters, wearing a bathrobe and slippers. He carries a steaming mug of coffee, a hip flask, and the Sunday paper. He moves slowly—he's nursing a hangover.*]

[*He sets the coffee and the paper on a table, then sorts through the paper. When he comes to a section he isn't interested in, he tosses it onto the floor. He isn't making a neat stack—just tossing each section over his shoulder and letting it land where it might. He doesn't look at where it lands. He doesn't care. He drinks some coffee, smacks his lips, then reaches for the flask and adds whatever's in it to the coffee. He tastes the coffee again, pours more liquor in. Tastes it . . . adds one more hit. Then he raises the flask to his lips and takes a pull.*]

[*He sits down, puts his feet up on the table, and buries himself in the paper, holding it up in front of him. The mug is within arm's reach. When he drinks coffee, he doesn't lower the paper, but reaches out and feels for the mug. The mug disappears behind the paper, then reappears. At one point when he reaches out, his hand lands on the flask instead of the mug. That, too, disappears behind the newspaper, then reappears.*]

[*There's a knock at the door. . . . Without coming out from behind the newspaper, BUTCH calls out.*]

**BUTCH**    It's open!

[BUTCH *remains behind the newspaper.*]

[HENRY BILLINGS *enters. He's everything* BUTCH *isn't—Mr. Straight and Narrow. He wears a suit and carries a briefcase. He keeps looking around. . . . He can't believe what he's seeing.*]

[*From behind paper.*]
Yeah?

**HENRY**    I'm looking for Butch Haggerty.

**BUTCH**    Yeah?

**HENRY**    Uh, are you Mr. Haggerty?

**BUTCH**    Yeah.

**HENRY**    I'm Henry Billings. From the city's assessor office.

[BUTCH *lowers the newspaper. He peers at* HENRY.]

**BUTCH**    Yeah?

**HENRY**    Yes sir.

[BUTCH *goes back to the newspaper.*]

**BUTCH**    What can I do for you?

**HENRY**    According to city records, this is supposed to be a church.

**BUTCH**    [*Behind newspaper.*] It is a church.

**HENRY**    I mean, a church that's open and running.

**BUTCH**    We are open and running.

**HENRY**    I was afraid you were going to say that.

[BUTCH *lowers the newspaper.*]

**BUTCH**    Something wrong?

**HENRY**    I'd say there is.

**BUTCH**    Yeah. You're probably in the wrong place. Must happen all the time. City bureaucracy being what it is.

[BUTCH *goes back to the newspaper.*]

**HENRY**   This is 515 Main, isn't it?

**BUTCH**   [*Behind newspaper.*] Uh-huh.

**HENRY**   Well, according to our records, this is supposed to be a working church.

**BUTCH**   It is a working church.

**HENRY**   *This* is a working church?

**BUTCH**   Uh-huh.

**HENRY**   I find that very hard to believe.

[BUTCH *lowers the newspaper.*]

**BUTCH**   Not religious?

**HENRY**   As a matter of fact, I attend services regularly. And I have never... What's the name of this church?

**BUTCH**   House of the Holy Moment.

[HENRY *consults a sheet of paper.*]

**HENRY**   That's what our records indicate. And when did you open your doors?

**BUTCH**   This morning? Few minutes ago. Went to bring in the paper.

**HENRY**   I mean, when did you open to the public.

**BUTCH**   I imagine that's in your records, too.

**HENRY**   According to these records, you were supposed to open a year ago.

**BUTCH**   We did.

**HENRY**   You did.

**BUTCH**   Uh-huh.

**HENRY**   And are you holding services today?

**BUTCH**   Uh-huh.

**HENRY**   When?

**BUTCH**   Soon as people show up. We've had some attendance issues lately. For our Sunday services.

**HENRY**   And your other services?

**BUTCH**   Had a big one last night.

**HENRY**   On Saturday night?

**BUTCH**   The Catholic church does.

**HENRY**   Those are evening services.

**BUTCH**   Every Saturday.

**HENRY**   What time are *your* Saturday services?

**BUTCH**   Start when people get here. Go until . . . oh, sometimes all night.

**HENRY**   That sounds more like a party.

**BUTCH**   We're very informal.

[BUTCH *goes back to the newspaper.*]

**HENRY**   Where's the pastor?

**BUTCH**   We don't call it that here.

**HENRY**   Where's the minister?

**BUTCH**   We don't call it that here.

**HENRY**   Where's the leader of the flock?

**BUTCH**   Don't call it that, either.

**HENRY**   Who is the leader of the congregation? The head of the church.

[BUTCH *lowers the newspaper.*]

**BUTCH**   That'd be me.

**HENRY**   I see. If I may ask, what bible do you use?

**BUTCH**   Life is my bible.

**HENRY**   How convenient.

**BUTCH**   Are you mocking my religious beliefs? That's un-American.

**HENRY**   You say you're open. As a church.

**BUTCH**   Uh-huh.

**HENRY**   And you're ready to hold services.

**BUTCH**   Yep!

**HENRY**   Today.

**BUTCH**   You bet!

**HENRY**   [*Indicates* BUTCH's *attire.*] Like that?

**BUTCH**   We're very informal.

**HENRY**   As soon as someone walks through the door.

**BUTCH**   Ready when they are!

**HENRY**   Except no one's going to walk through the door, are they?

**BUTCH**   Something you're trying to say?

**HENRY**   Mr. Haggerty... By the way do you *have* a title?

**BUTCH**   Butch'll do just fine.

**HENRY**   What a surprise.

**BUTCH**   Informal group.

**HENRY**   All right... Butch... I think we both know what's going on here.

**BUTCH**   We do?

**HENRY**   Yes.

**BUTCH**   What's going on here?

[HENRY *takes out a sheet of paper and hands it to* BUTCH.]

**HENRY**   I'm sure you've done your research, and are aware of all this. So why don't I just talk you through it.

**BUTCH**   Why don't you.

**HENRY**   The city of Appleton has no property taxes on houses of worship, and very liberal deed restrictions. City ordinances make it possible, in fact extremely easy, for anyone to come here, declare they're starting a church, buy property, and pay no taxes.

**BUTCH**   Sweet.

**HENRY**   As a result, Appleton, a town with a population of 3,000, now has a total of 300 churches. Any response so far?

**BUTCH**   Must be a very religious place.

**HENRY**   Or a place where people are taking unfair, and in some cases, unethical, advantage of the city fathers' good intentions.

**BUTCH**   You wanted churches, you got 'em.

**HENRY**   We wanted legitimate churches.

**BUTCH**   Who says my church isn't legitimate?

**HENRY**   Mr. Haggerty…

**BUTCH**   Butch.

**HENRY**   Are you really trying to say this is a legitimate church?

**BUTCH**   You questioning my church? That's un-American. Anyway, you sure you have a beef? You got your churches. OK, a couple may be a little hinky… But you have all the standard players. Isn't that what you asked for?

**HENRY**   What we asked for was a town where religion was respected. Honored. Welcome. What we *have* is… people like you.

**BUTCH**   Don't follow you.

**HENRY**   I think you do.

**BUTCH**   You attacking religion? That's un-American.

**HENRY**   We are most certainly not attacking religion. We are, however, getting ready to do something about people who are using religion for the purposes for which it is not intended.

**BUTCH**   I were you, I'd have a talk with the people across the street. Y'know, the Temple of Macedonian Agnostics.

**HENRY**   I have talked with them. And they happen to be Macedonian Agnostics. Whatever that is. They *are* operating a house of worship.

**BUTCH**   D'ja check out the people down the block? The First Church of James? You might want to…

**HENRY**   I've spoken to them as well. They believe in the teachings of Jesus' brother. Which, although I myself am not familiar with, at least *suggest* a degree of credibility.

**BUTCH**   Well, you might want to talk to...

**HENRY**   I will eventually talk to everyone. Right now, I want to talk to you. Here, in this "church."

**BUTCH**   Need religious counseling?

**HENRY**   I need the truth.

**BUTCH**   Don't we all. Good luck with that!

**HENRY**   You haven't even bothered to fix the place up.

**BUTCH**   Small cash-flow issue. Off-shore banking isn't what it used to be. But we're starting a new fund-raising drive. I've got a chain letter they tell me is guaranteed to...

**HENRY**   Mr. Haggerty...

**BUTCH**   Butch.

**HENRY**   To call this a house of worship...

**BUTCH**   You saying it isn't?

**HENRY**   I'm saying who could possibly believe anything of a religious nature happens here?

**BUTCH**   Maybe we have different ideas of what's religious.

**HENRY**   I'm sure we do. But how can you call this place a church?

**BUTCH**   Spiritual things happen here. As often as I can manage it.

**HENRY**   And by spiritual things you mean...?

**BUTCH**   Insights...Epiphanies...Realizations...Recalibrations...Readjustments...Finding ecstasy. Or whatever else is available. People experiencing tongues. Don't underestimate the power of tongues. A well-used tongue can be a miraculous thing.

**HENRY**   These are your religious activities?

**BUTCH**   You have a pure moment...An instant of bliss...Clarity... Truth...Oneness...Understanding...Serenity...Isn't that a holy experience?

**HENRY**   Would I be terribly wrong in assuming that these experiences... these moments...involve drugs?

**BUTCH**   Something wrong with that?

**HENRY**   It's illegal!

**BUTCH**   Depends on the drugs. And the religion. Lotsa religions use drugs.

**HENRY**   Except...

**BUTCH**   Yours.

**HENRY**   You can't just take any belief...any behavior...and call it a religion.

**BUTCH**   Why not?

**HENRY**   It isn't the way it's done.

**BUTCH**   Maybe that's the problem. Maybe it should be.

**HENRY**   That would mean someone could commit murder and say it was their religion.

**BUTCH**   Maybe there shouldn't be any religion at all.

**HENRY**   That, coming from a man of god.

**BUTCH**   Who said religion has anything to do with god?

**HENRY**   What?

**BUTCH**   Why can't you believe in god, without believing in religion?

**HENRY**   *That's* what you believe in?

**BUTCH**   We're very open-minded. Open to all possibilities. Y'ask me, religion is the problem.

**HENRY**   What?

**BUTCH**   Just let people believe in god and leave it at that. Once you start bringing religion into it, things get all bollixed up. Too many rules...restrictions...Too many isms.

**HENRY**  That would mean doing away with *your* church.

**BUTCH**  That would mean doing away with all churches.

**HENRY**  That would upset a lot of people.

**BUTCH**  Maybe that's the problem.

**HENRY**  I didn't come here to discuss this.

**BUTCH**  What'd you expect to discuss in a church?

**HENRY**  I came to discuss your religious activities. And frankly, I . . . I don't know what to say.

**BUTCH**  Happens. Being faced with the ineffable and all.

**HENRY**  I don't know what to say because I don't know what to make of your so-called beliefs.

**BUTCH**  Are you knocking my religion? That's un-American. Unconstitutional, too. And if you're speaking for the city fathers, it may be grounds for legal action.

**HENRY**  I'll tell you what's ground for legal action. We're taking a good hard look at all the churches in town. And we don't always like what we're finding. You're a prime example of what I'm talking about. You claim this is a house of worship. Yet there is no sign whatsoever . . .

**BUTCH**  We have a sign.

[*He points toward the front door.*]

**HENRY**  That says Acme Furniture!

**BUTCH**  The day I moved in, I was thinking about buying furniture. I get here, that's the first thing I see, right over the door. I took it as a sign.

**HENRY**  And you intend to leave it there permanently?

**BUTCH**  We're making do with what we've been provided. That small cash-flow problem.

**HENRY**  This doesn't even look like a church. In fact, it looks like you're running a business.

**BUTCH**   Isn't every church?

**HENRY**   And it looks like your business is having parties.

**BUTCH**   Still in the start-up phase. Working out a few identity issues.

**HENRY**   And yet you decided to call yourself a church. Obviously, to take advantage of city laws.

**BUTCH**   Seems to me, you're the one trying to turn churches into a business. Looks to me like you're trying to make it your brand.

**HENRY**   We're doing no such thing! As I've pointed out, we wanted legitimate churches.

**BUTCH**   As I've pointed out, what makes you think this isn't a legitimate church?

**HENRY**   What made you move to Appleton?

**BUTCH**   I prayed on it. God said to come here.

**HENRY**   Mr. Haggerty...

**BUTCH**   Butch.

**HENRY**   What would you do if we did make churches pay taxes? Would you stay or leave?

**BUTCH**   I'd pray on it.

**HENRY**   I think you'd be on the first bus out of town.

**BUTCH**   If god told me to.

**HENRY**   Well, you might want to start praying. There are going to be some changes around here.

**BUTCH**   Well, that's good. There's that noise ordinance I wouldn't mind having lifted. Y'know, a lot of people are up and very active at 2 am. You shouldn't...

**HENRY**   I'm talking about changing the laws regarding churches.

**BUTCH**   Don't lean on St. Tiffany's Love Angels of the Miraculous Touch. Those girls really do have great hands.

**HENRY**   And unless people can show they're running a church in good faith . . .

**BUTCH**   You *are* anti-religion. I think maybe I should get my lawyer on the phone.

**HENRY**   We are not anti-religion. We are anti-dishonesty. We are anti-fraud.

**BUTCH**   What's that got to do with us? We're a law-abiding church.

**HENRY**   Well, if you can prove that . . . I am going to bring this up before the city council, and . . .

**BUTCH**   I'm grandfathered in.

**HENRY**   What?

**BUTCH**   You can change the laws, but it won't apply to churches already established.

**HENRY**   How do you know?

**BUTCH**   I prayed on it.

**HENRY**   Well, it appears your prayers were answered.

**BUTCH**   Hallelujah. I also took a look at the city bylaws.

**HENRY**   Maybe we'll have to change some of those, too.

**BUTCH**   You might want to consider how it'll affect the other 299 churches in town. I don't think you want a church uprising on your hands. Last time that happened, we had the Crusades. And the Inquisition wasn't much fun either. But your call.

**HENRY**   We have bigger things to worry about. With so many people claiming church status, our tax base is eroding. We need revenue for things like the police, fire, and schools.

**BUTCH**   Oh, you got a cash-flow problem, too.

**HENRY**   We certainly do. And we're going to . . .

**BUTCH**   Y'know, your problem isn't you have too many churches. Your problem is, they don't pay taxes. They paid taxes, you're be rolling in it. Come to think of it, why *don't* churches pay taxes?

**HENRY**   Because... That's the way it is.

**BUTCH**   Maybe you should look at *that*.

**HENRY**   Maybe you should think about what constitutes a house of worship.

**BUTCH**   Or maybe *you* should.

**HENRY**   As for your "church uprising"... Once we make our situation clear, I doubt that any church... any real church... any real religion... is going to argue with us.

**BUTCH**   You never know what a religion is liable to do. Specially one that's organized.

**HENRY**   We'll take our chances.

**BUTCH**   Another thing you may want to think about... You mess with the city bylaws... make it hard on the churches... you're gonna get tagged anti-religion in every paper, on every news show in the country. Think about what *that'll* do to your tax base.

**HENRY**   As I said, real churches... truly religious people... will be on our side.

**BUTCH**   As I said, what's holy to one person isn't always holy to someone else. You don't have to read much history to see that.

**HENRY**   But there are standards.

**BUTCH**   You telling me what I should consider holy? That's...

**HENRY**   Un-American?

**BUTCH**   Arrogant.
So let's see... You guys goofed, now you're trying to fix it. I'm down with that. You just have to figure out *how* to fix it. Without making it worse. Hey, I've done a lot of consulting work in this area. You want, I can whip up a quick proposal...

**HENRY**   No thank you.

**BUTCH**   Best thing to do might be, just make 'em pay taxes. 'Course, it wouldn't be retroactive. That'd be a bait and switch. So what you do is, keep your open-door policy on churches, but the new kids in town pay for it. At the rate you've been going, you'll be in the black in no time. See, I'm all over this. You should hire me. I can start tomorrow.

**HENRY**   Maybe you shouldn't tell us how to run our city.

**BUTCH**   Maybe you shouldn't tell me how to run my church. And be more careful about what you let churches do. And for god's sake, a few standards when you let people set one up.

**HENRY**   We can't tell people how to manage their religion.

**BUTCH**   My point exactly.

**HENRY**   Do you consider yourself a man of god?

**BUTCH**   Haven't we established that?

**HENRY**   Well...As a man of god, I'm going to ask you to be completely truthful with me.

**BUTCH**   What makes you think truth is part of my religion?

**HENRY**   Isn't it?

**BUTCH**   There you go again, telling me how to run my church.

**HENRY**   *Is* the truth important to you?

**BUTCH**   Is the Pope Catholic? Does Madonna believe in the Kabala?

**HENRY**   Then, I ask you, in the name of truth...*Is* this a church?

**BUTCH**   Yeah!

**HENRY**   Mr. Haggerty.

**BUTCH**   What? It isn't *your* idea of a church. It's *exactly* what I think a church should be. A place where people can find comfort. Be themselves. Have a moment of genuine reality. Of pure... whatever they're looking for.

**HENRY**   Without a bible? Without doctrine? Without a pastor?

**BUTCH**   That's *your* version of what religion should be. See, you guys want the churches, but you want 'em to be your brand of church. I'm more open than that.

**HENRY**   Yet a few minutes ago, you were telling me to look into the Macedonian Agnostics.

**BUTCH**   Yeah, that was wrong. I was being intolerant. Mea culpa.

**HENRY**   So that's that?

**BUTCH**   I've had a revelation. We're big on revelations. And redemption and forgiveness.

**HENRY**   Does your religion have a *name*?

**BUTCH**   We're not big on names.

**HENRY**   So you're a...a...

**BUTCH**   We don't believe in labels.

**HENRY**   Every religion has a name.

**BUTCH**   They believe in labels.

**HENRY**   So anyone can come in here, and claim they're in church?

**BUTCH**   Yeah.

**HENRY**   And that helps them?

**BUTCH**   Maybe it does, maybe it doesn't. The path can be long and difficult.

**HENRY**   Yet a minute ago you said people find what they need here.

**BUTCH**   Well, it can be short and easy, too.

**HENRY**   That sounds like an enormous rationalization.

**BUTCH**   Whatever floats your boat. We don't judge.

**HENRY**   I think I've seen everything I need to. I'll be making my report to the city council next week. We'll see who stays open and who doesn't. Good day.

**BUTCH**   Lemme ask you something. Which churches you going to shut down?

**HENRY**   What do you mean?

**BUTCH**   All of 'em? The ones with low attendance? Or just the ones you don't like?

**HENRY**   That isn't fair.

**BUTCH**   Got that right.

**HENRY**   We would never shut down a church just because we didn't like it.

**BUTCH**   Isn't that what you're trying to do to me?

**HENRY**   What I'm trying to do is ascertain that you *are* a church.

**BUTCH**   Well, we are.

**HENRY**   How do I know?

**BUTCH**   I just told you.

**HENRY**   And why should I believe you?

**BUTCH**   I'm a man of god.

**HENRY**   I think that in this case, we may have to use different criteria.

**BUTCH**   And who's gonna determine those?

**HENRY**   The town leaders.

**BUTCH**   Based on?

**HENRY**   What's good for the town.

**BUTCH**   Your idea of what's good for the town is what got you into this.

**HENRY**   Hopefully we'll do a better job this time.

**BUTCH**   Maybe you should pray for guidance.

**HENRY**   We'll probably do just that.

**BUTCH**   We've got a special service that...

**HENRY**   Thank you. I'm sure we'll do fine on our own. Good day.

**BUTCH**   As long as you're here... Wanna make a donation?

**HENRY**   I really should leave now.

**BUTCH**   Leave the door open on your way out. Air-conditioning's not up to snuff.

**HENRY**   Good day, sir.

**BUTCH**   On your way out, you think you can bring in that food
delivery?

**HENRY**   Good day, sir!

**BUTCH**   It's for our after-service brunch.

[HENRY *leaves.*]

Hey... let go and let god.

[*He goes back to the newspaper.*]

[CHARLIE *enters. He walks slowly, with the weight of the world on his shoulders.*
BUTCH *keeps reading the newspaper.*]

**CHARLIE**   [*Looking around.*] I thought this was a church.

**BUTCH**   It is a church.

**CHARLIE**   This is a church?

**BUTCH**   We're a very informal group.

**CHARLIE**   Oh. Well, when do services begin?

**BUTCH**   When people get here.

**CHARLIE**   You *are* an informal group. Mind if I sit?

**BUTCH**   Suit yourself.

[CHARLIE *sits down and sighs heavily.*]

**CHARLIE**   I just don't know what to do.

**BUTCH**   It's early. You got all day.

**CHARLIE**   I mean... I think I'm at the end of my rope.

[BUTCH *lowers the newspaper.*]

**BUTCH**   Something on your mind?

**CHARLIE**   I don't know *what* I'm going to do.

**BUTCH**   What do you want to do?

**CHARLIE**   You don't want to know.

**BUTCH**   Probably not.

[*He goes back to the newspaper.*]

**CHARLIE**  I have such dark thoughts.

**BUTCH**  Welcome to the club.

**CHARLIE**  Some of them...If I told you, I'm sure you'd consider them terrible sins.

**BUTCH**  Probably not.

**CHARLIE**  Destructive...Evil...Inhuman.

**BUTCH**  Lemme know when you get to the terrible sins.

**CHARLIE**  When I say destructive, I'm not talking about hurting other people. Just...myself.

**BUTCH**  How badly?

**CHARLIE**  As bad as I can.

**BUTCH**  That could be pretty bad.

**CHARLIE**  It couldn't be worse than it is now.

**BUTCH**  You really do have something on your mind.

**CHARLIE**  Sometimes I feel like I'm *losing* my mind.

**BUTCH**  Been *there*!

**CHARLIE**  I don't know what to do. Where to go.

**BUTCH**  So you came here?

**CHARLIE**  I'm going to every church in town. Did you know there are 300 churches in Appleton?

**BUTCH**  Yeah, just heard.

**CHARLIE**  I went through the phone book and made a list. There are only 297 in the phone book. You're not one of them.

**BUTCH**  We're an unlisted church.
[*He lowers the newspaper.*]
How did you find us?

**CHARLIE**  I went to the city assessor's office.

**BUTCH**  Who are the other two?

**CHARLIE**   Other two?

**BUTCH**   Unlisted churches.

**CHARLIE**   [*Takes out a sheet of paper.*] The Second Coming Car Service, and Messiah Mike's House of Stereo.

**BUTCH**   You might go there. A high-end wide-screen plasma TV can do wonders for the spirit.

**CHARLIE**   I did. It didn't help.

**BUTCH**   Have you tried St. Tiffany's Love Angels of the Miraculous Touch? Those girls have great hands.

**CHARLIE**   Several times. Nothing.

**BUTCH**   Did you ask for Monique?

**CHARLIE**   She's got *really* great hands.

**BUTCH**   Nothing?

**CHARLIE**   Zip.

**BUTCH**   You really *are* in trouble.

**CHARLIE**   I'm going through this list church by church.

**BUTCH**   There's a lot of that going around.

**CHARLIE**   If nothing helps by the end of the list... I don't know what I'll do.

**BUTCH**   What's the problem? Money? Women? Booze?

**CHARLIE**   Everything.

**BUTCH**   Think you could you be a little more *vague*?

**CHARLIE**   Why would you want me to be more vague?

**BUTCH**   Hey, Mac...

**CHARLIE**   Charlie.

**BUTCH**   Charlie, I'm trying here. Least you can do is meet me halfway. What's got you in such a tailspin?

**CHARLIE**  Everything. I get up in the morning, I can barely get out of bed. I get out of bed, I can barely make it to the kitchen. I get to the kitchen, I can barely pour a cup of coffee. I pour...

**BUTCH**  I think I got it. You leave the house?

**CHARLIE**  Barely.

**BUTCH**  And then you barely make it across the street.

**CHARLIE**  I have to barely get down the block first.

**BUTCH**  Got a job?

**CHARLIE**  Yeah.

**BUTCH**  Payin' your bills?

**CHARLIE**  Yeah.

**BUTCH**  Got friends?

**CHARLIE**  Yeah.

**BUTCH**  Got a *special* friend?

**CHARLIE**  I get by.

**BUTCH**  And no fatal diseases.

**CHARLIE**  I'm an ox. My therapist says I'm clinically depressed, but I don't buy it.

**BUTCH**  So you just like to whine a lot?

**CHARLIE**  I now what you're going to say. I don't appreciate my blessings.

**BUTCH**  I was thinking more you're a big crybaby. But that's another way to put it.

**CHARLIE**  I know there are people much worse off than I am. But there's this dark cloud over me, all around me, and it's sucking the life out of *my* life. Everything just feels completely hopeless.

**BUTCH**  Have you tried these?

[*He takes out a bottle of multi-colored pills.*]

**CHARLIE**    What's that?

**BUTCH**    Better living through chemistry.

**CHARLIE**    Everywhere else, the first thing they tell me to do is pray.

**BUTCH**    We're very big on better living through chemistry.

**CHARLIE**    I tried that. It helped, but every time I turned on the evening news...

**BUTCH**    Tell me about it! D'ja try *not* turning on the evening news?

**CHARLIE**    And not reading the newspaper? And not going online? Not being part of the world?

**BUTCH**    Works for some.

**CHARLIE**    You call that living?

**BUTCH**    I call that self-preservation.

**CHARLIE**    How can we live this way? How can we live in a world like this? If that's what we've created, there *is* no hope.

**BUTCH**    *That's* what's got you? You want the world to be better?

**CHARLIE**    Is that too much to ask?

**BUTCH**    You *do* have a problem.

**CHARLIE**    See? It's hopeless.

**BUTCH**    Want a drink?

**CHARLIE**    [*Waves him away.*] This time of day, it makes me sleepy.

**BUTCH**    I've got these mushrooms...

**CHARLIE**    I already had breakfast. And eating's not the answer.

**BUTCH**    Maybe there is no answer.

**CHARLIE**    I'm glad to finally hear one of you admit it. Every church I walk into, they tell me what I should do. Pray...Meditate... Fast...Go on a retreat...Volunteer...Get married... Withdraw...Get reborn...Read the Bible...Give money... You're the only one honest enough to admit you don't have an answer. Well, you and the Macedonian Agnostics.

**BUTCH**  No, I mean it. Maybe there is no answer.

**CHARLIE**  None at all?

**BUTCH**  Nope.

**CHARLIE**  How'd we get in such a mess?

**BUTCH**  Hey, we're people...

**CHARLIE**  You mean, like, to err is human?

**BUTCH**  I mean, like, we're people. Deeply flawed. Weak, stupid, backward, primitive, stupid, selfish, greedy, shortsighted, cruel, stupid, easily manipulated, power-hungry, narrow-minded, prejudiced, stupid, arrogant, self-centered, and did I mention stupid?

**CHARLIE**  And?

**BUTCH**  You want more?

**CHARLIE**  And what's the answer?

**BUTCH**  Did I mention we're also stubborn?

**CHARLIE**  So what's going to save us?

**BUTCH**  Who said anything's going to save us?

**CHARLIE**  You mean, we're doomed?

**BUTCH**  Looks that way at the moment.

**CHARLIE**  Then what do we do? What do *I* do?

**BUTCH**  You live with it.

**CHARLIE**  What!?

**BUTCH**  You got a choice? Don't answer that. Of course you got a choice. You always have a choice. You can always chuck it in and check on out. If that's what you want to do.

**CHARLIE**  That's a sin.

**BUTCH**  Who told you that? Don't answer that.

**CHARLIE**  So, I'm right. It really is hopeless.

**BUTCH**   You're the one who walked in here with that idea.

**CHARLIE**   So it's *not* hopeless?

**BUTCH**   Of course it's hopeless. Don't you watch the evening news?

**CHARLIE**   Then I might as well...What'd you say? Chuck it and check out.

**BUTCH**   Your call.

**CHARLIE**   If it's hopeless, why not?

**BUTCH**   Well, here's how I see it...You take a good hard look at the way things are, you're not gonna like what you see. An advanced race came down today, they'd do everything they could to put us out of our misery. And by the looks of things, it's gonna get a lot worse before it gets better. *If* it gets better. A betting man would not give us great odds. We seem determined to out-lemming the lemmings. You don't like unhappy endings, you might wanna walk out on the movie.

But...Bad as things are, there's also a lot of fun to be had along the way. The smell of a new car...That first line of coke... Chocolate...Hawaii...The smell of roses and lavender... Tongues...Orgasms...Beauty...The first moment when you're drifting off to sleep...Waking up from a bad dream...And whatever else floats your boat. Now...Why give all that up? I don't know about you, but I'm sticking with it.

**CHARLIE**   What if you don't enjoy any of that?

**BUTCH**   Are you listening? How can you not...You can't find *one* thing?

**CHARLIE**   What if the cloud's so dark, that...No.

**BUTCH**   Oh...It's *that* bad. Been *there*. Plan B...It all just keeps coming at you. So fast, and thick, and heavy, that all you can do is hunker down, tuck your head between your knees, cover your ass, and kiss it good-bye. It's a tornado with your name on it, and any second it's gonna take you out and not look back. And there's not a damned thing you can do about it. Or maybe not. And there's not a damned thing you can do about it. So you hunker down and you wait to see what's gonna happen.

But... While you're waiting, you can do one thing. You can howl and scream back. With the shit flying so thick it's a wonder it hasn't ripped your head off, you can take a deep breath and scream "Fuck you!" as loud as you can, as often as you need to.

And you scream and you scream and you scream... And with any luck, you're still there screaming when it's finally done with you and blows past. You may be a mindless screaming idiot howling into the wind, but it's gone and you're still there. Even if you are hunkered down with your head between your knees and your hands clutching your ass.

And you pick yourself up, brush off the shit, and pick up where you were. Or start over if you have to. If you want to. And if you don't... If you wanna just chuck it in... You can do *that*. But you're doing it on *your* terms. *You're* making the decisions.

[*Long pause.*]

**CHARLIE**   That's it?

**BUTCH**   Sometimes that's the best you can do.

**CHARLIE**   That's it?

**BUTCH**   That's all I got.

[*Long pause.*]

**CHARLIE**   If that's all you have to say... [*Bellows.*] FUCK YOU!!!!!

**BUTCH**   Well, it's not for everyone.

[*Pause.*]

**CHARLIE**   You're right. It *does* help.

**BUTCH**   Then again, it's amazing where a good "Fuck you" can leave you.

**CHARLIE**   Wow! I haven't felt like this since the Church of the Smiling Shepherd suggested I spend some time with the sheep.

**BUTCH**   Glad I could help.

**CHARLIE**   So...When does the service begin?

**BUTCH**   What service?

**CHARLIE**   I came here for Sunday services.

**BUTCH**   This is it.

**CHARLIE**   What is?

**BUTCH**   This is.

**CHARLIE**   This is the service?

**BUTCH**   Yep.

**CHARLIE**   I can't believe it.

**BUTCH**   D'ja get what you came for?

**CHARLIE**   Yeah!

**BUTCH**   Church is out, son.

[*He goes back to his newspaper.*]

**CHARLIE**   I don't know how to repay you.

**BUTCH**   Donations are always welcome.

**CHARLIE**   Can I come back?

**BUTCH**   Welcome to the congregation.

**CHARLIE**   OK. See you next Sunday.

[*He starts to leave.*]

**BUTCH**   [*Waving* CHARLIE'*s list of churches.*] Hey, you forgot your list.

**CHARLIE**   Don't need it any more.
      [*He gets to the door...Stops.*]
      Hey...
      [BUTCH *lowers the paper.*]
      FUCK YOU!!!

**BUTCH**   Back atcha!

**CHARLIE**   That's amazing! See you next Sunday.

**BUTCH**   Hey, Charlie...

**CHARLIE**   Yeah?

**BUTCH**   Why don't you try our Saturday night services. I think you'll really like those.

**CHARLIE**   What time are they?

**BUTCH**   Start when people get here. Go until...oh, sometimes all night.

**CHARLIE**   Sounds like a party.

**BUTCH**   We're very informal.

**CHARLIE**   Yeah...OK.

**BUTCH**   See you on Saturday.

[CHARLIE *leaves.* BUTCH *goes back to the paper...*]

• • •

# The Disruptive, Discursive Delusions of Donald

Michael Roderick

# Michael Roderick

Michael Roderick started Small Pond Entertainment five years ago, when he found that it was virtually impossible for an artist to be at their best when they also had to produce. He developed a system for the advancement of a producing organization to be the umbrella for shows that lacked producers. Over the years Small Pond has become a major name in the NYC theatre community, having presented shows in numerous venues and with hundreds of different artists. As artistic director, Michael has produced over thirty shows since his arrival in New York in September 2002. He has also been the organizer of networking events that have included representatives from The New York Musical Theatre Festival, Fractured Atlas, and RWS Casting and Associates. He holds a BA in secondary ed English and theatre performance from Rhode Island College and an MA from NYU in educational theatre colleges and communities. Michael also teaches English at LaSalle Academy, where he is the head of the drama program. He has written fifteen plays, and his play *I'll Do It Tomorrow* was chosen for inclusion in *Best American Short Plays 2004–2005*, published by Applause Books. He also plans on eventually publishing a book about his first year teaching, called *Stage Fright*, as well as a young adult novel, titled *Norin's Quest: Beyond the Gates of Lavender*.

## cast

DONALD LUCKRET
BERNICE JONES
BO GARON
DAYNA HARRISON
SHIRLEY MASTERS

. . .

## scene one

[DONALD LUCKRET's *apartment. It is 3:20 a.m.* DONALD *is lying with his girlfriend* BERNICE *when the phone rings. The bed and the answering machine are the only things lit. The phone rings twice and then the answering machine picks it up. We hear* DONALD's *voice after a long beep.*]

DONALD    [*voice-over*] Hello. If you are calling for Mark Wurlitz and Jane
    Donaldson, they are not at this number. It recently came to my
    attention that their number ends with a five and ours ends with a
    three, so if you dialed wrong, no biggie. Just hang up now. If
    you're calling me, Donald, or my girlfriend Bernice, we can't
    come to the phone right now, so leave a message and we'll get
    back to you. Of course, if you don't leave a message, I think that's
    just rude, except if you were calling for Mark Wurlitz or Jane
    Donaldson, because then it would be okay for you to hang up
    because I told you that you could. But then there's always the
    possibility that you're just hanging up because this message is too
    long, which it is. Maybe if I hired a psychic to locate your chi from
    the call—but what if you were a salesman or, oh my God, what if
    you're Shirley. Oh, you are, I can feel it. Stop calling me. [*Beep.*]

SHIRLEY    [*voice-over—singsong voice*] Donald . . . [*There is a noise made by a
    squeaky toy.*]

[BO GARON *and* DAYNA HARRISON *enter. They are both wearing black trench coats.* BO *is tall, well built and has a scruffy beard.* DAYNA *is also tall with reddish brown hair and is very plain-looking. Both individuals are wearing mismatched sneakers, one black and one white. The same is true for their gloves.* BO *lights a cigarette.*]

**BO**  Why isn't he talking?

**DAYNA**  It's called sleeping. I mean, c'mon, Bo, you've done this enough times to know they're always asleep when we get here.

**BO**  I just heard him yacking away a minute ago. Are you trying to tell me he just passed out when we came over?

**DAYNA**  That was the answering machine, you dope!

**BO**  Oh.

**DAYNA**  I mean, let's get it together here, Bo. You've been a recruiter for how many years? Never mind. So you at least realize the potential of this candidate?

**BO**  Which one?

**DAYNA**  Him! The one sleeping next to the girl. He's a possible soul catcher.

**BO**  A what?

**DAYNA**  That's it. Get out your manual.

**BO**  Fine. [*Takes out manual.*]

**DAYNA**  Now read. Page one, c'mon.

**BO**  Welcome to Soul Scrubbers Incorporated. The middleman between eternal damnation and complete redemption. As a recruiter you will be responsible for finding candidates for our most important position, the Soul Catcher. Oh, that's what—

**DAYNA**  Go on. Didn't you read this when you were instated?

**BO**  No, I just used the coupons in the back.

**DAYNA**  You took full use of employee benefits without ever knowing the job you were doing? Why haven't you been fired?

**BO**  Hey! I may not have my names down, but I get the job done.

**DAYNA**  Okay, big shot. So what does the soul catcher do? [BO *cracks the book.*] Without looking at the book.

**BO**  Well, the soul catcher, um, yeah, well, uh . . .

**DAYNA**  You don't know. Okay, how did I get paired up with you? A soul catcher—catches souls. Wow, what a novel idea. Then they filter all the guilt out from people's sins by reliving those horrible moments that the person who died doesn't want to show to heaven. We at Soul Scrubbers Incorporated provide a human purgatory for all the bad stuff so the soul can get past St. Peter's defenses. We do all this for a small fee and the promise that the filtered souls will continue to spread throughout the upstairs office so that one day we may be able to buy Eternity Enterprises. That damn CEO Jesus keeps finding out about things and firing our guys. So we have to find more soul catchers to increase our employee output. Is that so difficult to grasp?

**BO**  I know about the socks.

**DAYNA**  Okay, whoopee. Everybody knows about the socks. So is he wearing white socks?

**BO**  I haven't checked.

**DAYNA**  The sooner we know, the better

**BO**  What if he's wearing black socks?

**DAYNA**  [*Gravely speaking.*] They never get dirty.

**BO**  The longer you wear them?

**DAYNA**  [*Sad, as if somebody died.*] The stronger they get. What about her?

**BO**  What about her?

**DAYNA**  Is her nightgown made of silk?

**BO**  Looks like polyester.

**DAYNA**  Damn.

**BO**  What's wrong?

**DAYNA**  You can't dye polyester.

**BO**  You mean, as long as she's in polyester, she won't—

**DAYNA**  Dye. Yes. I once worked for this woman who loved to dye and she told me "Dayna, polyester won't dye."

**BO**  So she can't die?

**DAYNA**  Nope, can't dye.

**BO**  You're sure?

**DAYNA**  Yes! It's a simple fact. Polyester won't dye.

[BO *pulls out a gun and shoots* BERNICE. BERNICE *stands up with blood all over her and drops to the floor, dead.*]

**BO**  Shit.
      [DONALD *wakes up.*]
      Shit.

**DAYNA**  Shut up! Shut up! I've got it.

[DAYNA *waves her hand and does the hokey pokey and* DONALD *falls fast asleep.*]

**BO**  How did you do that?

**DAYNA**  Not important. Is he wearing white socks?

**BO**  [*Fumbling under the sheets.*] Umm, uh . . .

**DAYNA**  Is he wearing white socks?

**BO**  I can't tell.

**DAYNA**  For God's sake! Look!

**BO**  Okay, okay. I'm looking. Oh no.

**DAYNA**  What?

**BO**  He's . . .

**DAYNA**  What?

**BO**  He's . . . [*Growing fear.*]

**DAYNA**  Damn it, what?

**BO**  He's not wearing socks.

**DAYNA**  No! This won't work at all. Damn him.

**BO**  I think it's time for plan B.

**DAYNA**  Yep, looks like it. So he did this yesterday after he—

**BO**   Yeah. So what, I'm bringing him back to *then*.

**DAYNA**   That would probably be best.

**BO**   Okay.

> [*Does three jumping jacks and howls like a wolf.* BERNICE *gets up and walks offstage.* DONALD *gets up backwards and walks almost offstage.* SHIRLEY *enters. She is attractive and perky. She is wearing a cute little sundress with a sweater over it. She is probably mid-twenties. They are both frozen. Time has now reversed.* BO *and* DAYNA *exit.*]

> [*As he exits.*] I hope he makes it.

**DAYNA**   [*As she exits.*] Me too.

[DONALD *and* SHIRLEY *unfreeze.*]

**DONALD**   I'm really glad I came over.

**SHIRLEY**   Me too.

**DONALD**   It's just so hard to find a sweet girl, you know?

**SHIRLEY**   It's hard to find a nice guy. But there you were, smiling at me from behind the parrot display.

**DONALD**   Yeah, that was kind of embarrassing.

**SHIRLEY**   You mean, when it repeated what you said about me?

**DONALD**   I thought I was alone. I mean, after that damn parrot blared, "My God, you could bounce a quarter off the ass of that clerk," I thought that you would think that I was some sort of male chauvinist and come over and slap me and kick me out of the store, making it impossible to ever buy a pet for the rest of my life, but you didn't flip out. You winked at me. Why?

**SHIRLEY**   Because nobody thinks of me like that. Hell, it was a compliment. I'm always being looked at like I'm somebody's little sister. I'm always called cute, not sexy, and you're the first guy to look at me like that and say something like that, even if you never meant to, it's still okay.

**DONALD**   This is great. I was so worried that I'd end up with some total psycho, so I decided not to go to any clubs or rock concerts or any hangout where you can meet strange women, and I'm talking strange. I figured that a pet store was such a safe place, you know? I mean, there aren't psychos working in places like that. There are just nice people and you're so nice.

**SHIRLEY**  Thank you. I have to admit I'm very attracted to you, Donald. I know you're probably just a really nice guy who just happened to give a girl a compliment without realizing it and you're probably very committed to some wonderful girl and you'll probably give me a soda and send me on my way in a second but—

**DONALD**  [*Kisses her.*] There. Whoo.

**SHIRLEY**  [*Thunderstruck.*] You kissed me.

**DONALD**  [*Kisses her again.*] Oh my god! I did, didn't I? I don't know if I should be doing this. I mean, I've been with the same girl for five years. You'd think I had a little more self-control. [*Kisses her again.*] I want you.

**SHIRLEY**  This is a little sudden. Are you sure you want *me*?

**DONALD**  Oh yeah. I mean, no. I mean. I just want to know what I'm missing. I mean, Bernice is wonderful . . . but you are very, very, beautiful. You look pretty young too. Oh, was that an insult? I'm sorry. I didn't mean it like "Hey, give Lolita a lollipop and send her home" young. I just meant that. Oh geeze. I don't know what I mean. I don't know what I want. I just think that maybe there is something else out there in this world and I should go for it. No, that's not what I mean. I mean. [*Looks at her and sizes her up.*] Wow. Do you do aerobics or something? You are in such great shape! Oh, what the hell!

[*Kisses her again, this time more passionately.*]

**SHIRLEY**  Could you do me a favor? [*Takes out a squeaky toy.* DONALD *looks at it.*] Squeeze this.

[DONALD *squeezes the toy halfheartedly.* SHIRLEY *lets out a slight erotic moan. He squeezes a little harder, and she gets louder.*]

**DONALD**    What in the world?

**SHIRLEY**    Oh. The first time I, um, lost it [*Giggles.*] it was on top of the squeaky toys in the pet store after closing and ever since that time, every time I hear a squeaky toy I get so hot!

**DONALD**    Oookay.

**SHIRLEY**    Squeeze it again, Donald.

**DONALD**    I'm not so sure about this. I mean, you're this sweet, wholesome girl. I mean, you work in a pet store for God's sake.

**SHIRLEY**    The hours are good. I'm not as nice as you think I am, Donald. Now squeak that thing.

**DONALD**    [*Squeezes it. She moans.*] This is really strange. I mean, really really.

**SHIRLEY**    Squeeze it again!

**DONALD**    [*Scared.*] Okay, okay!

[*Squeezes it again. She moans even louder.*]

**SHIRLEY**    Donald...you've been a naughty boy.

>   [SHIRLEY *rips open her dress and underneath she is wearing a dominatrix outfit with cartoon characters all over it. She retains all the cute Mary Sunshine qualities she had at the beginning of the scene and now also has a look of power and determination. She puts* DONALD *in a headlock.*]
>
>   [*Sugary sweet.*] I really like you, Donald. Have I told you that? You're great. You're a lot of fun. Squeeze the damn toy. [*He squeezes it.*] Oh God, that's better. Now who's the master?

**DONALD**    Ow! That hurts.

**SHIRLEY**    [*Puts him in a wrestling hold.*] Who's the master?

**DONALD**    You are!

**SHIRLEY**    [*Loosens up.*] Good. Now, I'm going to tie you up with these!

[*Takes out a pair of black socks.*]

**DONALD**    No! Not the black socks. Aaahhhh!

[*They both freeze. BO and DAYNA enter.*]

**BO**  He's still barefoot.

**DAYNA**  I see that. Well, skip him ahead.

[*They exit. SHIRLEY walks out backwards. BERNICE walks in and freezes. DONALD unfreezes and lies down in the bed. BERNICE unfreezes.*]

**BERNICE**  Donald? Donald? Where are you? [*Looks at herself.*] What the hell? I'm bleeding. Wow. There's a lot of blood. I've been cut or something. Donald?

Donald, where are you? [*She turns around.*] Oh, there you are! Didn't you hear me screaming? [DONALD *is still asleep.*] Wake up! There's blood on me, you idiot.

**DONALD**  [*Wakes.*] Huh?

**BERNICE**  Blood.

**DONALD**  Blood?

**BERNICE**  Yes.

**DONALD**  What happened to you?

**BERNICE**  I don't know. There was this loud bang and then I was covered in blood.

**DONALD**  Wow. That's weird. Well, are you in any pain?

**BERNICE**  No.

**DONALD**  Then maybe it's not your blood.

**BERNICE**  Of course it's my blood! How could I be covered in blood and it not be my own?

**DONALD**  Ever see the movie *Carrie*?

**BERNICE**  Yeah, that's it. I'm covered in pig's blood, you moron!

**DONALD**  Well, I don't know.

**BERNICE**  You sure don't.

**DONALD**  You're sure it doesn't hurt?

**BERNICE**  Yes.

**DONALD**  Positive?

**BERNICE**  Yes.

**DONALD**  Absolutely, without a doubt sure that—

**BERNICE**  Yes! Yes! I don't feel anything at all.

[DONALD *climbs out of bed and goes to* BERNICE.]

**DONALD**  [*Touches her.*] You're cold.

**BERNICE**  What?

**DONALD**  You're cold, Bernice. Cold as a Popsicle.

**BERNICE**  I'm still with you, aren't I? I can't be that cold.

**DONALD**  No, I mean, cold as in dead.

**BERNICE**  Oh, so I'm dead to you now? Is that it? I give you all this affection and you say I'm dead? What in the world are you saying? You know what, I don't need this. I'm leaving. [*Walks towards audience and then falls backwards.*] What? Donald, I can't move.

**DONALD**  What?

**BERNICE**  I can't move.

**DONALD**  Oh. What's the matter?

**BERNICE**  I can't move at all. I can't feel my arms, legs, ears, all of it.

**DONALD**  What the hell is going on!

[BERNICE *drops to the floor inanimate, and* DONALD'*s body is suddenly taken over by a strange force that propels him into his bed. He is knocked out.* BO *and* DAYNA *enter. They get into the bed and "sandwich"* DONALD.]

**DAYNA**  [*Taps* DONALD'*s foot.*] Wakey-wakey. Rise and shine.

**DONALD**  [*Wakes up.*] Who the hell are you?

**DAYNA**  Not important.

**DONALD**  Who says?

**DAYNA**  Me. That your wife?

**DONALD**  No, that's my girlfriend.

**DAYNA**  Unfortunate. She looks more like a wife.

**DONALD**  Who are you?

**DAYNA**  That doesn't matter.

**BO**  Who wrote *Moby-Dick*?

**DONALD**  Herman Melville.

**DAYNA**  Nope, Kevin Spacey.

**BO**  What is the name of the actor Dayna just mentioned?

**DONALD**  Kevin Spacey.

**BO**  No, Herman Melville.

**DONALD**  Wait a minute, I just said Herman Melville.

**DAYNA**  No. You just said Kevin Spacey.

**DONALD**  But you never said Herman—

**BO**  Shut up! We're asking the questions. Who wrote "The Metamorphosis"?

**DONALD**  Franz Kafka.

**DAYNA**  Wrong. Tennessee Williams.

**DONALD**  Huh?

**BO**  Exactly.

**DAYNA**  Yes. Excellent answer! We get more of these and we'll be all set. Boxers or briefs?

**DONALD**  Julia Roberts.

**BO**  Good, I think he's getting it!

**DAYNA**  Quickly now. Why ask why?

**DONALD**  Um, beer?

**DAYNA**  Ooh, so close, but no cigar.

**BO**  Once upon a—

**DONALD**  Time! Yes, time.

**DAYNA**   No! Midnight dreary. I can't work with him. He's a fool. Cut to the last part.

**BO**   What color socks do you wear?

**DONALD**   I don't wear socks.

**DAYNA**   [*Slaps him.*] What color?

**DONALD**   None. I sleep barefoot.

**BO**   [*Punches him in the stomach.*] What color?

**DONALD**   I don't wear—

[*At this point* BO *and* DAYNA *get out from underneath the covers and pull the sheet off of* DONALD.]

**DAYNA**   Go to your sock drawer.

**DONALD**   [*Desperately.*] I don't have a sock drawer.

**BO**   [*Takes out his gun.*] Go!

**DONALD**   Oh. You mean, the dresser? Well, I'll just head right on over. Now no need to get out of control.

**DAYNA**   Just do it.

[DONALD *walks over to his dresser and opens one of the drawers. He pulls out a pair of white socks and a pair of black socks.*]

**BO**   OK. Now put on the white ones.

**DONALD**   That's it! You can just shoot me if you want, I don't care! I have to know what the hell is going on. Who are the two of you? What are you doing in my apartment? Why is Bernice lying on the floor like a zombie? Is this my apartment? Am I frigging dreaming? That must be it. This must all be a dream and you are all just the product of my mind. You are really not here. Lalalalalalala.

**DAYNA**   [*Does a funny little dance and* DONALD *freezes.*] Good. He's quiet.

**BO**   Why can't I do that?

**DAYNA**   You'd hurt yourself. [*Points to Bernice.*] You already shot her.

**BO**   You said she couldn't die.

**DAYNA**   No, I said that polyester wouldn't dye.

**BO**   Huh!?

**DAYNA**   Dye, as in fabric dye, genius! You know very well that soul catchers are chosen by three very important criteria. First, the ability to make a clear-cut decision about what they want out of life; second, they need to be wearing a garment that can change color because you know that these people have to absorb the colors of the sins and the guilt and so on and so forth, And third, they have to be dead by some stupid coincidence. Do I have to explain everything for you? Eternity Enterprises gets the entire stock of natural-cause death cases as well as murders. She's a murder. Thanks! This brings our income way down.

**BO**   Oh, dye! That makes a lot more sense now.

**DAYNA**   Were you listening at all? Never mind. Here's what we're going to do. You remember what you did before?

**BO**   Yes. I sent him back in time two days. He was having an affair, she was sleeping. I shot her the day after that and he ended up getting stuck in the 3:20 a.m. time slot when he . . . well, you know.

**DAYNA**   I'm impressed. Now, we'll unfreeze him and see if we can recruit him. If not, we send him back. How does that sound?

**BO**   Then can we eat? I'm starving.

**DAYNA**   You realize he's going to be a very mixed-up candidate at the end of this. We shifted both his time and reality, thanks to you. How could you forget about the dye rule? It's right there in your manual. Rule #262 states that any female cannot be a soul catcher if she wears polyester because the dye of the sins just washes out and there's no color change.

**BO**   Can I ask you a question?

**DAYNA**   If you promise it won't be stupid.

**BO**   Why the hell are all of these celestial things based on garments? There's the dye rule, and then there's the whole thing with the black socks and the fact that they keep a person inanimate forever, while white socks absorb sins, not to mention that rule about the safety pins. Who would ever believe that you could save somebody's life with a safety pin?

**DAYNA**  You know Soul Scrubbers Inc. is owned by a seamstress in New Jersey! What did you expect? If it were owned by a guy who ran a burger joint, fate would be decided when you chose fries or onion rings. All things you'd know if you read your manual.

**BO**  Can we just finish this?

**DAYNA**  Fine. [*She snaps her fingers and* DONALD *unfreezes.*] Hello, Donald.

**DONALD**  What? La—

**BO**  Before you start doing that again, will you hear us out?

**DONALD**  Huh?

**DAYNA**  Do you remember anything that has happened in the past twenty-four hours?

**DONALD**  Of course. I left Shirley's after getting the beating of my life and I couldn't believe what a mistake I had made. I got back in my car and took the wine that I had brought for a romantic evening— which turned out to be a wrestling match. I should have been enjoying it . . . but I wasn't. I got in the car and I just started drinking. I started driving back and I finished the wine and threw the bottle out the window of my car. I heard it smash and I thought, Oh shit! Somebody could run over it and pop their tires and spin into a telephone pole that could get knocked over and land on a house with a family of five in it and some poor girl would have to explain to her friends that her family was demolished from a falling telephone pole and she'll be in therapy for the rest of her life and probably get a strong medication that her pet poodle Fifi would get a hold of and the dog would die and land on her cat who would also die and she seeing this horrible animal blood bath would be so distraught that she'd probably commit suicide and the one guy who loved her all her life, but she never knew it, would come running in just like in the movies and trip on all three carcasses and probably impale himself on the TV antenna at which point her landlord could come in and have a heart attack and then I'd be the one who was responsible for some guy's four flat tires, a city's telephone pole, the house of a family of five, the death of two cute and cuddly animals, the suicide of some innocent young girl, the complete ruination of her relationship with her would-be boyfriend—not to mention his death and the poor landlord's heart attack. I'd be a mass murderer! So you can see why I had to go back. I had to clean up that glass. So I got out of the car and started brushing it to the side of the road, and I don't remember what came next.

**BO**    A Mack truck.

**DONALD**    What?

**DAYNA**    A Mack truck turned you into road pizza.

**DONALD**    Did it hit anything besides me?

**BO**    Well, actually, it veered off the road, hit a telephone pole, which proceeded to land on a house owned by a family of—

**DAYNA**    Bo! Not now.

**BO**    Fine.

**DAYNA**    You don't remember anything else, Donald, because you're dead.

**DONALD**    Oh man. Talk about irony. What was all that stuff you were asking me before?

**BO**    Questions about your life. You see, you're a prime candidate to be a soul catcher.

**DONALD**    What's a soul catcher?

**DAYNA**    [*Freezes him.*] Bo! He's not supposed to know. He has to make the decision before he dies, remember?

**BO**    Great, so what do we do now? He's already dead.

**DAYNA**   But we can send him back! He's very indecisive, though, what do we do about that?

**BO**   An interpretive dance about banana-cream pie?

**DAYNA**   No, that only works on pathological liars. Why don't we just talk to him?

**BO**   OK. Suit yourself

**DAYNA**   [*Hops on one foot and does a karate move.*] Hello again, Donald.

**DONALD**   Could you guys stop doing that? I keep losing my train of thought. I was about to ask a question but I forget what it was.

**BO**   [*Gives* DAYNA *the thumbs-up.*] Donald, why did you go to Shirley's?

**DONALD**   I don't know. I guess I just was worried that there was something better out there and I was missing it.

**DAYNA**   You worry a lot, Donald. Do you know why we asked you about *Moby-Dick*? You had all the right answers on that quiz in fourth grade and you second-guessed yourself. Thought that maybe your answers were too plain. You ended up with an F.

**DONALD**   Oh, I get it. You guys must be my conscience, right?

**BO**   Not even close. You second-guessed yourself in college too. Tennessee Williams wrote "The Metamorphosis"? You knew it was Franz Kafka! Why don't you trust your decisions? The only time you ever trusted yourself is when you started dating Bernice.

**DAYNA**   It's pretty simple, Donald. It's very important to us that you are satisfied with what you have and not second-guess yourself. Do you understand?

**DONALD**   I'm happy with Bernice, I just don't want to make a mistake.

**BO**   You've been making them all your life because you're afraid of making them.

**DONALD**   Wow. Are you guys counselors?

**DAYNA**   [*Freezes him.*] I'm sorry I had to shut him up. Do you think he's ready to go back?

**BO**  Oh yeah. I think he's going to make some good decisions from now on. Hold on, let me just fix her. [BO *goes over to* BERNICE *and safety-pins her nightgown. Suddenly she's alive. She walks over to the bed and covers herself up.*] 3:20?

**DAYNA**  3:20. Make the right decisions, Donald, please.

[BO *and* DAYNA *go to opposite sides of the room. The scene unfreezes.* DONALD *goes to the sock drawer.*]

**DONALD**  Which socks should I wear, honey?

**BO and DAYNA**  Yes!

**BERNICE**  How about the black ones?

**BO and DAYNA**  No!

**DONALD**  Oh Geez. Never!

**BO and DAYNA**  What?

**BERNICE**  Why don't you want to wear them?

**DONALD**  It all goes back to the fifth grade. I use to wear black socks every day and one day I wore them with shorts because I was afraid of having cold ankles when I played kickball. I figured the black socks would absorb the heat of the sun and my ankles would be nice and warm. Well, a couple of kids thought I looked pretty funny and they beat me up and threw me in the ice cream cooler, and sure enough, I got frostbite on both ankles. The black socks were too thin. If I had worn the white ones, I wouldn't have gotten beat up. So I'll never ever wear black socks, touch black socks, or sing the song "Black Socks" again.

**BERNICE**  Donald, you are weird. Come to bed.

[*Lights come up on* SHIRLEY *in the darkness. She is looking at her watch and pacing impatiently while clutching a squeaky toy and a portable phone.* DONALD *looks over at her. She is like an apparition. He takes a pair of pristine white socks out of the drawer and puts them on. The lights fade down on* SHIRLEY *as her head sinks down.* BO *and* DAYNA *give each other a high five as* DONALD *gets into bed with* BERNICE.]

**DONALD**  Yeah. I think that's probably a good idea.

**BO**   So what do we do now?

**DAYNA**   Report to the boss.

**BO**   Do you think he'll be a good soul catcher?

**DAYNA**   Well, he's not with that other girl, so he made one good decision. Why not believe he'll make more?

**BO**   Let's get out of here. Sounds good.

[*Lights go down and the phone rings again. The answering machine clicks on. It is* BERNICE'*s voice.*]

**VOICE-OVER**   Hi. You've reached Donald and Bernice and just in case you're wondering, Mom, Donald finally proposed! Please leave a message except if you're looking for Mark Wurlitz and Jane Donaldson, in which case just hang up now. Thank you.

*Beeeeeeeep!*

• • •

# The Perfect Relationship

Jill Elaine Hughes

# Jill Elaine Hughes

Jill Elaine Hughes' plays have received productions and staged readings at thirty-plus small and medium-sized theatre companies in New York City, Los Angeles, Chicago, Seattle, Atlanta, Boston, Phoenix, Ohio, Canada, the United Kingdom, and elsewhere. In 1999, she also founded the nationally renowned Stockyards Theatre Project, Chicago's only theatre company dedicated exclusively to women's theatre and performance art, and served as its artistic director/producer for five years. She served three years as president of Chicago Women's Theatre Alliance (2000–2003) and formerly served as treasurer on the executive board of the International Centre for Women Playwrights (ICWP). Her plays and monologues have been excerpted and anthologized by Smith & Kraus, Applause Books, and Meriwether Publishing, and she has written plays for the high school drama market, which are published and licensed by Brooklyn Play Publishers. In addition to her theatrical endeavors, Jill Elaine is also a fiction writer, essayist, and humorist, and has contributed to many newspapers and national magazines, including the *Chicago Tribune*, *Chicago Reader*, *Missouri Review*, *New Art Examiner*, *Dialogue*, *Cat Fancy*, *Black Gate*, and many others. She also has completed five novels of contemporary women's fiction, some of which are published by Virgin Books, an imprint of Random House, under her pseudonym "Jamaica Layne."

Ms. Hughes resides in Arlington Heights, Illinois, with her husband and son.

## characters

MARY ANN, attractive blond woman, early 20s, giddy

CHRISTINE, quirky brunette, early 20s, fashionably dressed

ORCHID, a New Age–looking artist, mid-20s, hosts the women's biweekly relationship support meetings

## setting

ORCHID's living room—comfortable, with New Age décor.

• • •

[MARY ANN *and* CHRISTINE *are in* ORCHID's *living room for their biweekly relationships support group.* MARY ANN *and* CHRISTINE *are seated, munching on cookies;* ORCHID *is circling them, wafting incense smoke over their bodies.*]

ORCHID    As you'll remember, I said in our last meeting that we were going to try something new this week. What I'm doing right now is perfuming your auras, just allowing the incense to *reside* in your aura.

MARY ANN    Um, is that supposed to help us?

ORCHID    Of course!

CHRISTINE    How?

ORCHID    Well, Christine, your aura is the energy field that surrounds your body. It is the emotional energy that you produce, and if you are in a bad emotional state, like you both are, then your aura is going to smell bad. It needs perfume. Incense helps with that.

MARY ANN    I can't smell my aura.

CHRISTINE    I can't smell my aura, either.

ORCHID    Well, Mary Ann, Christine—let me tell you. I can smell both your auras, and they stink.

MARY ANN    Can you smell your aura?

ORCHID    Of course. My aura is very fragrant. Why do you think my parents named me Orchid?

**CHRISTINE**   I thought it was because they were hippies who took too much acid.

**ORCHID**   Well, my parents were very in touch with the spiritual-energy side of life, and drugs did help with that—but remember, ladies, we are all here to talk about your relationship problems. I'm just trying to open you both up. Now let's take a deep, cleansing breath in, deep, cleansing breath out—

[MARY ANN *and* CHRISTINE *breathe deeply, then both start coughing.*]

**ORCHID**   What's the matter?

**MARY ANN**   [*Coughing.*] Too much incense—

[ORCHID *extinguishes the incense in a glass of water.*]

**ORCHID**   Okay, well, then I think your auras are probably perfumed enough now, so let's move on to our rap session. Mary Ann, why don't you tell the group about your week?

**MARY ANN**   Well, it was an okay week, I guess.

**ORCHID**   Go on…

**MARY ANN**   Well, mostly I just went to work, came home, usual routine. It's still pretty hard to get out, you know, after—[*Chokes up.*]

**ORCHID**   It's okay, Mary Ann. We all support you.

**MARY ANN**   Well, you know, it's hard for me to go out, you know, after the incident.

**CHRISTINE**   I thought we weren't supposed to call our traumatic relationship experiences "incidents" when we're in group.

**ORCHID**   That's right, Christine. Now, Mary Ann, why don't you try restating what you just said without using the word "incident."

**MARY ANN**   [*Snuffling.*] Okay. Well, it's been hard for me to go out, you know, since the incident—well, since I found out that my last boyfriend was really a married Episcopalian minister—well, technically he wasn't a minister yet, but he was married and just about to finish seminary, and he felt that he had to come clean with me about who he really was and then break up with me so that he would have a clean soul when he went out to minister to his flock and everything—

**ORCHID**    Good, Mary Ann. Oh, that's very good that you can talk about it with such detail now. Keep going.

**MARY ANN**    But even though it's very hard for me to go out and do anything, since my last boyfriend, "Father Ray"—that's not his real name, of course—like, totally lied to me and betrayed me and dumped me and everything—but this week, I did go out, once. I went to the Kopi Coffeehouse on Clark Street and had a large chai tea with steamed milk, and I did see one guy that was kind of cute, and I waved at him, but he didn't see me, so he didn't wave back or anything, but that's what I did this week. Plus I had four cleansing cries!

**ORCHID**    Excellent! Mary Ann, that's just excellent! Going out, making an effort with the opposite sex—totally okay that it didn't get acknowledged this time, mind you, it's the act of trying that counts—and four cleansing cries! Wow, Mary Ann. Very, very good work. Let's all give Mary Ann a round of applause for her wonderful progress.

[ALL *applaud*, CHRISTINE *unenthusiastically.*]

**ORCHID**    So, Christine, why don't you tell us about your week?

**CHRISTINE**    Well, nothing much happened, really—

**ORCHID**    Now, now, Christine. You know the rule. During rap session we must all describe our weeks, describe what happened, good, bad or indifferent. Even if it's mundane things like just going to the dry cleaner's or something. Remember—every little step we take in our lives could lead to that Perfect Relationship!

**CHRISTINE**    Yeah, well, whatever.

**MARY ANN**    That's a nice attitude.

**ORCHID**    Ladies, ladies! Now let's not get snippy. We are here to grow, remember?

**MARY ANN**    Sorry.

**CHRISTINE**   I'm not, like, trying to be difficult or anything, I'm just—I'm just really fed up right now.

**ORCHID**   Okay, Christine, good, let's just get everything out in the open. What are you fed up with?

**CHRISTINE**   Well, for one thing, I've been so depressed lately that I've run out of clean underwear.

**MARY ANN**   Huh?

**CHRISTINE**   What I mean to say is, I've been so depressed lately that I can't get anything done around the house, you know? I just come home from work and turn on the television and watch reality shows on cable while I drink whole bottles of red sangria, okay? And for the past couple days I haven't even been going to work. I can't remember the last time I went to a Laundromat, or a dry cleaner's, or anything. I can't bear the sight of anyone except my cat and the guy on the sangria label. How am I supposed to take "little steps toward the Perfect Relationship" when my apartment is so full of garbage and dirty laundry I can't even get into my kitchen anymore? Huh?

**ORCHID**   Now, Christine, it sounds like you're just having a little bit of a setback this week, but—

**CHRISTINE**   Oh, I think I'm way beyond "setback" here, Orchid. My apartment is filthy and full of dirty clothes to the point that when I look at how bad it is, I get even more overwhelmed, to the point that the only solution I can think of is to charge more clothes and underwear on my credit card instead of actually having to go to a Laundromat and face the possibility that I might run into my ex-boyfriend while I'm there!

**MARY ANN**   Why are you running out of clean underwear when you can just go buy more?

**ORCHID**   Now, Mary Ann, that's not positive reinforcement—

**CHRISTINE**   Because my credit cards are fucking maxed out, okay? Because I lost my job, okay? Because I am so pathetic right now that the only time I can muster enough strength to leave my apartment is to come here. Because I have been wearing the same filthy underwear for a week. Okay?

[ORCHID *and* MARY ANN *are stunned and do not speak for a few beats.*]

**MARY ANN**   I guess it's not our auras that stink, then.

**ORCHID**   Well. Okay. So. Christine. You just ahhhh—you just made quite a statement.

**MARY ANN**   I'll say.

**CHRISTINE**   Oh, will you just fucking can it?

**MARY ANN**   Can this, bi—

[ORCHID *gets up and places herself between* CHRISTINE *and* MARY ANN.]

**ORCHID**   Ladies, please let's just remember why we're here. Why are we here? I asked you both a question. Why are we here? You know the answer.

**MARY ANN**   To heal ourselves—

**CHRISTINE**   To find the Perfect Relationship, yada, yada, yada.

**ORCHID**   Good. Now that's what I want to hear. So, Christine, you're having a—difficult time right now. I think what you need to do is revisit the source of your depression. Just face it, dead-on. Let's talk about what happened between you and—what do you call him again?

**CHRISTINE**   "Steve." Not his real name, of course.

**ORCHID**   Right. "Steve." Tell us what happened between you and "Steve."

**CHRISTINE**   But I already talked about this in group, like, eight times before—

**ORCHID**   Well, yes, but I like I said, I still think you need to revisit it. So you can break through this cycle of crippling depression that you're in.

**MARY ANN**   Yeah, and so you can get some new underwear. Phew.

**ORCHID**   Mary Ann, let's be supportive of Christine while she gets ready to tell her story.

**CHRISTINE**   Okay, well, I think you all know my pathetic relationship story, being as I've already told it in here I don't know how many times before, but here goes. "Steve" and I met when I was in graduate school down at the University of Chicago. He was on faculty at the divinity school, specializing in like Biblical literature or something. He wasn't religious at all—he viewed the Bible as, like, nothing but a historical document for studying the ancient world or something. So anyway, we got involved, we dated for, like, eight years, you know, nothing big, just spending almost every weekend together for, like, eight years, and when I finally asked "Steve" if we were ever getting married, he told me no, because he was already married! He'd been married for the entire time we'd been dating!

**MARY ANN**   What I still don't understand is, how can you date a guy for eight years and not know that he's married?

**CHRISTINE**   Well, you dated a married man too and didn't know until he told you!

**MARY ANN**   Not for eight years!

**ORCHID**   Okay, ladies, okay. Now Christine, you've revisited what happened with Steve. Why don't you try talking about how that's affecting you right now?

**CHRISTINE**   I already did.

**ORCHID**   Well, you did kind of talk about how you're having some very strong depression, so strong that it's affecting your home and your—personal hygiene, obviously. You talked about how you're afraid that if you go to the Laundromat you'll run into Steve. Why is that?

**CHRISTINE**   Well, it's kind of a really weird thing, I'd rather not talk about it—

**ORCHID**   It's okay, Christine. Nothing is too weird to discuss in group.

**CHRISTINE**   Well, this is pretty damn weird.

**MARY ANN**   Weirder than not changing your underwear in a week?

**CHRISTINE**   Look. Why don't you just shut up?

**ORCHID**   Okay, I'm sensing a little conflict in the room. Why don't we do some deep, cleansing breaths, try to clear the air a little. Deep, cleansing breath in, deep, cleansing breath out—

**MARY ANN**   Can you burn some more incense or something? I keep smelling Christine's underwear every time I breathe in.

**ORCHID**   No, I think that we all need to experience Christine's—uh, aura together, so that we can all—uh, empathize with her—uh, situation. You know, actually, I do have some orange spray around here somewhere that might help us—uh, experience Christine's aura a little more intimately—

[ORCHID *finds a can of natural orange air freshener behind the couch and sprays it liberally.*]

There. Now doesn't that make you feel so much closer to Christine's aura? Christine, now that we've all had some—uhhh, cleansing breaths, why don't you tell us about this "weird thing" that is causing your little, tiny, emotional block right now?

**CHRISTINE**   Well, my ex-boyfriend—you know, "Steve"—he kind of has this odd fetish.

**ORCHID**   Oh, I see.

**MARY ANN**   What kind of a fetish?

**CHRISTINE**   He, ummm—he, ummmm—he sort of, ummmm—

**ORCHID**   Go on...

**CHRISTINE**   He's sexually fascinated with the underwear of middle-aged obese women. He isn't sexually fascinated with middle-aged obese women themselves—just their underwear.

**MARY ANN**   Just their underwear?

**CHRISTINE**   Yep. He liked the smell. It turned him on. Something about the combination of fat-woman smell with menopause hormones or something—it made him feel primal. Anyway, that's how he explained it to me.

**ORCHID**  Uh-huh. Well. That's very interesting. So—did he need to, uhhh—experience the—scent of middle-aged obese women in order to—ahhh, achieve satisfaction?

**CHRISTINE**  Yep.

**MARY ANN**  Well, if he wasn't, like, dating middle-aged obese women, how did he get hold of their underwear?

**CHRISTINE**  Well, for a long time he just placed ads in the *Chicago Reader* Adult Services personals asking for middle-aged obese women to mail him their dirty underwear, and that did work for a number of years, but, ummm—then he sort of got into trouble with the postal service. You know, after 9/11 they got pretty strict about sending organic material through the mail. So, then he just started hanging out in Laundromats late at night and stealing them out of washing machines when you know, the fat middle-aged women weren't looking. He has to switch Laundromats every day so that the managers don't get suspicious.

**ORCHID**  Uh-huh. So, I guess this is why you aren't going to the Laundromat to do any of your own wash?

**CHRISTINE**  Well, yeah, because given the way he rotates Laundromats every single day, and there only being so many Laundromats on the North Side of Chicago, the chances of us running into each other at one of them are actually pretty good.

**MARY ANN**  You know, you could just send your laundry out. They have services, you know.

**CHRISTINE**  Well, that would be fine, if I actually had any money, but—

**ORCHID**  Christine, I think you've just made an important breakthrough.

**CHRISTINE**  What? No I didn't.

**ORCHID**  Yes, oh yes, you most certainly did! You just faced head-on why you are so emotionally crippled that you aren't even changing your underwear! You articulated it, put it out there, right in front of us, without being afraid! That's wonderful, Christine! Good for you! Let's all give Christine a hand!

[ALL *clap*, MARY ANN *unenthusiastically.*]

**MARY ANN**   Breakthrough, schmakethrough. Now maybe if you actually bathed, that would really be something.

**CHRISTINE**   I bathe—I'm just not changing my underwear right now, that's all.

**ORCHID**   Now, ladies, we're almost at the end of our rap session, so let's just try to remain positive for a little while longer, okay? And since you've both made such good progress today, I have an extra-special treat for both of you.

**CHRISTINE**   What's that?

**ORCHID**   Well, I know that in group it can seem a little one-sided that I am the one that drives the conversation all the time, that I'm always the one that chooses the topics for discussion. So today, for our final two topics of discussion, I'm going to let each of you choose what we talk about. So, you both get choose a topic!

**MARY ANN**   It can be anything we want?

**ORCHID**   Yes! Assuming of course that it remains within the sphere of our relationships.

**CHRISTINE**   What about your relationships, Orchid? Can it be about your relationships?

**ORCHID**   I don't see why not.

**CHRISTINE**   Okay. Well, then for my topic, I choose that Orchid tells us all about her worst relationship, ever. She has to tell us about her Relationship from Hell.

**ORCHID**   Okay, then. Mary Ann, what about you? What topic do you want to see discussed?

**MARY ANN**   Well, Orchid can talk about her relationships first, but when she's done, I want everyone—including Orchid—to tell us the real names of our Worst Relationship men. You know, no more fake names like "Father Ray" and "Steve." The real deal.

**ORCHID**   I'm comfortable with that as long as everyone else is.

**CHRISTINE**   Hell, now that you all know about my underwear I don't see why you can't know "Steve's" real name. That's fine. Orchid, go ahead and tell your bad relationship story.

**MARY ANN**   If you even have one to tell.

**ORCHID**   Oh, like any other human being on this small planet, I have had my share of relationships, believe me. Some good, some bad, some indifferent. But there was one relationship in particular, one in particular that led me to become a New Age healer hosting these weekly group sessions to help other women break past their crippling emotional firewalls and find the Perfect Relationship. But in order for me to do that, first I had to have the Relationship from Hell.

**CHRISTINE**   You had the Relationship from Hell? Ha. That hardly seems possible.

**ORCHID**   Oh, it's definitely possible.

**MARY ANN**   But how? You're like—perfect. You never have any problems.

**ORCHID**   No, no, no! Not true.

**CHRISTINE**   So when did your Relationship from Hell happen?

**ORCHID**   Well, I was in massage therapy school, and I met who I thought was a wonderful man—another massage therapy student—who well, let's just say he did not turn out to be who I thought he was going to be. In fact, he turned out to be much different from the man he said he was.

**MARY ANN**   Who did he say he was?

**ORCHID**   He said that he was the latest incarnation of Hare Krishna.

**CHRISTINE**   And he wasn't?

**ORCHID**   No.

**MARY ANN**   Who was he, really?

**ORCHID**   Well, no one, actually. He was an amnesia patient, so he didn't even know who he was. One day when I went to meet him for coffee, he didn't remember who I was. He completely forgot that we were in a relationship! When I kissed him hello, he got scared and ran away. That was the end.

[*There is a pause.* MARY ANN *and* CHRISTINE *show noticeable disappointment.*]

**CHRISTINE**    That's it?

**MARY ANN**    That's your Relationship from Hell? That's not a Relationship from Hell!

**CHRISTINE**    That—that's nothing! That's like—that's like saying World War III has broken out when you run out of coffee.

**ORCHID**    It was very traumatic for me. It took me years to get past it.

**CHRISTINE**    Well, what the hell am I doing here telling you all about my ex-boyfriend's underwear fetish when all you've got as your Boyfriend from Hell is some sweet, innocent, little Hare Krishna amnesia victim? Jesus, it wasn't even his fault he forgot who you were!

**MARY ANN**    Yeah, he only forgot you because he had a disease! Our ex-boyfriends were evil, manipulative, adulterous liars! Yours just lost his memory!

**ORCHID**    [*Tearing up.*] Well, it might not seem like a lot to you, but it hurt me very badly. And I'm afraid I can't tell you his real name, since I never found out what his real name was. I just knew him as Hare Krishna Doe.

**CHRISTINE**    Well, everybody has to give the real names of their Boyfriends from Hell. We all agreed.

**MARY ANN**    I guess you could just make up a real name for him. Make up a name that he might have had in real life.

**ORCHID**    Well, in compromise, I will tell you the name of the absolutely wonderful man I'm with now. How's that?

**CHRISTINE**    That's fine. Who's he?

**ORCHID**    Well, he's a born-again Christian—except he's the liberal kind of born-again Christian, not one of those kooky right-wing evangelist types. He's very into the Earth as God's temple, that sort of thing. His name is the Reverend Doctor Evan Eagle.

**MARY ANN**  What?

**CHRISTINE**  What did you say his name was?

**ORCHID**  I said, his name is the Reverend Doctor Evan Eagle.

**CHRISTINE**  Oh. My. God.

**MARY ANN**  What is he, about six-foot-two, salt-and-pepper blondish hair, ice-blue eyes, wears Dockers with a hole in the left knee?

**CHRISTINE**  Chipped left incisor?

**MARY ANN**  Scar on his right thigh, right below the groin?

**CHRISTINE**  Loves pâté de fois gras?

**ORCHID**  [*Wary.*] Yes. Yes, that's him, exactly. Are both of you clairvoyant or something, because I don't remember either of you telling me that you were clairvoyant before—

**MARY ANN**  The Reverend Doctor Evan Eagle was my Relationship from Hell.

**CHRISTINE**  Mine too.

**MARY ANN**  You know, the married Episcopalian minister?

**CHRISTINE**  Who I guess was also the supposedly agnostic married Biblical scholar who liked to sniff old-lady underwear?

**MARY ANN**  While at the same time being a New Age Christian who picks up New Age healers?

**CHRISTINE**  Jesus H. Christ. The man gets around. To think that the Reverend Doctor Evan Eagle would want to get into your nasty pants, Mary Ann—

**MARY ANN**  Oh, look who's talking, Little Miss Crusty Crotch!

**CHRISTINE**  Oh well. Mary Ann, we both slept with the same lying Bible-thumping fucker, I guess we might as well try to be friends. Truce?

**MARY ANN**  Truce. Orchid, you have got to dump this guy. Now. He's playing you like an eight-track tape.

**CHRISTINE**   Definitely. Dump the bastard, before you end up like us!

**ORCHID**   But—but, no! He's—the Reverend Doctor, he's wonderful! He understands me completely! He knows me better than anyone ever has before! He knows me better than I know myself! He's—he's—

**MARY ANN**   The Perfect Relationship?

**CHRISTINE**   The Perfect Man?

**ORCHID**   Yes! Yes! Don't you see? I took little steps and found the Perfect Relationship!

**MARY ANN**   Have you ever considered going into group therapy?

**CHRISTINE**   [*Sarcastic.*] Yeah, because I know this great New Age healer lady.

**MARY ANN**   Yeah. Healer my ass. Christine, what do you say you and me go to Big Chicks and get wasted on Mai Tais? My treat. We can pick you up some new underwear on the way.

**CHRISTINE**   Yeah, let's go. I'm outta here.

[MARY ANN *and* CHRISTINE *exit.*]

[ORCHID *slumps on the sofa defeated. After a beat, she makes a face and begins sniffing herself.*]

**ORCHID**   Oh. Oh Goddess. Oh, sweet mother Goddess, my aura stinks!

[ORCHID *lights incense and frantically begins wafting incense smoke over herself.*]

**ORCHID**   Every little step leads to the Perfect Relationship. Every little step leads to the Perfect Relationship. Every little step leads to the Perfect Relationship. . . . FUCK!!!

[*Curtain.*]

• • •

# The Perfect Medium

## Eileen Fischer

# Eileen Fischer

Eileen Fischer also writes stories, reviews, poems, and essays. Her publications have appeared in a wide range of periodicals and books. Her play *A Hunger Artist*, adapted from Kafka's short story, was produced many years ago at the Yale Summer Cabaret. Eileen Fischer is a professor of humanities at NYC College of Technology, CUNY. She holds both a master's degree and a doctorate in dramatic literature and criticism from the Yale School of Drama.

## dramatis personae

**HESTER DOWDEN**
**OSCAR WILDE**
**JOSEPH FRANKLIN**

London, 1923
1 Interior Set
3 Characters

The script is loosely based on the pamphlet *Psychic Messages from Oscar Wilde*, edited by Hester Dowden, 1924.

## music for Eileen Fischer's *The Perfect Medium*

Composed by Charles Porter
CD Version 7

| | |
|---|---|
| Track 1: (0:50) | Page 238. Opening. Gaps of silence at end of track are to intersperse Hester's opening lines with the music: "Over here."—[*Music hit.*]—"Over here."—[*Music hit.*]—"I SAID, OVER HERE." |
| Track 2: (0:43) | Page 239. Hester plays a phrase on the piano, then says during the gap of silence, "And as for the automatic writing, one day the messages simply started." She then plays the second phrase. |
| Track 3: (1:08) | Page 239. June 8, 1923. Séance music. |
| Track 4: (0:20) | Page 243. June 18, 1923. Séance music. |
| Track 5: (0:19) | Page 244. June 19, 1923. Séance music. |
| Track 6: (0:20) | Page 248. July 2, 1923. Séance music. |
| Track 7: (0:19) | Page 252. July 4, 1923. Séance music. |
| Track 8: (0:34) | Page 261. Hester plays part of a waltz on the piano. |
| Track 9: (0:11) | Page 266. Hester plays a fragment. |

| Track 10: (0:44) | Page 269. July 12, 1923. Séance music. |
| Track 11: (0:37) | Page 273. July 23, 1923. Séance music. |
| Track 12: (0:58) | Page 275. Following Oscar's lines, Hester plays the piano until she screams, "DON'T STOP." |
| Track 13: (0:50) | Finish, page 278. To accompany the moths that fly from Oscar's mouth until just before Hester's final words. (Consists of 28 seconds of moth music followed by 22 seconds of repeating material.) |
| Track 14: (0:06) | Page 279. As lights fade to black. |

• • •

[*A well-appointed Victorian sitting room in London. Downstage-center, a round table and two chairs. Much moody atmosphere here: flickering candles, shadows, dark furniture, a chaise lounge, a piano. Then total blackout. From the blackness, a voice—*]

**HESTER**   Over here. [*Music: track #1. Pause.*] Over here. [*Music: track #1. Pause. Then with annoyance.*] I said, over here.

[*Lights gradually up on* HESTER DOWDEN, *a sturdy-looking woman, 55 but looks older, in a high-collared, white-on-white embroidered blouse with a full-length dark green wool skirt. Her black and gray hair is in a bun. She wears reading glasses and takes them on and off and moves them up and down her nose. The glasses are attached to a chain around her neck. She is seated at the table covered with a cream-colored lace cloth.*]

Yes. On me. Look at *me*. Let us begin. . . . Twenty-three years ago Oscar Wilde left the present life and crossed to the other side. It may seem incredible [*To audience.*] to you that he should attempt to send his thoughts back again to a world where his infamy exceeded his good fame and fortune; but here it is, 1923, and Oscar Wilde chooses to send us messages today. [*Pompously.*] Are the messages genuine? Does Oscar Wilde still exist? [*Slight pause.*] And where exactly is he? . . . The public must judge these matters. We will return to them again and again. Yes. . . . We will. You'll see. Again and again. [*Pause.*] Do you understand? Oscar Wilde, the famous Irish writer, the international *bon vivant* and gadfly came to me, Hester Dowden. He spoke to me, here, twenty-three years after his bodily death. Yes...it is complicated. Yes...it seems unusual...yes. But it is true. It happened. Everyone must believe me. Without belief, without faith, what have you? [*Pause.*] Those to whom Oscar's words came [*Pats herself proudly.*] can only transmit them to the world.... As for me, I've been a psychic investigator for many years, starting back in Dublin. Now I see clients for private readings here in my London home, and I instruct students in psychic investigations as well. What else can one do? An independent woman must make do. And I do. I do, indeed.... Were you wondering how these messages were received? Let me help. They came through automatic writing and sometimes the messages came through the Ouija board—two well-known methods of psychic communication. [*She crosses to the piano and plays softly.*] And as for the automatic writing, one day the messages simply started. [*Music: track #2.*]

[*Brief blackout. Lights up on a screen above, which projects the following words: Automatic Script, June 8, 1923. At downstage table now, along with HESTER DOWDEN sits JOSEPH FRANKLIN, 45-ish, dark hair with thin mustache, wiry and skittish, in white shirt, tweed jacket, and cravat. Séance music: track #3.*]

[*Both HESTER DOWDEN and JOSEPH FRANKLIN hold writing tablets and pencils. Throughout the automatic writing scenes, they write intermittently. JOSEPH FRANKLIN writes OSCAR WILDE's words while HESTER DOWDEN rests her hand on JOSEPH's hand. Music plays.*]

[*From offstage a wonderful voice purrs seductively—.*]

OFFSTAGE VOICE    Lily. My little Lily. No, the Lily was mine—a crystal thread, a silver reed that made music in the morning.

HESTER    [*Looking around perplexed.* HESTER *exchanges glances with* JOSEPH. *Lights flicker.*] Who is that? Where is the voice coming from?

[OSCAR WILDE *enters.*]

**OSCAR**    Pity Oscar Wilde... one who in the world was a king of life. I must complete forever the circle of my experience. Long ago I wrote that there was a twilight in my cell and a twilight in my heart, but this is the twilight of the soul. In eternal twilight I move—

**HESTER**    [*Abruptly.*] Are you Oscar Wilde?

**OSCAR**    Yes. I am. Oscar Wilde himself.

[OSCAR *wears a white silk shirt, a paisley ascot, and a burgundy velvet smoking jacket. He is very tall, has big hands and fusses throughout with white gloves; he smokes gold-tipped black cigarettes and wears a bit too much makeup. His hair is dyed poorly, yet he appears shabby chic. Scrim use with* OSCAR WILDE *onstage possible at times.*]

**HESTER**    [*Unnerved, to* JOSEPH.] Really! Oh my, my, Mr. Franklin. This is wonderful. Messages from Oscar Wilde are coming through.

**JOSEPH**    But he's long dead.

**HESTER**    He's on the other side, Mr. Franklin, in Summerland. But hush now. Let us be certain it is Oscar Wilde. [*To* OSCAR.] Tell me the name of the house you lived in, in Dublin.... Tell me where your father used to practice.

**OSCAR**    Near Dublin. My father was a surgeon. These names are difficult to recall.

**HESTER**    Not at all difficult if you are *really* Oscar Wilde.

**OSCAR**    I used to live near here. Tite Street. T-I-T-E. Tite Street.

**HESTER**    [*To* JOSEPH.] There is a Tite Street near here. He spelled it correctly. I didn't know where he lived in London. Did you?

**JOSEPH**    No. I know very little about Oscar Wilde.

[OSCAR *strolls about the room throughout this episode.*]

**HESTER**    [*Businesslike.*] Let us see... Oscar Wilde, what *was* your brother's name?

**OSCAR**    William—Willie.

[HESTER *nods in agreement at* JOSEPH.]

**JOSEPH**    Why have you come during our automatic writing session today?

**OSCAR**    To let the world know that Oscar Wilde is not dead. His thoughts live on in the hearts of all those who, in a *gross age*, can hear the voice of beauty calling on the hills or mark where her white feet brush the dew from the cowslips in the morning.... Now the mere memory of the beauty of the world is an exquisite pain. I was always one of those for whom the visible world existed.... I worshipped at the shrine of things seen. There was not a blood stripe on a tulip or a curve on a shell or a tone of the sea but had for me its meaning, its mystery, and its appeal to the imagination.... Soon the full moon will swim up over the edge of the world and hang like a great golden cheese... [*Agitated. Screaming.*] STOP! STOP! STOP! STOP! This image is insufferable. [*To* HESTER.] You write like a successful grocer who has now taken to writing poetry.

**HESTER**    [*To* JOSEPH.] Who said *that*?

**JOSEPH**    I'm not sure I understand what is going on here.

[JOSEPH *and* HESTER *seem stunned.*]

**OSCAR**    [*Downstage now.*] I find the words in my medium's mind. [*Points to* HESTER.] Try again. [*Pause.*] Like a great golden pumpkin hanging in the blue light. There. That *is* better... but it is a little rustic, no? Still, I adore rustic people. They are so near to nature, and besides, they remind me of all the simple pleasures I somehow missed in life.

**HESTER**    [*To* JOSEPH.] Rustic! Oscar's family was quite sophisticated—his father a renowned surgeon and his mother, Lady Wilde, as you probably know was famous for her revolutionary political beliefs in Ireland.

**JOSEPH**    Yes. I know. And later she wrote poetry.

**HESTER**    *Mediocre* poetry.

**OSCAR**    [*Starting to exit upstage-right.*] Please do not insult my mother. I loved and honored her.

**JOSEPH**   We are not insulting her.

**HESTER**   Spell out the name by which your mother called herself.

**OSCAR**   S-P-E-R-A-N-Z-A . . . She called herself Speranza. Yes. It is quite true what I have said. I lived for the beauty of the visible.

[*Brief blackout.* OSCAR WILDE *vanishes. Lights up on* HESTER DOWDEN *and* JOSEPH FRANKLIN *at the downstage round table.*]

**HESTER**   It is true. Beauty and pleasure were central to Oscar's life. Beauty also destroyed his life. It gave him wings and then terrible chains. [*Pause.*] But I must say, I am encouraged, Mr. Franklin. For a professor of mathematics with no special interest in literature, and for a man who is only a beginning student in psychic matters, you provided a very receptive and harmonious atmosphere. You helped greatly.

**JOSEPH**   I'm astounded myself, Mrs. Dowden.

**HESTER**   You seem to possess the powers of a medium.

**JOSEPH**   Really? Can it be so? Perhaps it only appears so . . . But hearing this from you, Mrs. Dowden, coming from you, a well-known psychic medium, this flatters me. I *am* eager to continue automatic writing lessons with you. I want to work with the Ouija board, as well.

**HESTER**   We will use the Ouija board some other day.

**JOSEPH**   Have we truly made contact with Oscar Wilde?

**HESTER**   Evidently, my dear man, since the communicator, Oscar Wilde, in this instance, volunteers information that is not in the minds of the mediums. And here, Joseph, I may call you that, Mr. Franklin, may I not?

**JOSEPH**   Yes, of course, as you wish.

**HESTER**   If we, as the mediums of the moment do not have the information in our minds, and if the information proves to be correct, then, yes, the communicating voice may indeed be that of Oscar Wilde.

**JOSEPH**   I must confess to you, Mrs. Dowden, that I have not read Oscar Wilde's work except for the novel *Dorian Gray*....And I've never seen any of his plays performed.

**HESTER**   That's even better for us, Joseph. I've read some of his work and have always had interest in his plays, but I most certainly have *not* read a page of his work in the past twenty years. Not since the scandals—

**JOSEPH**   Most curious. Of course I know a bit about his terrible court trials and his flamboyant reputation, but when did you say Oscar Wilde died?

**HESTER**   1900.

**JOSEPH**   That's twenty-three years ago.

**HESTER**   Yes. He died in Paris. In exile. [*Pause.*] Unrepentant...

**JOSEPH**   Sipping champagne on his deathbed.

[*Blackout.*]

[*Séance music: track #4. Light upstage on* OSCAR WILDE. *Screen projection above reads: Automatic Writing Script Obtained June 18, 1923.*]

**OSCAR**   Being dead is the most boring experience in life. [*Pause.*] That is, aside from being married or dining with a schoolteacher. [*Pause.*] Do you doubt my identity? I am not surprised since sometimes I doubt it myself. I might retaliate by doubting yours.

[OSCAR *crosses downstage to where* HESTER *and* JOSEPH *sit at the table, immobile in dimmer light. He smokes gold-tipped black cigarettes.* OSCAR *wears a red velvet jacket, ruffled white shirt, white gloves, and a lily in his lapel.*]

I have always admired your professional organization, the Society for Psychical Research. They are the most magnificent doubters in the world. They are never happy until they have explained away their ghosts. And one suspects a genuine ghost would make them exquisitely uncomfortable....

[*Lights fully up on* HESTER *and* JOSEPH, *who now become animated.*]

**JOSEPH**   You *are* a ghost, then, are you not?

**OSCAR**   Mr. Franklin, for example, is he romance or reality? [*Winks to* JOSEPH. JOSEPH *becomes pleasantly flustered.*] Is he fact or fiction? If it should be decided that he is fact, then, of course, we should strenuously doubt it. Fortunately, there are no facts over here. On earth we could scarcely escape them.

**JOSEPH**   I'm a fact, Oscar, certainly. But so are you. . . . In a manner of speaking.

**OSCAR**   A factual ghost? An imaginary ghost? You decide.

**JOSEPH**   This is baffling.

**HESTER**   [*To* JOSEPH.] It is difficult. Have patience. Let us ask him some questions. Perhaps his answers with lend some clarity.

**JOSEPH**   Please explain, Mr. Wilde, how you—

**OSCAR**   Don't degrade me by forcing me to give you *facts*.

[*Brief blackout. Séance music: track #5. Lights up. Screen projection now reads: Communication Received at the Ouija Board, June 19, 1923.* HESTER *and* JOSEPH *sit at table with a Ouija board between them. Their fingertips rest on a planchette. During this episode* HESTER *seems to go in and out of a trance; she moans periodically. At other points,* JOSEPH *appears to be in a mild trance.*]

**OSCAR**   [OSCAR *upstage now. Lights on* OSCAR.] Yes. It is Oscar Wilde here again. I have come, as you asked. . . . I am *naturally* an interesting person—not only do I flaunt the colors of literature, but I have the lurid flame of crime attached to me also. My dear lady, do you realize that you are talking to a social leper?

**HESTER**   [*Condescendingly.*] Yes, we do.

**OSCAR**   [*Drinks from a champagne flute.*] I do not wish to burden you with details of my life, which was like a candle that had gutted at the end. I rather wish to make you believe that I was the *medium*, yes, I, too, can be a medium of sorts, a medium through which beauty filtered and was distilled like the essence of a rose. . . . But let me explain that to me you are a mere illusion, and in reality, you are less alive than I am. For I am still a living soul and vibrant mind, and I have as great a feeling for beauty as I had when I wore a top hat and let my hair stream from beneath it. As you know, the desire for beauty is merely a heightened form of the desire for life.

**JOSEPH**   [*To* HESTER.] I'm beginning to understand. But is he a living soul?

**HESTER**   Very much so. Be patient. He will need to reveal more.

**JOSEPH**   Who are you communicating through today?

**OSCAR**   Through Mrs. Dowden. You [*Gesturing to* JOSEPH.] are a tool. You are the light that lets me peep again into the world, which seems so dazzling now that Divine Justice finds it His pleasure to keep me in dim twilight.

[*Pause.* OSCAR *strolls about with champagne flute and cigarette.*]

Cigarettes. [*To* JOSEPH.] A cigarette is a perfect pleasure. Is it not? It is exquisite and it leaves one unsatisfied, wanting more. What more can one want?

**HESTER**   [*Imperiously.*] A great deal more, as you well know, Oscar Wilde.

**OSCAR**   She's rather practical, and—

**HESTER**   Let's discuss my friend and colleague in psychical research, Mr. William Butler Yeats.

**JOSEPH**   Did you know Mr. William Butler Yeats?

**OSCAR**   I knew Yeats very well—a fantastical mind, so full of inflated joy in himself.

**JOSEPH**   Surely you admired his work.

**OSCAR**   A little drop of beauty that was spread with infinite pains over the span of many years.... Yeats will *not* be terribly interested to know that I still have a voice that speaks and a mind that communicates. But he tried to help me, his brother in art who fell from too much beauty, or rather the desire for truth and beauty.

[*Lights fade on* OSCAR.]

**HESTER**   Wait! Give us proof of your identity.... He's gone. [*To* JOSEPH.] I'll need proof of his identity if I am going to make anything of this.

**JOSEPH**   What do you mean, "make anything of this"?

**HESTER**   A book. I mean a book, of course.

**JOSEPH**   But how could you? How could you simply use Wilde's words? And for what reason?

**HESTER**   His words came unsolicited to *me*, in *my* house, so I can use them as I see fit. I am, after all, a journalist as well as a psychic investigator.

**JOSEPH**   But to publish them? Why?

**HESTER**   The publicity it will engender, Mr. Franklin, shall advertise my business. What a glorious opportunity. New clients will want readings and lessons with me. And the book might earn more money than my first book, *Voices from the Void*, earned.

**JOSEPH**   Surely money does not motivate you.

**HESTER**   It doesn't, really.

**JOSEPH**   I'm convinced one should not publish and publicize that which comes to one so, so strangely, so mystically. Maybe Wilde's words should remain private and mysterious.

**HESTER**   Nonsense. You've heard him speak. I've heard him. Why shouldn't I prosper because of it? Moreover, it might set Oscar free.

**JOSEPH**   It doesn't feel right to me. I do not wish to prosper on his account.

**HESTER**   You won't. Please, let me worry about it.... Oscar Wilde came to me for good reasons, I'm sure. Don't overly concern yourself with this, Joseph. It's my affair, truly, not yours. You are as Oscar Wilde said himself—

**JOSEPH and HESTER**   [*Simultaneously.*] A tool.

**HESTER**   And nothing is wrong with that. Psychic abilities take many forms.

**JOSEPH**   The commercial aspect troubles me.

**HESTER**   It shouldn't. I've told you—you won't prosper.

**JOSEPH**   But you will?

**HESTER**   The world will. Posterity shall be enriched. Publicizing Oscar Wilde's messages does not constitute a commercial venture at all.

**JOSEPH**   So now it's a good deed?

**HESTER**   That's exactly what it is. Indeed, a good deed. That you know this, Mr. Franklin, confirms my intuition that you have psychic capabilities of your own. You are what we sometimes call a sensitive.

**JOSEPH**   A sensitive. I like that.

**HESTER**   Yes. A sensitive as a psychic perceives material through means other than the ordinary five senses.

**JOSEPH**   And a sensitive senses non-physical forces as well?

**HESTER**   Most certainly. Understand this: Authentic mediums do not predict the results of horse races.

**JOSEPH**   Now *that* would be profitable—

**HESTER**   And crude.... We are not fortune-tellers and crystal-ball gazers. Mediums authenticated and validated by the Society for Psychical Research, a very respectable organization, do not engage in the races, I assure you.

**JOSEPH**   But yet you race to publish Oscar's words.

**HESTER**   No. I'm not hurrying this experience along. Oscar will reveal himself at his own pace like a blooming flower.

**JOSEPH**   A lily, I'm sure.... And in the meantime, I shall remain—

**JOSEPH and HESTER**   [*Simultaneously.*] A tool.

[*Brief blackout. Lights upon* OSCAR *first, upstage, then on* HESTER *and* JOSEPH.]

**OSCAR**   Please do not ask me for proof of my identity again and again. That's *so* tedious. I am Oscar Wilde. Period. And I do not wish to visualize my medium as an old spinster nosing around into the other world.

**HESTER**  Then don't. I'd drop the name-calling if I were you.

**OSCAR**  Touchy. Touchy. Short-tempered, too. Don't tell me you are thin-skinned, Mrs. Dowden, because I know—

**JOSEPH**  There. There. Both of you...calm yourselves.

**OSCAR**  I am infinitely amused by the remarks you darlings make.... You know, here I have no body, no physical body; therefore, one of my most interesting occupations is now impossible. [*Pause.*] It is not at all agreeable to be a mere mind without a body.... Over here that amusement [*Winks to audience.*] is quite out of the question.

**JOSEPH**  [*With a touch of disappointment.*] Out of the question?

**OSCAR**  Yes. Adorable or not, we know far too much about each others' ideas. [*To* JOSEPH.] But Hester no longer has interest in physical adoration. She's [*In mock whisper.*] fifty-five years old. Now she has other interests, other needs—

**HESTER**  [*Abruptly.*] Don't provoke me, Oscar.... It is unwise.... Have you seen your mother lately?

**OSCAR**  Yes. I have seen her. She has not really improved in the process of dying.

[OSCAR *crosses upstage, preparing to leave.*]

**HESTER**  Will you visit us again?

**OSCAR**  I will come again gladly. I like to remind myself now and then of the fact that there are people who regard this little globe as the whole of what is reality.... [*Slow fade.*] Poor dears.

[*Séance music: track #6. Light upon screen projection above; it reads: Communication Through* HESTER's *Hand at the Ouija Board, July 2, 1923. Then lights up on* HESTER, *alone, at the Ouija board table.* OSCAR *wanders about and examines objects in her sitting room. He twirls a walking stick with a gold pommel.*]

**OSCAR**  If it gives you pleasure to speak to one who is in a manner *soiled* in the eyes of the world, I will continue to talk to you and spin my webs of thought around you.

**HESTER**   Do you see me?

**OSCAR**   Yes. I can see you quite clearly. As you know, I have only dimness around me. . . . My mind is now a rusty lock into which the key grates with a rasp. It does not move as lightly as it used to. As sprightly—

**HESTER**   Do you see this room?

**OSCAR**   Yes. A little. Dimly.

**HESTER**   How do you manage when Mr. Franklin and I sit together?

**OSCAR**   I can control his hand. I can only control your mind. Your hand is guided by your mind. I shall readily speak to you because it seems to me that these glimpses of the sun keep me from growing too moldy here below. Hamlet speaks of his father's ghost as "old mole." The clumsy way in which he addressed the shade of his father used to wound my feelings of delicacy and selection. But now that I am a mole myself, I fully appreciate this expression.

**HESTER**   I have sent your messages to Mr. Yeats.

**OSCAR**   Yeats? Why?

**HESTER**   Yeats uses automatic writing with his wife George.

**OSCAR**   Does he? How amusing. Droll, actually.

**HESTER**   They have had much success with these methods.

**OSCAR**   I find most success vulgar.

**HESTER**   That's ridiculous. You sought success like a hunter—a hungry hunter.

**OSCAR**   Ha. Well said, madame. . . . Permit me to point out, that you, too, pursue your goals with great enthusiasm. I sense what you're up to.

**HESTER**   I'm not up to anything, Oscar.

**OSCAR**   It takes a self-promoter to know one.

**HESTER**   Rubbish.

**OSCAR**   Then why did you share our communication with Yeats?

**HESTER**   I thought he could help us.

**OSCAR**   Us? No. You thought he could help you.

**HESTER**   Yeats remains sympathetic to you, Oscar. You know that.

**OSCAR**   I do recall the letters of support he solicited from the literary men of my time for the court. That was most gracious. Extraordinarily so.

**HESTER**   It was. Indeed. But let us move on—

**OSCAR**   [*He interrupts* HESTER.] No. Now that I think about it, didn't your father, Prof. Edward Dowden, refuse Yeats a letter of support on my behalf?

**HESTER**   I, I, [*Flustered.*] I'm not sure.

**OSCAR**   I'm certain. Your father would not write to support me during the trial.

**HESTER**   Father must have been otherwise engaged. He was a very busy man, an esteemed scholar. Surely he wanted to offer testimony—

**OSCAR**   He didn't. [*Pause.*]

**HESTER**   I'm very sorry. Father was always kind and generous.

**OSCAR**   Was he? Are you revising your own history, Hester? Or do you not value honesty when it comes to *your* personal life?

**HESTER**   [*Sighs in frustration.*] Now you doubt my integrity? ... My self-awareness? That's ludicrous. I am a professional psychic investigator. Please, Oscar, I implore you, please explain why you chose to convey these messages through *me*.

**OSCAR**   I like to speak to you because you remind me of the time when I, too, was a creature hampered by that garment you call a body. I really do not miss it much.... Well, sometimes I do.... My dear lady, what will it be for you to lose your little shape, to have no shape, to be a fluid and to merely stream about in such an undecided way that it is like drifting before a heavy tide?

**HESTER**  I don't know. I don't know what it will be like. But you didn't select me because of my body. I am certain of that.

**OSCAR**  We commingle. Yes. Lovely word, commingle, is it not? [*Pause.*] *My mind* is not really as repulsive as you would expect. There is the brilliant orange of my thoughts and the deep rose red of my desires, which cling to me still. They are perfumed and smell sweet to me. But there is somehow a sense that they are getting a little stale. This condition of twilight is bringing out a delicate, mossy mold.

**HESTER**  You are a malcontent now.

**OSCAR**  So far, I cannot be said to have found the afterlife a state of bliss. But I will someday. You'll see.... Nonetheless, my mind is quite clear today. I am in excellent condition for exploiting the English language. Try me. Give me themes to weave patterns on. It's my pleasure.

**HESTER**  Certainly.... Tell me about your time at Trinity College, Dublin.

**OSCAR**  I almost forgot that time when I was chained within the walls of the university. I was like a carrier pigeon that had flown by mistake into a nest of sparrows. I was a giant among pygmies.

**HESTER**  And *I*, Oscar, what about *me*? I can't stop thinking about this. Why did you select *me* as your medium? I must know.

**OSCAR**  That, Hester *cherie*, is not easy to explain. Clearly, this question disturbs you.... I try to let my thoughts fly through your brain.

**HESTER**  Fly. That's no explanation.

**OSCAR**  *Soooo* stubborn, Hester. You are a rebel of sorts....

**HESTER**  I bridge the spiritual and physical world for you, don't I?

**OSCAR**  You do.... All right, then, perhaps this will satisfy your curiosity. Communicating through a medium resembles writing plays for the stage. Would you agree?

**HESTER**  Interesting. Yes. I believe I do. Playwriting, you say. That's sharp. Very well. Let me see where all this goes.

**OSCAR**   Goes?

**HESTER**   Yes. Never mind, Oscar.

**OSCAR**   I need a medium with certain traits.

**HESTER**   Traits!

**OSCAR**   It is true.

**HESTER**   Please don't be impertinent. Don't judge my character. Don't. And I won't judge yours. [*Pause.*] But I assume you'd like to know a legend has sprung up concerning you—

**OSCAR**   Only one? Don't be silly, dear.

**HESTER**   Can't you ever be serious?

**OSCAR**   Serious! What have the gossip mongers concocted?

**HESTER**   [*Imperiously.*] It is believed by some that you did not die when you were supposed to have died.

**OSCAR**   Men are ever interested in the remains of those who have had the audacity to be distinguished and when, add to this, the corpse has the flavor of crime, the carrion birds are eager to light upon it. . . . And hence this legend has a charm. . . . It is really delightful to think that when one has striven and conquered London—for I conquered London partly through my supposed crime—it is delightful to think that after the carcass has been conveyed to its modest hole, a legend is woven around its decaying particles. This legend is merely an accident due to the fact that I am still talked about.

[*Lights slowly down on* OSCAR.]

**HESTER**   [*As if musing to self.*] And would that I be talked about, too . . . Oscar takes fame for granted. Not me. I struggle for everything— for dignity, for my reputation, for autonomy. Nothing is a given in my life. *I must take.* [*Pause. Now poignantly.*] No one takes care of me. No one.

[*Brief blackout.*]

[*Séance music: track #7. Screen projection above reads: Communication Through Hester's Hand at the Ouija Board, July 4, 1923.*]

[*Lights up on* HESTER *at the Ouija board with her fingertips on the planchette.* OSCAR *prowls about the room, smokes, and reclines on the chaise lounge.*]

**OSCAR** [*Languidly.*] I am a little astray as to what special subjects are of interest to you today.

**HESTER** We are interested in—

**OSCAR** We? How royal of you, Mrs. Dowden. Or is it the editorial we you use?

**HESTER** I mean, Mr. Joseph Franklin and myself, as well as my friends from the Society of Psychical Research who help transcribe your words from the Ouija board. . . . I prefer communicating through the Ouija board. Automatic writing with Joseph Franklin's hand makes me feel uneasy.

**OSCAR** Very well, then; you sound like you are becoming a cottage industry. Do tell. What *are* we interested in?

**HESTER** We are interested in drama.

**OSCAR** If you tempt me to speak of drama, I shall weary you with my complaints and my fancies. I had different thoughts from my fellows when my plays were produced. Consequently, I cannot absorb their attitudes to the stage.

**HESTER** To whom do you refer? George Bernard Shaw?

**OSCAR** My dear lady, how do *you* approach the theatre? What side of your nature does it repel or attract?

**HESTER** I, I, I'm not sure.

**OSCAR** Consider whether our task should be to aim at representing life in its rather crude and disgusting shape, or whether the stage— like the other platforms from which we try to bring home the essence of things to the masses—should be reserved for the exposition of beauty in some form.

**HESTER** But one can't only dramatize the beautiful.

**OSCAR** I do not intend to listen to your modern criticism simply because you have the misfortune to live in an age of harshness.

**HESTER**   Yes. We have harshness and abrasiveness.

**OSCAR**   In abundance. While in my lifetime I strove to bring beauty home to the hearts of men. But in your present time, the main endeavor of the so-called artist is to torture the senses.

**HESTER**   Since you feel that way about it, tell me about your *beautiful* plays, Oscar.

**OSCAR**   *Touché.* My idea in writing a play was to weave a pattern of humanity. I have never swerved from my ideal. I have served the theatre in my own way. And from my own standpoint, I succeeded...

**HESTER**   You have, although it took ten years after your death for the public to read and embrace your work.

**OSCAR**   [*Sighs.*] *C'est dommage.* I fear that once a manuscript is published or performed it becomes public property. I *rarely* think that anything I write is true....But I can believe anything provided that it is *incredible*....It affords me great pleasure when I reflect that I escaped this age of *rasp*. Yes, my dear. [*With exaggeration.*] *RASP.*

**HESTER**   *Le mot juste, bien sur.*

**OSCAR**   *Mais oui, naturellement.*

**HESTER**   We are great admirers of your plays.

**OSCAR**   [*To audience.*] Again her royal we. I bend deeply to your compliment, madam. My plays were scarcely drama. Well, not conventional dramas. I wove character into pattern. I illustrated the surface of human beings. I did not delve into the heart, that organ *so frequently maligned* did not interest me much.

**HESTER**   That is surprising.

**OSCAR**   Why? It seemed to me people received more from each other by accepting the outsides than by probing into the intestines. [*Pronounced "intesteins."*]

[*He playfully pokes her belly. They laugh.*]

**HESTER**   That being the case, I assume you hold George Bernard Shaw in high esteem.

**OSCAR**   Shaw might be called a contemporary of mine. We had almost reached the point of rivalry, in a sense, when I was taken from the scene of action. . . . I had a kindly feeling towards poor Shaw. He had such a keen desire to be original that it moved my pity. But he was without any keen appreciation of the lovely or the graceful.

**HESTER**   Unkind words.

**OSCAR**   No. Astute words. I have a very great respect for his work. . . . After all, he is my fellow countryman. . . .

**HESTER**   *Our* countryman, Oscar.

**OSCAR**   Countryman or not, Mr. Shaw is so eager to prove himself honest and outspoken that he spouts a great deal more than he is able to analyze. He overturns the furniture and laughs with delight when he sees the canvas bottoms of the chairs he has flung over.

**HESTER**   Dear Oscar, you are most amusing today.

**OSCAR**   I am glad that a poor ghost can bring laughter to your eyes.

**HESTER**   And one more question on Irish literature, if I may. What is your opinion of James Joyce's *Ulysses*?

**OSCAR**   I have smeared my fingers with that vast work, but I understand that if I'm to retain my reputation as an intelligent "shade" who is open to the new, then I must peruse this *Ulysses*.

**HESTER**   I have not read more than a dozen pages of the book.

**OSCAR**   It does not suit your style, Hester, does it?

**HESTER**   Not at all . . . [*Some offstage noise.*] I believe Joseph Franklin is arriving now. I'll let him in. Perhaps you two can entertain yourselves while I attend to some business with my automatic writing transcriber, Miss Geraldine Cummins. Quite like Mr. Franklin, Miss Cummins is a very devoted student of mine.

**OSCAR**   But of course, madam.

[OSCAR *bows ceremoniously.* HESTER *exits.* JOSEPH FRANKLIN *enters but does not see* OSCAR *upstage in dim shadows.* JOSEPH *hangs his hat, jacket, and pours himself a cup of tea. He then primps before the wall mirror and paces about while he softly hums the "séance music."*]

**OSCAR**   You have a charming voice, sir.

**JOSEPH**   [*Startled. Looks about.*] Oscar?

**OSCAR**   Naturally. Were you expecting anyone else?

**JOSEPH**   [*Laughs.*] Around here one never knows what to expect.

**OSCAR**   That's true. It is always something at Mrs. Dowden's salon.

**JOSEPH**   Some people call her Mrs. Traver-Smith, you know. That was her married name.

**OSCAR**   *Pauvre* Hester. She did not marry well, did she?

**JOSEPH**   I don't know. I don't know the details.

**OSCAR**   I do. It's a typical story, another woman abandoned.

**JOSEPH**   You sound cynical.

**OSCAR**   No. Truthful is more like it. First Hester's mother died at an early age. Then her much adored father abandoned her for his new wife.

**JOSEPH**   That's sad.

**OSCAR**   Then Hester was forced to give up her previously promising classical music career.

**JOSEPH**   She never told me about this.

**OSCAR**   She will. And after that—how many devastating abandonments are we up to now?

**JOSEPH**   Her mother, her father, her music—

**OSCAR**   Then she suffers the indignity of a miserable marriage to Dr. Travers-Smith—who eventually leaves her and her two children.

**JOSEPH**　That's a lot of loss.

**OSCAR**　Yes. Loss and absence inform her character.

**JOSEPH**　I didn't realize she suffered this much.

**OSCAR**　She still suffers, albeit silently and discreetly for the most part.

**JOSEPH**　Hester Dowden is quite an admirable woman. I am proud to take psychic lessons with her. At the university—I am a professor of mathematics, did you know that?

**OSCAR**　Yes. Go on.

**JOSEPH**　At the university we do not have characters like her.

**OSCAR**　I don't imagine you do.

**JOSEPH**　Studying and working with Hester and her colleagues from the Society for Psychical Research has opened my eyes—

**OSCAR**　Were they closed?

**JOSEPH**　You know what I mean. This is a more exciting world than academia.

**OSCAR**　All worlds are preferable to academia. [*Pause.*] Our old girl has pluck, though. I'll give her that.

**JOSEPH**　She has some intentions you might not admire, Mr. Wilde. I don't know if I should tell you this, but—

**OSCAR**　Oh, go ahead. What can you possibly be afraid of? Nothing shocks me.

**JOSEPH**　Hester plans on sharing your messages with the world.

**OSCAR**　Is that so?

**JOSEPH**　Yes. I try to talk her out of it. I try to expose the indecency of it—

**OSCAR**　But to no avail. Indecency does not deter Hester Dowden.

**JOSEPH**　Are you not appalled?

**OSCAR**　No. That's not the word. I'm tired; I'm hurt; I'm lost; but, no. I am not appalled.

**JOSEPH**   Surely you don't want her to profit from your pains?

**OSCAR**   I can't say I see it that way, Mr. Franklin.

**JOSEPH**   I'm not sure I understand.

**OSCAR**   This is tricky. But Hester will do what Hester must do. Much in the same way that I will do what I must do.

**JOSEPH**   And what must you do?

**OSCAR**   I must get out of here. Be gone—

**JOSEPH**   Where, exactly, are you, Mr. Wilde?

**OSCAR**   Why—I'm—

[*Lights out on* OSCAR. *Pause.* JOSEPH, *alone, resumes humming séance music. Brief blackout. Lights slowly up on* OSCAR *upstage and* HESTER *and* JOSEPH *downstage.*]

**OSCAR**   [OSCAR *now wears a fur coat over his velvet jacket.*] If no one minds, I think I'll have a glass or two of absinthe to chase the tea. [*He pours himself absinthe and smokes.*] Wonderful fluid absinthe. I adore it.... There is no difference between a glass of absinthe and a sunset....

**HESTER**   No difference? Please—

**OSCAR**   Don't quibble, Hester. Rejoice that you are watching a spirit drinking spirits.... Would you like some?

**HESTER**   No, thank you. I believe absinthe is in the same family as Plato's hemlock. I prefer self-preservation.

**OSCAR**   You don't say.... No taste for self-destruction?... Personality must be accepted for what it is. You mustn't mind that an artist is a drunk; you should mind that drunks are not always artists...

**JOSEPH**   Very clever.

**OSCAR**   Extraordinarily so. But absinthe, my dears, is fickle. Some days it offers grand oblivion; other days it does not make one drunk at all. In the end, though, absinthe provides consolation, much needed, warming consolation.

**HESTER**   Were the women in your life also a consolation?

**OSCAR**   Dear lady, I feel rather melancholy tonight. Perhaps I'll reasonably babble about lost illusions—

**JOSEPH**   Did women inspire your work?

**OSCAR**   I was the editor of the magazine *Woman's World* for years. This work permitted me to finance my household comfortably for my wife and young children. And this *Woman's World* position bought me time to give birth—so to speak—to my stage plays. [*Pause.*] Women were ever to me a cluster of stars. They contained for me all, and more than all, that God has created.

**HESTER**   Most interesting, Oscar. Perhaps a bit surprising to hear this, as well.

**OSCAR**   Do I insult you if I maintain that woman must ever be to man the force that is creative? That was what made her hateful in my sight—hateful and sweet as a too powerful vintage.

**HESTER**   Surely all women were not the same to you.

**OSCAR**   I gathered them as flowers might be culled from a rich garden. All their varied perfumes came to intoxicate me and made my days both sweet and bitter.

**JOSEPH**   Like muses for your work—

**OSCAR**   [*From chaise.*] Don't talk to me about work. It is the last refuge of the mentally unemployed, the occupation of those too dull to dream. [*Rises and pours himself another absinthe. Returns to chaise.*] To be eternally busy is a sign of low vitality. So, my friends, live to do nothing and be happy.... Eschew work and be fine.... No one should ever do anything. At least no woman should. The woman who was content to merely *be* was always charming, but the woman who *did* was often detestable.

[*Blackout.*]

[*Lights up on* HESTER *at downstage table. She fusses with manuscript pages and notebooks.*]

**HESTER**   Method. Method. Impose a method.... Chronological messages and then expert commentary.... Yes. That's it—

[*Yawning and stretching sounds. Then lights up on* OSCAR. *He reclines on the chaise and sounds tipsy.*]

OSCAR   Have some absinthe, Hester. Go on. Let your hair down.

HESTER   I didn't realize you were with me.

OSCAR   I'm always with you, Hester. Am I not? We'll be together for eternity.

HESTER   You're tipsy!

OSCAR   No. I'm in-intoxicated. We're like an old married couple. We are.... wedded. Welded.... Wilde Welded.... Use that title.

HESTER   Title?

OSCAR   Don't play coy with me. Not now.

HESTER   [*Packs up her books and papers.*] I won't.

OSCAR   [*Rises from chaise and makes matador moves.*] You've become quite the matador—swirling capework and all.

HESTER   And you're speaking gibberish.

OSCAR   Nothing wrong with that. You, Mrs. Hester Dowden, soon to be *internationally renowned* medium and psychic investigator, yes, you, Mrs. Dowden, will organize my words.

HESTER   I'll edit and arrange them.

OSCAR   Like a matador. On second thought, perhaps you are more like the bull. [*Makes bull moves.*] Head down, determined, fearless—

HESTER   Oh, stuff and nonsense!

OSCAR   Someday the world will admire your courage, your bullishness—

HESTER   *You* are the stubborn bull, Oscar. Not I.

OSCAR   Maybe we're both bulls or, both matadors. At the *corrida's* moment of truth, the bull and the matador become one—

HESTER   [*Rises and makes matador moves.*] But then the bull dies—

OSCAR   Yes. The animal is finally free of the arena's cruel conventions.

**HESTER**  While the matador receives the crowd's adulation—

**OSCAR**  Now you've got the spirit.

**HESTER**  The public applauds wildly—

**OSCAR**  Wildly. Ha! That's rich—

**HESTER**  [*Recovers her usual physical reserve.*] We are getting ahead of ourselves.

**OSCAR**  Ha. Ha. [*Nearly hysterical.*] Getting ahead. That's what we want.

**HESTER**  Stop it. Compose yourself.

**OSCAR**  [*Collapses on chaise.*] More absinthe—more—

**HESTER**  That's enough for now, Oscar.

**OSCAR**  Enough is never enough.

**HESTER**  There. There. Rest awhile.

**OSCAR**  Awhile—

**HESTER**  There. There. I'll sit right here. I won't leave you.

**OSCAR**  [*Child-like.*] You won't leave me?

**HESTER**  I won't leave you. Close your eyes.

[*Blackout.*]

[*Lights up on HESTER at the piano. She plays a tune while JOSEPH waltzes around the room. Music: track #8.*]

**HESTER**  I'm worried about Oscar and uncertain what I should do with his messages.

**JOSEPH**  Do! You persist in believing that you must do something with this, don't you?

**HESTER**  Oscar was not particularly musical, you know, even though his sensitivity to the sounds of words was always strong. I believe his brother Willie was the musical one. . . . I made several attempts to get Oscar to speak about music with no success. . . . It is a pity since music is my dearest subject and has been since childhood—

**JOSEPH**   I know. I enjoy your music very much.

**HESTER**   I've composed a new piece. I shall call it *Purgatory*.

**JOSEPH**   *Purgatory?*

**HESTER**   Yes. *Purgatory*. Oscar is trapped in purgatory.

**JOSEPH**   Wasn't he always?

**HESTER**   Perhaps. But not like this. Remember when he spoke to us of his twilight state?

**JOSEPH**   I do.

**HESTER**   Well, he's stuck. Think about it. His spirit cannot move on.

**JOSEPH**   I am not sure I understand. What binds him? Does his obsessive love of beauty bind him?

**HESTER**   Partially. Yes. It is complicated, I know. Oscar cannot free himself from the weight of his misdeeds and desires.

**JOSEPH**   Can anyone do that?

**HESTER**   I think so. For Oscar, though, it is, at present, too difficult. He is condemned.

**JOSEPH**   *Now?* Condemned to what? He served two years of hard labor in jail. Surely that's condemnation enough.

**HESTER**   Perhaps the sentence was sufficient for the courts. But Oscar now imprisons himself on the other side. He condemns himself to be the same.

**JOSEPH**   He cannot help but be himself.

**HESTER**   Precisely. Yes. Oscar would do everything all over again in exactly the same way. The illicit passions, the plays, the notoriety, the danger... everything. Oscar can't untie the fraying threads of his character.

**JOSEPH**   I wonder if any of us can untie such knotted threads. Probably not.... But I know I'd like to help him.

**HESTER**   How? You've succumbed to his charms. What can you do for him other than write down his messages during our automatic writing sessions? And that, Joseph, is quite an achievement in itself, you know.

JOSEPH  [*Deflated.*] Yes. But I would prefer to liberate him.

HESTER  That's very kind of you. But Oscar must find his own salvation. No one saves anyone else. [*Connivingly.*] Isn't it curious that more than half of Oscar's words came to *me* when I was sitting *alone* at the Ouija board?

JOSEPH  Yes. And you succeeded quite well at the Ouija board, perhaps even better than at our writing sessions.

HESTER  In one Ouija session alone, the planchette flew from letter to letter with lightning speed—at the rate of 60 to 70 words per minute. Miss Geraldine Cummins, the transcriber I mentioned, sat on the other side of the room hidden behind a screen and wrote Oscar's words down as soon as I received them.

JOSEPH  That's remarkable. Similarly, I have recently discovered that semi-hypnotic states, or partial trances, seem to create powers we do not ordinarily possess.

HESTER  That's quite true. I have no exceptional clairvoyant gift, yet at the Ouija board I develop the power to get at facts that are not present in my ordinary consciousness.

JOSEPH  That must be the subconscious mind. I believe in it.

HESTER  Do you? [*Imperiously.*] In cases of double mediumship, the communications can not be attributed to either medium alone.... In my experience, the ideas expressed are *more definitely* connected with the person who lays a hand on the writer's hand than with the actual automatic writer.

JOSEPH  [*Rises to pour himself champagne.*] Are you insinuating that your role in our automatic writing and Ouija sessions is more important than mine?

HESTER  I am. And I trust this does not offend you.

JOSEPH  It doesn't. Nonetheless, these messages from Oscar remain a joint production of ours, are they not?

**HESTER**  There. There. I do not mean to diminish your input, Joseph.

**JOSEPH**  [*A bit fed up.*] *That's* a relief.

**HESTER**  The case of Oscar Wilde's messages is the third instance of successful double mediumship which has come to me during the many years I have worked with the Society.

**JOSEPH**  Double mediumship or not, it is quite obvious to me that Oscar has lost neither his pride nor egotism even though he complains repeatedly of the dimming of his senses.

**HESTER**  We should not expect his messages to be in a style equal to his best work of the 1890s.

**JOSEPH**  Why not?

**HESTER**  The difficulties of psychic communication are here compounded by the fact that he ended his life a complete wreck, dissolute—

**JOSEPH**  And loveless—

**HESTER**  Yes. Without the love he craves. . . .

**JOSEPH**  Everyone craves love. Everyone needs love.

**HESTER**  I don't. [*Pause.*] Not anymore.

**JOSEPH**  Why is that?

**HESTER**  Oh, Joseph. . . . Must we now have a melodramatic scene that reveals distressing emotions? [*Pause.*] I have had my romantic passions. I think that people are granted a *finite* love quotient, a personal ration, if you will. Yes, just so much love is allotted per person. And once one fully experiences one's share, one uses it up. It disappears.

**JOSEPH**  Can't you be granted more?

**HESTER**  I've had my share already, Joseph. Maybe more than my share. And that is probably something others cannot say. [*She drinks the champagne* JOSEPH *pours for her.*] My portion was wonderful, plentiful. But now—it is gone.

**JOSEPH**   Won't destiny offer you more romance? Erotic love?

**HESTER**   I'm afraid not. [*Pause.*] Of course, on the brighter side, my children offer loving comfort.

**JOSEPH**   Perhaps your fate will change.

**HESTER**   Character *is* fate. You know that.

**JOSEPH**   I've heard it said, but I'm not sure it is true. . . . You're a willful woman, though. You've got initiative—

**HESTER**   I have faith that my fate will bring professional success. This will please me. It will justify my life's work.

**JOSEPH**   Instead of yearning for love you now yearn for fame?

**HESTER**   A very twentieth-century exchange, wouldn't you say? But it needn't be an either/or proposition. Unfortunately, though, it seems to be one for me.

**JOSEPH**   That's not a happy destiny.

**HESTER**   Happiness! No one in their right mind seeks happiness.

**JOSEPH**   Oscar did.

**HESTER**   No. He sought sensual indulgence and excess—the illusion of happiness.

**JOSEPH**   Oscar still seeks love.

**HESTER**   And that's why he remains in bondage.

**JOSEPH**   What do you mean?

**HESTER**   Until Oscar gives up his quest for perfect, undying, physical love, he will remain bound in purgatory, yearning for an ecstasy that is unattainable.

**JOSEPH**   You can't be sure of this.

**HESTER**   I am. I just know it. Oscar must forsake eroticism.

**JOSEPH**   He'll never do that. He can't.

**HESTER**   He must. Until he does, punishment will always find him on the other side. [*She returns to the piano.*]

**JOSEPH**   Yet Oscar persists. That he specifically chooses to send messages through us is significant. He needs something from us.

**HESTER**   Of course he does. Oscar needs *me*. He needs me. [*Music: track #9. Then speaks emphatically.*] *I am convinced* that Oscar Wilde is actually speaking at these sittings.

**JOSEPH**   I am trying to keep an open mind on this point. It is quite likely that Oscar's spirit is communicating with us.... On the other hand, I doubt this is a case of subconscious plagiarism—

**HESTER**   Because?

**JOSEPH**   Because Oscar's style is *too* easy to plagiarize.... Surely we can create a style similar to Oscar's. Others could, too, I'm sure.

**HESTER**   Perhaps you are correct. The inevitable nonbelievers will wonder whether it is really Oscar Wilde at his best or whether his wit is tarnished....

**JOSEPH**   Does that matter as long as it is Oscar speaking?

**HESTER**   The simplest theory for others is that Oscar Wilde erupts from the subconscious memories of one or both of the mediums who produce the messages.

**JOSEPH**   Since I know so little of his work I cannot be accused of recalling it. You know more about it than I do.

**HESTER**   If Oscar Wilde arises from my memories, he is one of hundreds of literary people who interested me over the years.

**JOSEPH**   True—

**HESTER**   So why should my subconscious mind amuse itself by plagiarizing his style rather than the style of another writer who has captured my attention more fully?

**JOSEPH**   Again. Because Oscar's style is easier to recreate and imitate—

**HESTER**   The mediums must produce as much irrefutable evidence as possible.... Later on, I should think, as the mediums in question [*Points to self and* JOSEPH.] we have an obligation to provide explanations and critiques.

**JOSEPH**   I don't want to write about Oscar. I told you. I do not wish to exploit him at all. I'm *very* fond of him.

**HESTER**   As am I.

**JOSEPH**   Then let's liberate him, Hester.

**HESTER**   [*In exasperation.*] How grand of you! That is out of your control. . . . Joseph, please, be more realistic. . . . You can't liberate Oscar Wilde. You can't. . . . We can vindicate him at most, no more than that.

**JOSEPH**   I'm not sure what you mean by vindication in this case.

**HESTER**   The public demands clear explanations from Oscar's mediums. Too much subtlety and obscurity confound them. Of this I am certain. Much in the same way that an actor is the best and most intimate critic of the drama, a medium who has instinctively *felt* results can provide a point of view arrived at by no other person.

**JOSEPH**   The doubters will say—

**HESTER**   [*Testily.*] There are doubters everywhere. They always get in the way of true psychic research. And they foolishly impede my career, as well.

**JOSEPH**   You must address them, then. Do not ignore them. Didn't your friend Mr. Yeats say, "We were all skeptics once?" . . . I suppose you must impress upon them that every medium is neither a fraud nor a conjuror who could make an easier living performing on the music hall stage.

**HESTER**   *Music hall*! Do you know that I grew up longing to become a concert pianist? I trained for years, and my dear father was most encouraging . . . at first.

**JOSEPH**   Your father was a formidable man

**HESTER**   He was.

**JOSEPH**   Everyone at the university knew Professor Edward Dowden, the Shakespeare scholar.

**HESTER**   Yes. Father was very well known for his writings on Renaissance drama. It is true. After my love for father, music became the grand passion of my life.... [*Wistfully.*] A pity nothing became of all that. I had such high hopes...

**JOSEPH**   What happened?

**HESTER**   My intensity was greater than my talent. [*Pause. Summoning forced bravado.*] Years later, back in Dublin I had to earn enough to support myself and my children, so I turned to journalism out of necessity.... Then I eventually became a psychic investigator. During these years, spiritualism became respectable.

**JOSEPH**   I know. Even mathematicians find spiritualism fashionably attractive... but, please, Hester, forgive my boldness, tell me what happened to your husband.

**HESTER**   [*Slight pause while* HESTER *pours champagne for herself and refills* JOSEPH's *glass. She crosses to a mirror and rearranges her hair while speaking.*] Dr. Travers-Smith? Ha. The renowned physician. The healer of the sick. After sixteen years of marriage, he abandoned me and the children for his young girlfriend.

**JOSEPH**   I'm sorry, Hester.

**HESTER**   Don't be.... Let's get back to work. That's much more important to me now.

**JOSEPH**   This Oscar business of yours will stir up a fuss.

**HESTER**   Let it.

**JOSEPH**   I urge you to plan ahead for your detractors because you don't seem willing to let this business go—

**HESTER**   [*Shouting.*] BUSINESS! You *repeatedly* call my Oscar work *business*! Please don't patronize me. I do not fear for my reputation.

**JOSEPH**   Perhaps you should—

**HESTER**   [*With conviction.*] No. No. *I refuse to let anything deter me from publishing these psychic messages.* In fact, I now feel confident we have been receiving communication from the discarnate mind of Oscar Wilde.

**JOSEPH**   Discarnate as in disembodied or disconnected?

**HESTER**   Both. Discarnate spirits in a phase of life different from our own.

**JOSEPH**   Considering our psychical studies together for the past few months, I now believe in the existence of angels, and tutelary spirits, so communication from the discarnate mind of Oscar Wilde seems perfectly possible.

**HESTER**   Yes. It is. Wilde himself speaks to us. It is the obvious and simple explanation.

**JOSEPH**   A simple explanation in this very complex case might be best—

**HESTER**   Especially if I want a worldwide audience. I know full well that people will set aside explanations that do not easily excite their imaginations.

**JOSEPH**   People are slow to admit the possibility that we survive death.

**HESTER**   Of course they are. It is a difficult and troubling proposition for those not attuned to spiritualism.

**JOSEPH**   Survival excites me.

**HESTER**   As it should.

**JOSEPH**   As a professor who teaches advanced theorems and proofs, I must say that we cannot *prove* survival.

**HESTER**   Proof of survival varies. If I were asked to state what I consider proof of an afterlife, I would reply reconstruction of personality.

**JOSEPH**   [*Laughs.*] Well, our visiting Oscar certainly has personality. Only the insensible will deny that.... Once we review the evidence without prejudice, we can come to our own conclusions.

**HESTER**   [*Adamantly.*] The proof we demand is that *mind as spirit* survives.

[*Brief blackout. Séance music: track #10.*]

[*Projection above reads: Ouija Board Communication Through Hester's Hand, July 12, 1923. Lights up on Ouija board round table.*]

**HESTER**  Are you there, Oscar?

[*Music stops.*]

**OSCAR**  [*Voice from darkness.*] There? No. I'm here. You, dear Hester, are there.

**HESTER**  You sound gloomy.

**OSCAR**  [*In light now.*] No. I'm pensive.

**HESTER**  That being the case, perhaps this is a good time to discuss your life in prison.

**OSCAR**  I do not object at all. It was a most enthralling experience.

**HESTER**  Surely you jest. Enthralling.

**OSCAR**  No. When I say enthralling, I mean that my circuit of the world's pain would not have been adequate without that supreme misery. I, who worshipped beauty, was robbed not only of the chance of beholding her face, but I was cast in on myself. . . . No diversions, not one pleasure. And there, in the barrenness of soul, I languished until my spirit rose once more and cried aloud that this was an opportunity to seize.

**HESTER**  Opportunity, indeed. [*Under her breath, as if musing to herself.*] I feel that way, too.

**OSCAR**  If I may be a little autobiographical—

**HESTER**  Yes. Of course. Feel free.

**OSCAR**  It seemed to me that I had died—metaphorically, in this particular instance—and passed across the bitter stream to that place of dimness where now I am confined. Yet within me, despair never found lodging. It was impossible, surely, that all beauty had deserted me. . . . I had been sentenced monstrously, but by whom?

**HESTER**  By the powers that be. The small-minded, the self-righteous, and the unimaginative condemned you.

**OSCAR** And what comfort, Hester, that you do not condemn me.

**HESTER** I have no call to do so.

**OSCAR** Promise me that you will never judge me.

**HESTER** You know I won't.

**OSCAR** Nor I you.

**HESTER** I will present your messages as you bestowed them upon me.

**OSCAR** That's the way, old girl. Keep my legend glowing for posterity.... And I'll reciprocate by rescuing you from the doldrums of domestic obscurity.

**HESTER** Obscurity strikes me as an overstatement, Oscar. Don't forget, I have my medium practice here in London and publications to my credit.

**OSCAR** Nonetheless, dearie, [*With great exaggeration.*] I adore overstatements.

**HESTER** I don't.

**OSCAR** Please indulge my rhetorical habits. You know I can't restrain myself in such matters.... [*Reclining on chaise.*] I shall now continue my extraordinary discourse about my prison sojourn.

**HESTER** As you please.

**OSCAR** While incarcerated I realized how absurd it was to have been hounded down by little men and called unclean by Pharisees and Philistines.... How imbecilic! I had a greater place in the world's scheme than they had ever dreamed of. And then I finally understood that all trials are trials for one's life. [*Pause, then winks ironically.*] Please note the profundity of *that* gem.... This brought me a certain quiet—

**HESTER** Was the quiet calming?

**OSCAR** My soul was healing, but my vision of the visible was blind. Let me elaborate. In my cell there was dimness and pain. I suffered because the world was faithless to me. I suffered because all that gave me life and gave glorious value to my life was shut away from me. But there I later learned what I could never learn when beauty was my playmate.... I learned the force and use of indignation.

**HESTER**   I have experienced indignation myself. It surges in the bloodstream.

**OSCAR**   Yes. It gave me life again, a scarlet life, flashes of scarlet on a somber background.... I became a vital man again. In prison I discovered for the first time what strength is lodged within a man.

**HESTER**   Are you in jail now, so to speak, because of what you were sent to prison for?

**OSCAR**   Well said. . . . The world divides what it is pleased to call our sins from our good deeds. This cleavage is possibly the end result of total ignorance.... My life cannot be patched up. My life, my love, was always doomed. I acted accordingly. My love was neither ignoble nor unnatural. I ran to my own ruin, did I not? What a mad dash it was.... Sometimes I think the artistic life is a long and lovely suicide... and I am not sorry that it is so.

[*Pause.*]

**HESTER**   No regrets?

**OSCAR**   None to speak of, my dear. Some of us relish our tragic roles. We thrash about as if we were drowning; but, in truth, we are swimming along to our predetermined calamities.

**HESTER**   Why did you not change course if you knew it would all end disastrously?

**OSCAR**   That is not how tragedy proceeds, Hester. If one's life is cast in the tragic mold, then inevitability trumps transformation.

**HESTER**   Such anguish! Is there no end to it, poor man?

**OSCAR**   There is no justice here or in the world. For justice is the full completion of experience, nothing more.

**HESTER**   Indeed, Oscar. I couldn't agree more.

**OSCAR**  I don't regret for a moment having lived for pleasure. It was glorious, truthful, and edifying. There was no pleasure I did not experience. I threw the pearl of my soul into a glass of wine. [*Pause.*] I wither here in the twilight, but I know that I will rise again to ecstasy. I will. [*Shouting.*] I MUST. PERPETUAL ECSTASY. I WILL RISE TO ECSTASY....

[*Cross fade. Séance music: track #11. Lights up on* HESTER *and* JOSEPH *at the downstage table. They have tablets and pencils.* HESTER *puts her hand on top of* JOSEPH's *hand while he writes throughout much of the episode. Above screen projection reads: Automatic Writing Script, July 13, 1923.* HESTER *wears a black satin sleep mask for a while over her eyes.*]

**OSCAR**  Are you summoning me?

**JOSEPH**  Yes. We are ready for you.

**OSCAR**  Fine. And how are you, Mr. Franklin?

**JOSEPH**  Quite well, thank you. If no one objects, today, Mr. Wilde, I would like to ask you about my fiancée, Miss Theodora Raleigh.

**HESTER**  [*Rips off her black eye mask and bangs her fist on the table.*] What are you saying, Joseph? This is intolerable.

**JOSEPH**  I thought Mr. Wilde would be kind enough to contact my fiancée for me.

**HESTER**  Your fiancée? I didn't know you had one.

**JOSEPH**  Last year she, uh, she . . . crossed—

**OSCAR**  She's in Summerland, now, Prof. Franklin. Summerland.

**HESTER**  I'm sorry for your loss, Joseph. Truly. I am.

**OSCAR**  My condolences, sir. [OSCAR *pours drinks for all, raises glass to toast.*] To love—

**HESTER**  [*Reassuringly to* JOSEPH.] As you well know, Oscar is not visiting us to communicate with Miss Raleigh. He's here for very specific reasons of his own.

**JOSEPH**  I understand that. But I just need to know Theodora is not in any pain. And I must pledge my undying love to her—

**OSCAR**  Perhaps you should have whispered that vow while she was entwined in your embrace.

**JOSEPH**  I didn't. And I regret it bitterly.

**OSCAR**  Berating yourself won't help. I do not wish to *further dispirit you*, but connecting with your Miss Raleigh is not within my purview. Perhaps Hester can help you with that. Her spiritual expertise might offer you the solace you seek.

**HESTER**  [*To* JOSEPH.] I can assist you. But this is not the right time. Trust me. We have much work to do while Oscar graces us with his presence.

**JOSEPH**  All right. I'm sorry.

**HESTER**  Let us get on with it, then, gentlemen. Please resume, Oscar. You were telling us about prison.

**OSCAR**  [OSCAR *strolls upstage, smoking and drinking champagne.*] Ah, yes. Prison. Society sent me to prison and then into exile. The world that had welcomed me so gladly later thrust me out of its care.... The world had no place for me. I was alone.... When I walked in public places I was asked to leave. People viewed me as a monster of vice.

**HESTER**  [*To* JOSEPH.] They did, indeed.

**JOSEPH**  [*Shakes head.*] Insufferable!

**OSCAR**  I lost my wife and my children. I lost my lover.... And I found it impossible to live without love.

**HESTER**  All things are possible.

**OSCAR**  So they say.... I lost everything except my genius.... Even some of my manuscripts were tampered with and spurned—

**HESTER**  But for the last few years you have become one of the most widely read writers in the English language.

**OSCAR**  That *is* lovely. My reputation does not worry me. My fame once preceded me.... Inevitably, it shall succeed me.

[*Lights slowly out on* OSCAR.]

**HESTER**   Fame.... Oscar acts as if fame is his entitlement.

**JOSEPH**   Well, Oscar is special. He always was, I suppose.

**HESTER**   Yes. The Wilde family has enjoyed great acclaim and success—

**JOSEPH**   Until Oscar landed in prison—

**HESTER**   The relentless ostracizing led to self-imposed banishment—

**JOSEPH**   The Europeans were not much kinder. Maybe the Americans would have treated him better.

**HESTER**   I doubt it. Hypocrisy dwells internationally.

**JOSEPH**   I hope Oscar will take comfort when he realizes that some of us consider him alive and free.

**HESTER**   He's not free. Not yet.

[HESTER *moves upstage to the piano and plays softly during the following five lines.* JOSEPH *paces about. Music: track #12.*]

**JOSEPH**   Why not?

**HESTER**   Oscar must evade his current phase of his existence.

**JOSEPH**   Meaning what?

**HESTER**   He must leave purgatory.... DON'T STOP. [*Music stops.*] Forward!

**JOSEPH**   Pardon me?

**HESTER**   I am going ahead with a volume called *Oscar Wilde from Purgatory*.

**JOSEPH**   So you've made up your mind, after all.

**HESTER**   Yes. I will let nothing stand in my way now.

**JOSEPH**   The unbelievers will rant against the improbability of our experiences with Oscar.

**HESTER**   So be it. My book will appeal to people responsive to psychic phenomenon. This will enhance my position in the Research Society; it will bring new students, *and*, I daresay, I will reap a modicum of fame.

**JOSEPH**   That modicum of fame builds upon Oscar's misfortunes. Surely, Oscar Wilde deserves better treatment.

**HESTER**   [*Angrily pounds piano.*] I did not cause his troubles. My book might *alleviate* his troubles.

**JOSEPH**   How?

**HESTER**   If, from the twilight, Oscar Wilde realizes that he is the subject of cultural discussion once again, it will please him that he can still make a bow to the public. . . . I have no doubt it will delight him.

**JOSEPH**   I'm not so sure of that.

**HESTER**   Believe me. And there's more to it—

**JOSEPH**   The greatest value of your publication is that people might eventually interpret Wilde's words from the other side as proof of survival.

**HESTER**   Yes. And let us hope the methods by which the messages arrived will not injure their chances of having a fair hearing.

**JOSEPH**   How can you possibly expect a fair hearing when this concerns Oscar Wilde?

**HESTER**   [*Frustrated but stubborn.*] I want a fair hearing. I must have one. Posterity demands it. And what is more, a literary ghost is a new departure in the psychic world.

**JOSEPH**   Please! I still sense exploitation here.

**HESTER**   [*Angry and sarcastic.*] I don't imagine you, a lovelorn mathematician, could appreciate the nuances of a literary ghost. But if you insist upon accusing me of exploiting Oscar, then I must reproach you for your supremely selfish and thoughtless request for Oscar to contact your fiancée. It was a dangerous move.

**JOSEPH**   Hester, I meant no harm.

**HESTER**   Ever since Oscar appeared to us, you played the role of the oh-so-ethical one. And yet you have the audacity to question my motives after you brazenly sought to use—*no, to abuse* Oscar for your own purposes!!

**JOSEPH**   No. I—

**HESTER**   You are an amateur in psychic matters.

**JOSEPH**   I don't pretend otherwise.

**HESTER**   Consider yourself officially suspended from your studies with me.

**JOSEPH**   But, Hester—

**HESTER**   Let us part ways for now, Mr. Franklin. It's best for all concerned.

**JOSEPH**   Your vehemence astounds me.

**HESTER**   [*Calmer now.*] Passion frightens you, Mr. Franklin.

**JOSEPH**   [*Exiting upstage.*] I shall call upon you in the future.

**HESTER**   Farewell, Mr. Franklin.

**JOSEPH**   Good-bye, Mrs. Dowden. I trust you will soon find it possible to forgive me.

[JOSEPH *exits. Light tightens on* HESTER, *now alone, pacing.*]

**HESTER**   [*To self and then nearly to audience.*] The soul and mind of Oscar Wilde still lives and will continue to develop *until he rises . . . again . . . to . . . ecstasy. . . . I, too, shall rise to ecstasy.*
[*Pause. She crosses to table and places her hand on the planchette.*]
Oscar? . . .

[*Lights up on* OSCAR *in chaise, drinking champagne and smoking.*]

**OSCAR**   Over here.

[*She does not turn to him.*]

**HESTER**   Oscar?

**OSCAR**   [*With annoyance.*] I *said*, over here.

**HESTER**   [*She approaches* OSCAR *and looks directly in his eyes. Long pause.*] I am publishing your messages. I have written a book about us.

**OSCAR**   You think you'll find salvation in professional success. . . . You won't.

**HESTER**  [*Voice altered as if entering a trance.*] You will rise again, Oscar Wilde. Your soul will heal.

**OSCAR**  That the world maimed my soul was terrible, and to have maimed the soul of my work was more terrible still. For my work is my link with the minds of living.

**HESTER**  Of course it is.

**OSCAR**  It is the golden thread that will draw me closer to the more joyous generations in the aftertime.

**HESTER**  I understand that. Perfectly.

**OSCAR**  I imagine you do. Perfectly.

**HESTER**  Yes, Oscar. Yes. Renounce your life of love and your work shall live forever.

**OSCAR**  There can be no life here, there, or anywhere without love. Believe me, Hester. All is atoned for.

**HESTER**  [*Chanting that intensifies.*] Let go, Oscar. Let go. Forsake love to be free. . . . *Forsake love. Then, only then, shall all love return without end.*

**OSCAR**  [*Pleading.*] I was always a lover. I did nothing wrong. [*Pause.*] Oh, Hester, please. . . . I can no longer drift in this emptiness. . . . Release me with your gift.

**HESTER**  [*Closed eyes. Chanting.*] Transcend. . . . Transcend. . . . Transcend. . . . Transcend. . . .

[*Lights down slowly on* HESTER, *and then lights tighten on* OSCAR's *face. As he utters his last line, a gobo effect surrounds his head, as if bits of confetti float about him.*]

**OSCAR**  Pray, spare me. . . . From my lips little moths flew.

[*Music: track #13, as the light effect lingers of moths fluttering from* OSCAR's *lips. While the lights fade slowly, new music becomes clearly repetitive and then sounds as if the needle was stuck on a recording. From the darkness, a voice . . .* ]

**HESTER**  Over here. [*Pause.*] Over here. [*Pause. Then with annoyance.*] *I said, over here.*

[*Lights gradually up on* HESTER DOWDEN, *a sturdy-looking woman, 55 but looks older, in a high-collared, white-on-white embroidered blouse with a full-length dark green wool skirt. Her black and gray hair is in a bun. She wears reading glasses and takes them on and off and moves them up and down her nose. The glasses are attached to a chain around her neck. She is seated at the table covered with a cream-colored lace cloth.*]

Yes. On me. Look at me. Let us begin. . . . Twenty-three years ago Oscar Wilde left the present life and crossed to the other side. It may seem incredible [*To audience.*] to you that he should attempt to send his thoughts back again to a world where his infamy exceeded his good fame and fortune; but here it is, 1923, and Oscar Wilde chooses to send us messages today. [*Pompously.*] Are the messages genuine? Does Oscar Wilde still exist? [*Slight pause.*] And where exactly is he? . . . The public must judge these matters. We will return to them again and again. Yes. . . . We will. You'll see. Again and again. . . . Without belief, without faith, what have you? [*Pause.*]

[*Lights slowly fade to black. A final projection appears above. It reads: Hester Dowden became a minor celebrity when her pamphlet* Psychic Messages from Oscar Wilde *was published in 1924. Simultaneous to projection disappearance, as lights fade, a few bars of triumphant music resound. Music: track: #14 .*]

• • •

# Outsourced

## Laura Shaine

# Laura Shaine

Laura Shaine is the author of six full-length plays. She debuted at Steppenwolf Theater with a main stage production of her play *Bang*, a dark comedy set in an underground condominium. *Bang* received a Jefferson Award nomination for Best New Play. *Beautiful Bodies* premiered at Olympia Dukakis' Whole Theater in New Jersey. *Beautiful Bodies* has gone on to frequent regional productions, one of which won the Stoney Award for Best New Play in Savannah, Georgia, in 2000. In 2003, the play began a national tour of Russia and remains one of the most popular plays in Russia and the former CIS nations. *Beautiful Bodies* has been produced in major productions in Ukraine, Finland, Bulgaria, Estonia, and Finland. In 2008, the play will open in São Paulo, Brazil. Her plays are published as *Plays* by Laura Shaine by Broadway Play Publishing and in numerous anthologies, including Vintage's *Take Ten*, *Plays for Actresses*, *Leading Women*, *Laugh Lines*, and in many of the Applause Books Best Plays series. In 2007, Laura's latest play, *Sleeping Arrangements* (adapted from her memoir) premiered at Theater J, in Washington, D.C., and *Web Cam Woman* premiered at 13th Street Repertory Theater, in March 2007. In 2008, *Bang* is scheduled for main stage production at Theater-in-the Square in Indianapolis, Indiana. Laura Shaine's many short plays, including *Flop Cop*, *Outsourced*, and *Happy Talkin'*, are widely produced across the United States and are especially popular in college one-act festivals.

## cast

**MAX FISCHY**, a desperate man, age flexible

**SONALI**, a young woman of melodious if somewhat mechanized vocal abilities, with a slight East Indian accent. She is unseen for the first portion of the play. She is later revealed.

• • •

[*A high-rise apartment studio, illuminated by a violet nocturnal urban glow. The hour of financial lunacy is at hand*—MAX FISCHY, *in his underpants, but wearing a formal businessman's tie on his bare chest, is talking into his chin-held portable phone. . . . He is having a sweated midnight emergency. Credit cards and credit checks fan around him. He occasionally, spasmodically, toys with body-improvement devices—of the rubber band variety. . . as he walks a spiral course, circling, stage right, in his anxiety.*]

**MAX**   [*Believing he is speaking to a machine.*] Max Fischy is the name on the account. That is "M" as in Man, "A" as in Apple, "X" as in what the hell has an X?—X-Files? Xerox? X! You know "X"! X-rated! Okay, now Fischy—"F" as in Frank, "I" as in Idiot, "S" as in . . . [*He starts to say "shit."*] "Shi-*ite*" . . . I said Shi-*ite* . . . Oh, all right . . . "S" as in Simple, is that *simple* enough for you? "S" as in *Stupid*! "C" as in Catastrophic H as in Hell! "Y" as in . . . You . . . ! Okay, *you* got that?

**SONALI**   [*Melodious but mechanical, with that odd electronic delay.*] The last four digits of your social?

**MAX**   Two-three-five-nine.

**SONALI**   Mother's maiden name?

**MAX**   [*Registering inner agony.*] Kornfield.

**SONALI**   [*With a seductive but mechanical breathiness.*] For identification purposes, we have matched your account to your home telephone number. This call may be monitored to guarantee your best service. My name is Kimberley—what can I do for you today?

**MAX**   I was just checking my balance electronically. . . .

**SONALI**  [*Breathy, with odd emphasis on "doll-ars."*] Your available balance is...sixty-two doll-*ars*, and forty-*two* cents.

**MAX**  ...I was thinking of a...credit increase. Could you see your way clear to granting me [*Wheeze.*] a...credit increase?

**SONALI**  I shall be a moment as I review your accounts.

[MAX FISCHY *twitches, turns up his CD player—we hear classical music, NPR station, Mozart.*]

**MAX**  [*To himself.*] I went to you because you said "Perfect credit not required. Bad credit, no credit okay." A few thousand will buy me time and I can just pay this down....I have to warn you, if *Shitti*-bank....No I didn't say "shitty"—I have a slight speech impediment—I mean, *Citi*-bank—can't see its way clear to giving me a credit increase, I am seriously considering taking my banking business and all my credit cards elsewhere....

**SONALI**  We are unable to authorize the credit increase you requested. You will be getting a letter of explanation in the mail.

**MAX**  Why not? I always pay my minimum. I am almost always on time.

**SONALI**  We cannot authorize a credit increase at this time. Is there anything else I can do for you tonight?

**MAX**  [*Under his breath, he is goofing, not thinking she is human.*] Yeah how about...[*Sexual slurring.*]...phonetic fellatio?

**SONALI**  Please spell that. We do not understand your response.

**MAX**  That is because I have hypoglossal neuralgia. A condition of pain through the mandibular and lingual nerves. I have trouble controlling my tongue. I know you may find this odd—but my mouth can become...electrical. It is too painful for me to kiss or be kissed, and you are probably responding to my speech impediment [*He slurs "impediment."*]

**SONALI**  Do you have any other liquid assets? I see you have your mortgage with us.

**MAX**  It's all liquid now, Kimberley. And I don't believe your name is Kimberley. I am not sure if you are a person, or an electronic voice. Can you clarify if you are human?

**SONALI**  We do not understand your response. Do you have any other liquid assets?

**MAX**  Okay, you're a machine, Kimberley. Where are you? Brooklyn or New Delhi, Bangladesh?...So I can speak more freely to you...
[*He drinks straight from a wine bottle.*]
My liquid assets are right here...runnin' in my gut...the background sound you hear is my intestines, knotting and then unfurling...the gut-slide of my financial ruin.

**SONALI**  You own your apartment.

**MAX**  The half-a-million-dollar hovel....I bought it ten years ago, it is a skinny little studio—a sliver of space, for fifty grand, and now it is my single asset...other than my sex appeal, which still seems to kick in, despite or perhaps even because of my hypoglossal neuralgia and irritable bowel syndrome....

**SONALI**  How much equity remains on your mortgage?

**MAX**  Actually, a thousand doll-*ars* [*He mimics her.*] remain, but I was hoping you could work with me on that....Come on, Kimberley—crunch some numbers for me, I'd appreciate that very much.

**SONALI**  Do you mind if we pull a credit card report? It will only take a second.

**MAX**  I mind but what the fuck. Go ahead, pull it, pull my...Yank my chain...just give me some dough....I am lying here, fake computer-generated Kimberley, like a guppy on the rug....Do you know what it is like not to have money? I mean, *none*? Money is oxygen. I can't breathe...the sound you hear is my near asthmatic wheezing....I am having a shortage-of-cash panic attack....I have all the symptoms—I am seeing stars—I am feeling the passing of every second—I am zooming, as if at Mach Ten toward the first of the fucking month....Debt is visible, Kimberley—it floats in the air, gives off a malignant sparkle like radioactivity—it combines with dust motes....I try to breathe. [*Wheeze, wheeze, wheeze.*] Can't you see your way clear to crediting me with a few grand?

**SONALI**   I have pulled your credit rating. I see you are just short of qualifying for our "Less-than-Ideal Credit."

**MAX**   But you said, "Bad credit okay." I saw your infomercial. How people can re-establish their credit with you. I spent my last credit balance on a Buns of Steel Master Buttock Toner, results guaranteed in two nights. . . .

**SONALI**   That charge of sixty-three doll-*ars* and ninety-nine cents was declined on your Citibank MasterCard. It exceeded your credit limit. Also the video on how to create and keep "a six pack . . ." You placed that charge at 3.45 a.m. Too late, Max, your finance charges had just been compiled, so everything tonight went over the line. . . . Why did you wait until so late, Max?

**MAX**   Oh, fuck! What are you doing to me tonight, Kimberley? [*He kicks an imaginary TV, tightens the tie at his neck.*] The late, late nights, my dear Kimberley, are for the nocturnal financially impaired, and yes, to give myself a boost, I became intrigued with the promise of "abs, abs, and abs, " and "buns, buns, buns." On other cable stations, people with abs and buns are having complicated but somehow dull sex. [*He clicks his remote.*] I don't like their facial expressions no matter how endowed they are . . . [*He clicks TV.*] so I come back to you, to . . .

**SONALI**   "Bad credit okay."

**MAX**   Yes—okay! Help me! I am saying "please" to you, even if you are an electronic voice with false financial fellatio phrasing—"sixty-two doll-*ars*! [*He mimics her.*] You can detect sincere desperation, can't you? And isn't there a ghost in the machine—who will give me a chance?

**SONALI**   I am researching some other possibilities for you. . . . How is it in New York tonight? Hot?

**MAX**   Very hot. How is it in Brooklyn, New Delhi or Bangladesh?

**SONALI**   I am in South Dakota.

**MAX**   Yeah, you are . . . Kim-*ber*-ley! I know where you are. I know what you are. I know this is outsourced and you are on the other side of the world, and your name is probably Sonali or Nabu or something, but you know everything about me, every purchase down to my last Zantac...

SONALI   *Xanax* at twelve tonight from an all-night pharmacy at 72nd Street and Amsterdam Avenue. What about your car, the Toyota Camry, with the $439–a-month car payment you missed, Max?

MAX   Shit! I forgot to move it! I left it on Tuesday and Friday no parking, and today is...

SONALI   Saturday night. Here, is already Sunday... [*She cracks a little.*] But I must work for another fourteen hours....
[*New tone.*]
You are listening to beautiful music. I can hear it here, Max.

MAX   [*Perked up.*] You are a person! And you admit—you are on the subcontinent! Omigod, I sincerely apologize about the fuck and the fellatio references, I thought you were a machine, my gosh, believe me, I am a gentleman! Don't hold those profane asides against me. I was letting off some steam! Look...listen...You mentioned you have to work fourteen hours a day, a night—this isn't so easy for you either.... I can only imagine your working conditions... help us both out! You have it at your fingertips there, in India or is it Bangladesh, to fix this nocturnal nausea....

SONALI   I don't know, I am running some numbers here... trying to find a way...

MAX   Just tap in an acceptance, a credit increase, and all will be well. I always land on my feet; look at my history—twelve years of near financial ruin, always a save at the end, then a burst of income...

SONALI   Your accounts have a high burn—money whooshing in and out, a back draft. I am looking at an event back in 2003, in which you had a minus balance...

MAX   That was the divorce. She left me as cartilage... picked clean... I had to buy her out of 23A, and that cost, big time.... Since then I have been alone... except for infomercials, the sex channels, and Karl Haas, but Karl Haas's dead now, but still on NPR, saying,

"Hello, Everyone." "Karl Haas—adventures in great music!"
Karl was ninety! I won't get to be ninety, will I? So I should
have some release from this pressure now, before I have a
financial aneurysm....

SONALI   That is such beautiful music....

MAX   Yes, I listen twenty-four hours a day, even as I watch TV—it calms
me....

SONALI   What is that selection?

MAX   Mozart. Something he wrote to restore serenity.

NPR ANNOUNCER   [*Recorded voice, offstage, with soft background music.*]...
You have been listening to ... [*Voice fades out.*] by Wolfgang
Amadeus Mozart. Conducted by Sir Neville Mariner at the
Academy of St. Martin's Lilies of the Field.

MAX   [*More desperate.*] *Where are you*—really?

SONALI   I told you—I am in Sioux Falls, South Dakota, the capital of
credit. Tell me the name of the musical selection Sir Neville is
conducting, please? Please ... the exact piece? I would like to hear
it again! Where does this beautiful music originate? Who is Sir
Neville Mariner? and where is this Academy of St. Martins in the
Fields? Where exactly?

MAX   Sir Neville Mariner conducts ... I don't know where the Academy
of St. Martins in the Fields is ... but I picture heaven, an
afterlife—Sir Neville, on the prow of a schooner, filled with lost
souls, cutting through a sea of lilies....

SONALI   Oh, oh, I am quivering, Max, I want to go there, with Sir
Neville Mariner ... to this moonlit field of lilies....

MAX   So you *are* a real woman. Who are you, really? Where are you,
really?

SONALI   Oh, I shouldn't say ... but oh, I can no longer deny the truth—
my name is not Kimberley, it is ... Sonali, and I am not in Sioux
Falls, South Dakota—I am on the subcontinent.

**MAX**  Oh, now we are approaching something vital—what do you look like?

**SONALI**  I am unbelievably gorgeous.

**MAX**  Don't you want to know what *I* look like?

**SONALI**  I know what you look like. I can see you.

[MAX *looks askance at the phone.*]

**MAX**  But I am not sending you a picture....

**SONALI**  You no longer have to *send* it.... I have the ability to see you.... You have a noose around your neck.

**MAX**  It's not a noose. It's a tie, from Abercrombie and Fitch. I paid $70 for this tie, in better days.

**SONALI**  You are attractive, Max. I agree. I may agree to meet you....

**MAX**  In South Dakota...?

**SONALI**  I could play with the numbers and arrange a...vacation...for us both.

**MAX**  And you are really unbelievably gorgeous?

**SONALI**  You maxed out, Max.... So what do you want me to do? This music, your image with the noose, you are making me a little, how do you say it in America—feel the moonlight madness? I will access your accounts, and pay off all your debts in one great clean sweep...we have a plan for this—it is called "Suck-hout..."

**MAX**  Suck-out?

**SONALI**  Suckhout was the name of the CEO who conceived of it.... It is an excellent plan for people without options; such as yourself... Max.... So shall I authorize this loan, at 29.9999% interest with a balloon payment due upon the next lunar eclipse?

**MAX**  I guess that's the choice. Yeah. Sure.

**SONALI**  So tell me the name of the music, Max.... I want to listen to it forever.... I see you now, you are less sweaty.... I call to you from across the continents, from across the oceans, the stars and new solar systems, Max. . . . I think I am coming to care for you, although I have never met you and . . . Oh, what is that music, you must tell me now!

**MAX**  It is called *Requiem*.

[*Mozart's Requiem soars.*]

[*Lights come up on* SONALI, *in Bangladesh—she enters—she is unbelievably gorgeous but dragging a hard drive tower by a leg shackle.*]

[*On opposite sides of the stage, the phone-and-tie-manacled* MAX *moves toward an invisible wall that divides him from the computer shackled* SONALI. *As the music reaches its crescendo, they appear to dance to the music, toward each other, and end pressing upheld hand-palms and kissing the invisible barrier.*]

**SONALI, MAX**  I love you.

**SONALI**  [*Recorded.*] Your transaction is now completed; please hold for your confirmation number. Your balance is six million dol-*lars and zero-zero-cents.*"

[*Blackout, Strobe light, sparks fly, end of play. Music.*]

• • •

# Dead Trees

Rick Pulos

# Rick Pulos

Rick Pulos is a writer, director, multimedia artist, and critic, who has worked in theatre, film, and broadcast television. He trained in film and theatre production at Yale University and the School of Cinematic Arts at the University of Southern California. He recently completed his master of arts in media arts at the Brooklyn campus of Long Island University with an emphasis on screenwriting. He teaches acting, theatre, and speech at Long Island University's Brooklyn campus.

**CITSEKO**, 50s, a Malawian carpenter turned coffin maker
**MOYENDA**, 20s, his son
**LIZAYA**, 60s, his mother
**BANDU**, 40s, his brother, a village leader

## time and place

Right now in Malawi, Africa

[*The main set of the play is a modest living room with coffins strategically stacked on the floor and leaning against the walls. There is an upstage swinging door that leads to the kitchen, a stage-right door that leads to CITSEKO's woodshop, and a stage-left door that leads to the rest of the modest home. There is a beautiful round table with three ornate chairs near the kitchen door. A series of overhead projections will create time and place. Note: Although not required to tell the story, the projections will enhance the experience for the audience.*]

## projection 1

[*As the audience enters.*]: A still image of a lone tree in a field in Africa with the words "This is happening now" in the sky above the tree.

# scene 1

## projection 2

[*As the house lights go down.*]: A series of excerpts from newspaper and Web articles:

*Land Where Only Coffin Makers Thrive*, "At the . . . 24-hour coffin workshop, business has never been so brisk." —Neil Darbyshire, Telegraph.co.uk, June 23, 2002

*Malawi Coffin Makers Cash in on AIDS Pandemic*, "The surge in AIDS-related deaths in Malawi . . . has contributed to a thriving coffin business." —Ed Stoddard, *Aegis*, June 2, 2004

*Malawi AIDS-Fight Changes Economy*, "For many local carpenters . . . being surrounded by death is good for business. —Jae Lynam, BBC News, July 3, 2007

[*The distinct sound of wood being cut by saws echo throughout the space as a new projection begins.*]

## projection 3

[*As the lights come up onstage.*]: A montage of trees falling to the floor of the forest, trucks carrying logs to a sawmill, and logs being transformed into lumber.

[LIZAYA *enters from the upstage door and looks around the living room. She stops at the table and reads a large sign propped up that reads "Father & Son Coffin Workshop." She then examines the coffins around the room and contemplates a way to reorganize them.*]

**LIZAYA**   I don't know what to do with this mess. Citseko! Citseko!

[*The woodcutting ceases and* CITSEKO *calls from offstage.*]

**CITSEKO**   [*Offstage.*] What! I'm busy!

**LIZAYA**   I need help getting these coffins out!

**CITSEKO**   [*Offstage.*] Out? Are you crazy? Don't move a thing.

**LIZAYA**   I'm not kidding this time. Moyenda will be here soon.

[CITSEKO *enters from the stage-right door wiping his sweaty brow with a handkerchief.*]

**CITSEKO**   Stop fussing about the living room.

[*She tries to lift one of the coffins alone.*]

**LIZAYA**   It looks like we live underneath the cemetery. Grab the other side.

**CITSEKO**   Leave it....

**LIZAYA**   Fine, but this does not look like a proper home.

[*She sits down at the table, rubs her hands on her dress.*]

**CITSEKO**   I think the heat is getting to me.

**LIZAYA**   You're just excited.

[*He peers out over the audience as if looking through a window.*]

**CITSEKO**   He should be here soon.

**LIZAYA**   Did you finish it?

**CITSEKO**   It's drying. Don't touch it.

**LIZAYA**   You know this is going to be a big change for Moyenda.

**CITSEKO**   What would he do without this house or without this business?

**LIZAYA**   I don't feel like arguing today. We should celebrate. How about some tea?

**CITSEKO**   That would be nice.

[*She exits.*]

**MOYENDA**   [*Offstage.*] Sir. Father. Hello!

[MOYENDA *enters with a bag on each arm.*]

**CITSEKO**   Son, let me look at you.
        [*Calling out.*]
        Mother! Mother!

[*They shake hands and then embrace.* MOYENDA *reads the sign over his father's shoulder and his reaction is immediate disappointment.*]

[CITSEKO *pulls away from their hug and looks* MOYENDA *up and down. He holds both of* MOYENDA's *hands. He pulls them closer for examination. His face sours as he examines* MOYENDA's *hands.*]

**CITSEKO**   [*Spoken sternly.*] Your hands are soft. America's made you soft. Just what I expected!

[LIZAYA *bursts out of the kitchen with the greatest speed a lady of her age can muster.*]

**LIZAYA**   [*Scolding.*] Now, you leave him alone.

**CITSEKO**   Look at this boy!

[CITSEKO *pulls* MOYENDA's *palms over to* LIZAYA *for inspection.*]

**CITSEKO**   No woman would marry a man who doesn't show signs of hard work!

[LIZAYA *shoots* CITSEKO *a disapproving look.* CITSEKO *releases* MOYENDA's *hands and steps back.*]

[*Satisfied by his retreat,* LIZAYA *takes* MOYENDA's *hands, looks him deep in the eyes and then hugs him.*]

**LIZAYA**   We've missed you, Moyenda. Now, you must eat, have tea and tell us all about your trip.

[LIZAYA *exits to the kitchen.*]

**CITSEKO**   Business is good.

**MOYENDA**   I can see that. I guess the business of the dead never dies.

**CITSEKO**   What is that supposed to mean?

[*There is an awkward silence for a few beats.* LIZAYA *enters with a tray of tea and bread.*]

**LIZAYA**   Tell us about the city, Moyenda.

**MOYENDA**   It's unbelievable. You would love it. People from everywhere all around. My favorite place is this place they call Coney Island. They have this boardwalk right on the beach. You can get candied apples and all sorts of things.

## projection 4

A montage of New York City with busy streets, snowy sidewalks, frenetic subways and a Disneyfied Time Square.

**LIZAYA**   Candied apples?

**MOYENDA**   Yes, coated with anything like caramel or even chocolate. It's like the happiest place anywhere.

**LIZAYA**   Did you hear that, Citseko?

[CITSEKO *grunts. They eat in silence for a few beats.*]

**LIZAYA**   More tea, Moyenda?

**MOYENDA**   No thank you.

**LIZAYA**   Citseko?

**CITSEKO**   I'm fine.

[*They continue to eat in silence.*]

**LIZAYA**    I think I'll make more tea.

**MOYENDA**    Oh! And Central Park. You'd have to see this place in autumn. I mean, it is so colorful and the air is perfectly cool. I'd sit out there for hours writing in my journal. Writing down anything that would fly into my mind.

[CITSEKO *stops eating and looks at* MOYENDA.]

**CITSEKO**    You said nothing about the new sign.

**LIZAYA**    Citseko!

[MOYENDA *scours.*]

**MOYENDA**    What do you want me to say?

**CITSEKO**    Thank you. [*Beat.*] I'm honored. Something. Acknowledge it at least.

**MOYENDA**    I don't know what you're expecting.

[CITSEKO *rises in a furry.*]

**CITSEKO**    Some respect. Some acknowledgement of the many sacrifices we've made for you.

**MOYENDA**    You've turned the living room into a cemetery!

[*Silence for a few beats.*]

**CITSEKO**    How dare you speak to me like this!

**MOYENDA**    Father, it's just, I don't recognize this house.

**CITSEKO**    What do you think paid for your education in America?

**MOYENDA**    I'm sorry. I just. I don't know what to say.

**CITSEKO**    This business, this house, this is all yours. And you refuse it? Opinions like yours don't feed a family, Moyenda. You can scribble things in that journal until you're gray, but it means nothing if you are hungry. Look, many people hate what they do but they do it because they have to. They have no choice.

**MOYENDA**    I thought the point of me going away was to have more choices.

**CITSEKO**    Not at the expense of what we've built here. This is your life. This your home.

**CITSEKO**    What will you do without this? What will your children do?

[CITSEKO *exits. Beat.* LIZAYA *lovingly looks at* MOYENDA.]

**LIZAYA**    Eat. Please. Don't worry about all this now.

[*The muffled noise of sawing emanates from the wood shop.*]

**BANDU**    [*Offstage.*] Hello! Mother? Brother?

**LIZAYA**    Come in, Bandu.

[BANDU *enters with fanfare; he's wearing a small hat and a long white traditional robe.*]

**BANDU**    Moyenda! It's all over the village. And it is true. You are back!

[MOYENDA *rises and bows to* BANDU.]

**MOYENDA**    Very good to see you Uncle.

**BANDU**    Mother. You tell me nothing. I know nothing of what goes on in this house. I hear more from gossip.

[LIZAYA *continues to eat. She barely acknowledges her eldest son.*]

**LIZAYA**    The town has nothing to do with MOYENDA's return.

**BANDU**    We are proud and we are happy. We want to hear all the great stories of America!

[BANDU *raises his arms like a politician at a podium.*]

**BANDU**    This is an occasion. The entire town has missed you. We must hold a celebration. A feast, a festival!

**LIZAYA**    I'm not sure that's such a good idea.

**BANDU**    Don't listen to the woman, Moyenda. This is your chance to truly return to your home.

[*He looks at* MOYENDA *with great affection.*]

**BANDU**    The women will fall all over you.

**MOYENDA**    That sounds just perfect.

[LIZAYA *stops eating suddenly.*]

**LIZAYA**   Moyenda, I don't think you know what you're getting yourself into.

**MOYENDA**   A few drinks. Some dancing, music. What could be so bad?

**BANDU**   Then it's all set. Tomorrow evening. All the arrangements are already made.

[*He turns to* LIZAYA.]

Mother. Tell Citseko the villagers are curious to see him. Good-bye.

[BANDU *exits exuberantly.*]

[LIZAYA's *disapproval is apparent in her sharp, efficient bites.*]

**MOYENDA**   You can't shun your neighbors. It's just not right.

**LIZAYA**   That's a terrible way to speak to me.

**MOYENDA**   I'm sorry.

**LIZAYA**   There are things you don't know. Things, unspeakable things, that people did. It seems like ages ago, but I feel it all the time, Moyenda.

[*She sips her tea and then deeply sighs.*]

**LIZAYA**   It's not your fault. I suppose you shouldn't suffer from things you have very little to do with.

[*She takes another sip of tea.*]

[MOYENDA *lifts himself up. His weariness shows in his sluggish rise.*]

**MOYENDA**   It's so hot. I need to lay down. Excuse me.

[MOYENDA *grabs his bag and looks around the living room in defeat and then exits.*]

[*Fade to black.*]

# scene 2

## projection 5

A dark figure carries a lone lantern down a dirt road while an eerie mystical music plays.

[MOYENDA *re-enters with a kerosene lamp that flickers brightly. He drops to his knees downstage left.*]

**MOYENDA**   Mother, I've tried to understand him but I can't. I don't get any of this. He's never done anything to me and all I want to do is hurt him. Why do I feel this way? Why is it like this? I must make a choice to save myself, otherwise I will die here in a way that I can not face. Please talk to me. Tell me what to do.

[*Beat.*]

There is so much I still need to know. And you had no time to explain to me anything that I must know and he has no interest in talking. It is all work. All painful.

[*Fade to black.*]

[MOYENDA *enters carrying the lantern and stands in the cold dark of the living room.*]

**MOYENDA**   Father.

**CITSEKO**   [*Offstage right.*] I'm working. Leave me alone.

**MOYENDA**   I wouldn't have bothered you but there's a visitor.

**CITSEKO**   At this hour? Send them away.

**MOYENDA**   A woman from near Nyasa. I can't remember her name but...I know her.

[CITSEKO *enters.*]

**CITSEKO**   Ah. Okay.

**MOYENDA**   I'll come too. You'll need help.

[*They move towards a coffin perched against a wall and move it off the stage in silence.*]

[*Fade to black.*]

# scene 3

## projection 6

Tears stream down a Malawian woman's face, dirt falls into a grave and the sun rises over a barren African field.

[CITSEKO *and* MOYENDA *enter the living room and collapse at the round table. A warm morning sun fills the space.*]

**CITSEKO**   That woman nursed your mother when she was carrying your brother. She walked two hours to us...each and every day...and kept coming...even after he was born...she kept coming until your mother, finally, was well enough to take care of him on her own.

**MOYENDA**   What happened to him? I don't even know. You never talk about it.

**CITSEKO**   Some things are better off left buried, Son.

[*Blackout.*]

## scene 4

[MOYENDA *is writing in his journal at the round table.* LIZAYA *enters and sets tea on the table.*]

**LIZAYA**   Good morning!

**MOYENDA**   I had strange dreams.

**LIZAYA**   That doesn't surprise me.

[CITSEKO *enters.*]

**CITSEKO**   I'm meeting with Mr. Banda today in the city. Do you know who that is?

**MOYENDA**   No.

**CITSEKO**   He runs one of the largest headstone factories in Blantyre. This is big business for us.

[*He waves his hands in the air.*]

**CITSEKO**   Huge!

   [*Behind him,* LIZAYA *lovingly mocks him by waving her hands in the air.* MOYENDA *snickers.*]

   Mr. Banda wants to meet me to pitch me a business proposition.

**MOYENDA**   Can we just not make all these decisions this week?

**CITSEKO**   I'll be back at sundown.

[CITSEKO *rises*. MOYENDA *glances at* LIZAYA.]

**MOYENDA**   We'll be down at the village center. Uncle Bandu is gathering everyone for a celebration to welcome me home.

**CITSEKO**   You agreed to this?

**MOYENDA**   I did. We'll be fighting the gossip for weeks if I hide in this house.

**CITSEKO**   Fine. I won't promise to come.

**MOYENDA**   Father, please. Don't embarrass me. You're expected. It should be fun.

**CITSEKO**   There's some cut wood outside against the wall. Stain it for me.

[CITSEKO *exits*.]

**LIZAYA**   I know you think he's hard but his heart is in the right place.

**MOYENDA**   Every day I was in this house after Mother died, he ignored me. He worked in that shop all day and all night. He never once brought me in there. It was like this dark, forbidden room in the house. And now he wants me to be a part of it, when I am so far from it, I can't even stand it.

**LIZAYA**   Times were tough then. You never knew how hard it was. Your father lived in that shop because it kept his mind busy.

**MOYENDA**   You don't talk about the past much.

**LIZAYA**   There's nothing to say. What's done is done.

**MOYENDA**   I just wish I understood things a little better, then maybe it would be easier for me to deal with this.

**LIZAYA**   You didn't live through the bad days. The real bad days. Life was like a dying garden. All you could do to think was to dream. You'd pray for your kids, hope for your neighbor's kids. People behave differently in bad times. Sometimes, your prayers are met with disappointment and you find your neighbors are raiding your lifeline without remorse. It was a sad time for us all,

Moyenda. A sad time for this house and this village. It's too hot for me right now. I'm going to my room.

[LIZAYA *exits. Fade to black.*]

# scene 5

## projection 7

A montage of villagers dancing and celebrating.

**VOICES OF VILLAGERS**   [*Sound cue.*] [*Singing.*] Good friend. Home again. Good times. On the rise. Welcome, good friend. Welcome, neighbor of mine.

[*Lights up.* BANDU *enters, followed by a festive* MOYENDA. LIZAYA *sits at the round table.*]

**BANDU**   Grand festivities!

**MOYENDA**   Glorious!

[BANDU *sits in between his mother and* MOYENDA.]

**BANDU**   You see. The town loves our family.

**LIZAYA**   The town loves feasting.

[LIZAYA *looks away with a wry smile.* BANDU *appears disgusted.*]

**BANDU**   Is your father planning to come?

**MOYENDA**   He's in Blantyre on business. You know how the ride from Blantyre can be bumpy and delayed.

**BANDU**   We can't wait too long for him. But for now. Enjoy. Tell more dazzling stories of the city.

**MOYENDA**   New York is on fire every night. A billion lights, almost a light for every person in the world. A light for every star in the sky. People talk on phones in the middle of the street. It's magical.

**BANDU**   We wanted your father to be here too. Your father and I were once like the moon and the stars. Things change, though. People see things in different ways.

**MOYENDA**  I understand... I think.

**BANDU**  Look at it this way. I love you. I really love you.

[BANDU *gets up and dances wildly.*]

**BANDU**  Now, lets have a grand time now.

[BANDU *dances in a goofy, drunk way towards offstage as* MOYENDA *follows him out.*]

[LIZAYA *sits and heaves with a difficult breath.* CITSEKO *enters.*]

**CITSEKO**  Everything is perfect. I've done good for my grandchildren. The business deal is all in place.

**LIZAYA**  So what! For WHAT? You never buy anything, we never go anywhere. More, more, more! Look at this place! Look at yourself. What's happened to you?

**CITSEKO**  Are you okay?

**LIZAYA**  I'm fine. I'm just tired. It's so hot in here. I'm on fire. I'm going to lay down.

[CITSEKO *is left alone in the silence of the living room.*]

[*Fade slowly to black.*]

## scene 6

[*A bed is rolled out downstage right. A kerosene light dims to soft glow.* MOYENDA *enters hesitantly.*]

**LIZAYA**  Come in. Sit with me, Moyenda, please.

[MOYENDA *quietly comes to her bedside.*]

**LIZAYA**  Your mother changed all our lives. She blew in here like a western wind off Lake Malawi. You look a lot like her, you know.

**MOYENDA**  Thank you.

**LIZAYA**  Your father wasn't a man until he had her. He was always my boy, but never a man.

[LIZAYA *coughs deeply.* MOYENDA *passes her a small bowl with water. She drinks.*]

**LIZAYA**  Thank you.

**MOYENDA**  But what happened? Why do you both hate the village so much?

**LIZAYA**  I don't hate anyone. I love my family. Like I said, your mother was a wind, a force, and she was also like the rain. Our gardens were alive when everything else here was dying or dead. We were able to eat and we held our prayers for everyone here. It was torture for a time. People believed she was some kind of witch. That we had dark magic. How else could you explain our good fortune?

**MOYENDA**  That's ridiculous.

**LIZAYA**  Not to us old folks, Moyenda. I wondered myself. Not about your mother, but about this land.

**MOYENDA**  The soil is moist, that's all. It's very logical.

**LIZAYA**  There was so much suffering, Moyenda. People needed something to believe in. And we were it. Even your uncle became suspicious.

**MOYENDA**  But that doesn't explain all this hatred. It just doesn't.

**LIZAYA**  No, you're right. That's not all. Your uncle came to your mother on behalf of the villagers. There was great pressure on him and then on her. Your father had no idea.

**MOYENDA**  They came here for food?

**LIZAYA**  Your mother thought that if she could save one family, even if it meant sacrificing herself, that she would rest easy in the afterlife. We seemed to have so much then compared to others.

**MOYENDA**  But what about this family?

**LIZAYA**  She was young, Moyenda.

[*She coughs uncontrollably and then finally passes to the next life.* MOYENDA *covers her face and slowly exits.*]

[*Fade slowly to black.*]

[*Lights up on the living room.* CITSEKO *stands in front of the most beautiful coffin seen yet.* MOYENDA *enters with his bags. He sets them down.*]

**CITSEKO**   You're leaving *now*.

**MOYENDA**   I've been leaving for years.

**CITSEKO**   I'm not sure what to say to that.

**MOYENDA**   I love you so much. But you have what you have. I'm looking for something else.

**CITSEKO**   That makes no sense.

**MOYENDA**   Listen. My life is not here. This is your history. I need to etch a road for myself to follow. I want you in my life. But not this way, Father. You are wounded. I am fresh and clean. I love you ... but I must go. We'll be together again. Someday.

[*He picks up his bags and exits.*]

# scene 7

[LIZAYA'*s coffin is noticeably gone.* CITSEKO *enters. He examines the living room with a stoic face. One by one he begins to move furniture out of the living room, finally taking the round table and chairs. He returns to the living room for one last look. The only items left are a few coffins. He exits.*]

[*Blackout.*]

# scene 8

## projection 8

Montage of fire burning all kinds of wood and then a house burns to the ground.

[*Blackout.*]

[*The sound of wood crackling loudly rises to a disturbing pitch.*]

• • •

# G.C.

Theodore Mann

# Theodore Mann

Theodore Mann, for Circle in the Square Theatre, has produced and/or directed over 250 productions on and Off-Broadway, along with his partner of forty-three years, Paul Libin. Productions include works by O'Neill, Williams, Shaw, Moliere, along with Greek classics, and more, and have starred such actors as George C. Scott, Colleen Dewhurst, Jason Robards, Al Pacino, James Earl Jones, Vanessa Redgrave, and Dustin Hoffman.

Circle in the Square Theatre was co-founded in 1951 by Mann and José Quintero. Their 1952 production of Tennessee Williams' *Summer and Smoke* is considered to be the birth of Off-Broadway. Mann also directs opera and oversees Circle's celebrated Theatre School. He is the author of a new book, *Journeys in the Night*.

## characters

GEORGE C. SCOTT
THEODORE MANN
JACQUELINE GAULTIER

## time

11:30 a.m., May, 1973

## place

Ted Mann's office, Circle in the Square Theatre on Broadway

[*At curtain* TED MANN *is seen standing behind his desk, tie askew, cradling the telephone on his shoulder while working on a poster on his desk. The walls behind him are covered with posters and photographs from past productions.*]

MANN   [*On the phone, voice on edge.*] Tony, we have to have those costumes! [*Listening.*] Rehearsals are tomorrow at two o'clock. And make sure the waist is tighter for Julie. And Nicole's Vanya clothes have to be distressed. You know: sloppy, dirty—just like him... [*Listening.*] But, Mr. Scott has very strong feelings about what Astrov wears, he needs to feel natural. George told me he spoke to you. And believe me, Tony, if he's not comfortable, you'll know about it and you better duck when he raises his arm. And I mean, DUCK—FAST! [*Listening.*] You are laughing, Tony, it's not funny. I don't want to set him off. You know how actors get tense when it comes to costume fittings. Up until now, George has been calm and so have the other actors.

[*Listening.*]

Tony, I'll call you later. Please get it done! [*Slowly emphasizing.*] George has to be comfortable in his costume or he won't wear it. You don't want him playing in street clothes.

[*Hangs up phone. He dials another call. He calls out stage left to his assistant.*]
Lorraine! Get me Don Josephson.

[*Pause. He continues to work on the poster.* MANN *mumbles to himself. Then to* LORRAINE, *offstage.*]

The ad agency.... [*Pause, the phone rings.*] Donald, when do I see the ad? Okay. What about the billing? No. No. George doesn't want to be on the top. No, no, if the billing is not right, he'll be very upset. Remember the time with that reporter? He almost strangled him, and would have if Paul hadn't stared him down eyeball to eyeball. George can be a pussycat if you don't twist his tail. What he wants is alphabetical! I know he's *the* star of this star cast, Cathleen Nesbit, Lillian Gish, Nicole Williamson, no that's not a woman, he's a big tall actor, Julie Christie, and wants it alphabetical, that's right. So it's Julie, [*With each name, he gives* DON *time to write it down.*] Lillian, Barnard, Kathleen, and the last name, just before the bottom, George C. Scott. All in the same size type. I know, yes. George is a star but he doesn't have to prove it in the *New York Times*. It's a full page, right? *Uncle Vanya* 100%, Directed by Mike Nicoles 50% Anton Chekov 50%, Donald, I know, but he is just as important. He's the playwright, don't tell anybody but he's the most important thing we've got. What do you mean—of course everyone knows *Uncle Vanya*, it is as popular as *The Christmas Carol*. [MANN *laughs.*] Actors 50%, yeah, yeah [*Slowly.*] George had agreed to that. Paul and myself above the title 25%, and don't forget the Circle logo down at the bottom. I gotta see a layout by five o'clock. I know you love music, Donald, remember the song, [MANN *sings.*] *"How come you do me like you do, do, do."* Hey, how'd you like the ad for Patricia's recital? That's right, Lincoln Center, June 15th. Oh, you're going to buy a ticket, great. No, no, there's no discount, Donald. I don't get a discount from you. Wonderful. She's my darling.

[*Hangs up the phone, goes to work, mumbling.*]

George C. Scott, what a guy. [*Phone rings.*] Yeah, Lorraine, what is it? Ms. Gaultier? Who's that? She's writing an article? For what paper? Oh yeah, the *Figaro* in Paris, I forgot all about it, send her right in.

[MANN *puts on jacket and straightens tie as* JACQUELINE GAULTIER *enters, a woman in her forties, nice-looking, with wavy brunette hair and long legs. She is wearing casual work clothes, jacket, blouse, skirt and high heels, simple and the best French style.*]

**MANN**   Ted Mann, how do you do? [*Extends his hand.*]

**GAULTIER**   [*French accent, she accepts hand.*] Jacqueline Gaultier.

**MANN**   Welcome, madame.

**GAULTIER**   [*She points to the ring on her left finger.*] My mother's.

[MANN *smiles.*]

**MANN**   [*Indicates for her to sit.*] Ah, mademoiselle. Would you like some coffee or tea?

**GAULTIER**   No thank you.

**MANN**   You live in New York City?

**GAULTIER**   No, no, Paris.

**MANN**   Oh, you came all the way for this interview?

**GAULTIER**   [*Nods her head.*] Yes, I arrived five days ago.

**MANN**   Seen any plays here?

**GAULTIER**   Oh yes, I saw Mickey Rooney in *Sugar*. I love Mickey Rooney, but he is so small, so cute.

**MANN**   I liked it.

**GAULTIER**   It's the first time I've seen him onstage. He is so small, but so cute, oh la la.

**MANN**   Any American plays running in Paris now?

**GAULTIER**   No—I just saw Jean Louis Berrault at the Odeon playing Marivaux's *Les Fausses Confidences* with his wife, Madeline Renaud.

**MANN**   [*Flirting.*] Oh, I love Paris. So romantic.

**GAULTIER**   You would be most welcome.

[MANN *thinks there is hope for a tango in Paris. She changes the subject.*]

**GAULTIER**   Oh, I saw your gospel show.

**MANN**   *Trumpets of the Lord.*

**GAULTIER**   *Oui, oui*, it was the best play in the festival.

MANN   Mr. Berrault saw the production Off-Broadway, and he invited me to bring the show to Paris. When the company got together in Paris it was like a family reunion, we ate collard greens and chitlins.

GAULTIER   *Je ne comprends pas.*

MANN   [*Speaking slowly.*] Collard greens—green vegetables like spinach, and chitlins are chopped-up chicken.

GAULTIER   Ah. *Oui, je comprends.*

[*Laughs. Opens up her purse and takes out her notepad and pencil.*]

GAULTIER   Sounds delicious. When I arrived in America there was a big story in the newspaper about Mr. Scott being detained by the police.

MANN   [*Laughing.*] Oh yes, some woman he didn't know got into his hotel room and she made a scene. Mr. Scott asked her to leave.... An argument broke out, banging doors, broken glass, and the hotel called the police. [MANN *covering for* SCOTT.] She was a naughty girl.

[*He doesn't want to talk about* SCOTT*'s difficulties. To distract her.*]

MANN   A couple of years ago the French government invited us to bring O'Neill's *Long Days Journey Into Night* to Paris and at the rehearsal, I noticed that the cyc was uneven.

GAULTIER   Cyc? *Qu'est ce que c'est?*

MANN   The cyclorama. You know, the thing that hangs across the back wall of the stage. There was a big wrinkle from top to bottom right in the middle. I asked the stagehands to straighten it. They insisted that could not be done. And then they regally informed me that all of Paris stops now and eats lunch. And they left. Nobody was around so I ran backstage and climbed up into the scaffolding and started to pull on the scrim. Then suddenly, out of nowhere, the stagehands were also up on the scaffolding, all six of them pulling in the opposite direction—they were so tight, one behind the other, they looked like a Bruegel painting. I pulled one way, they pulled the other way, and viola! The cyclorama was perfectly straight. They were all smiling and marched off humming the Marcie.

[GAULTIER *laughs, enjoying* MANN's *storytelling.* MANN *thinks he's making headway with her, pulls his shoulders back and smiles charmingly.*]

GAULTIER     [*Poised to write.*] This is your first season on Broadway and—

MANN     [*Interrupts.*] No, no, no, and by the way, mademoiselle, can I call you Jacqueline?

[*She nods her head affirmatively.*]

MANN     Well, please call me Ted.

[*They both smile.*]

MANN     We've done three plays before on Broadway, but now we have our own theater here. After we're finished with my interview, Jacqueline, I'll take you down and show you. It's quite different. The audience sits in a semicircle around the stage like in Shakespeare's time. We are the only theater in the round on Broadway.

[GAULTIER *writing feverishly.*]

MANN     You know the way theater started was somebody would get up on the back of a wagon and people would gather round a semicircle to watch them perform. The Greeks and Romans built their theaters bigger but with the same idea—people around on three sides of the stage.

GAULTIER     Ted, *trés interessent.*

MANN     Thank you.

GAULTIER     I would like to sit in on the rehearsal of *Uncle Vanya.* And then I would like to talk to Mr. Scott. Is that possible?

MANN     Oh, no, he never gives interviews while he is rehearsing.

GAULTIER     [*Persistent.*] Perhaps after the opening?

MANN     Perhaps.

**GAULTIER**  [*Still pushing.*] I heard that Mr. Scott and Mike Nichols had trouble in the filming of *The Day of Dolphins.*

**MANN**  [MANN *realizes that she has come to interview* SCOTT, *not him. Changing his friendly tone towards her.*] The trouble you are referring to, mademoiselle, must be because of the dolphins.

**GAULTIER**  [*Perplexed.*] The dolphins?

**MANN**  They can talk.

**GAULTIER**  [*Laughs.*] They can talk, I did not know.

**MANN**  [*Laughing it off.*] Neither did Mr. Scott. But there was no trouble, just the usual discussion that directors and actors have.

[*Phone rings.*]

**MANN**  [*Trying to be friendly again.*] Excuse me, Jacqueline. [MANN *picks up phone, very pleasant.*] Hello. Jane, how are you? Yeah. Well they are rehearsing right now. They'll be breaking soon. [*Terrified sotto voice.*] What?! What did you say?!

[MANN *moves downstage with the phone and* JACQUELINE, *sensing his need for privacy, gets up to look up at the posters and photographs behind his desk. Silent for a moment and then continues.*]

**MANN**  He doesn't want to play the matinees? [*Harsh whisper.*] Jane, we have to play the matinees. We need the money. [*Beat, laughing.*] Oh yeah, oh yeah, I know how George is once he has made up his mind. Try cracking a stone with your bare hands. [*Beat.*] All right, all right, no, no, I'll talk to him. If I survive I'll let you know. [*Beat.*] No, Jane, we sold too many tickets for the matinees. George has to play them. All right, if I'm still standing, I'll talk to you later. [*Pretending happiness.*] Sure. I'll call you back. Bye.

[MANN *hangs up the phone and returns to his charm persona.*]

**MANN**  Jacqueline, would you please excuse me? Unfortunately, I have some business to take care of.

**GAULTIER**  Of course.

**MANN**  Perhaps we can meet for lunch at Sardi's in an hour and finish the interview then.

**GAULTIER** *Tres bien*, Ted. Sardi's?

**MANN** 44th Street, between Broadway and 8th. I'll make the reservation. Jacqueline.

**GAULTIER** *A tout a l'heure*, Ted

[*She exits.*]

**MANN** *A tout a l'heure.* [*Mispronounced. He rushes back to the desk, picks up house phone and says briskly.*]

**MANN** Lorraine, make a reservation for two at Sardi's at one o'clock and get a message to the stage manager that I'd like to talk to Mr. Scott. [*Listening.*] No. [*Impatiently.*] The reservation is not for Mr. Scott, it is for me. Yeah, I know. [*Harshly.*] No, it's for two people, not one. One o'clock is the time, not the number of people. [*Listening.*] Look, look, forget about Sardi's and forget about the stage manager—[*As though speaking to a child*]—go down and talk to Mr. Scott and talk very gently to him. Don't get excited. You know he likes women. Do not order him. Use your charm. Tell him there is something I have to talk to him about, it will only take a minute and, sweet Lorraine, please speak gently—like you do to me—sometimes.

[*He hangs up and shouts to her.*]

**MANN** Don't raise your voice. Do not order him. And remember [*Raises his voice.*] don't raise your voice!

[*Wrenches his jacket off and unloosens his tie and mutters "Fuck, shit, piss, goddamn it, we need those matinees." Works on the* Vanya *poster on his desk. Phone rings.*]

**MANN** Hello, oh, my darling, [*Pause.*] Patricia, how are you? I miss you so much. Yeah, but this morning is a long time away—it's almost twelve o'clock! How're the kids doin'? [*Listening.*] Andrew is being kept at school, why? He said what to Mrs. Cohen? [*Listening.*] Oh, well, that's not so terrible. Well, the kids have their own lingo, don't worry about it. And, yes, Jonathan is with the all-stars this afternoon? Good. [*Listening.*] Oh, things here are fine, very calm and then wham! Chaotic. I don't have your schedule here, but aren't you supposed to be down in Philadelphia next week...

yeah, with Pavarotti. And just remember, when you are rehearsing with him don't let him grab your arm. Remember the bruises last time. Where are you now? [*Listening.*] Oh, at Lincoln Center. Tully Hall? Yeah, okay. Everything going okay? Mmmhm, mmmhm. How's the sound in the hall? Oh, good, good. Tully is selling tickets. . . . See you for dinner. . . . Oh, about eight o' clock. I know, I'll try to get there before the kids go to sleep. As you say, it's the quality of time not the quantity. [*Listening.*] I love you, my darling. [*He hangs up.*]

[GEORGE C. SCOTT *enters, carrying baseball cap and jacket over his shoulder, secured by his finger.*]

**SCOTT**  What is it, Teeddy? [SCOTT'*s pronunciation of "Teddy."*]

**SCOTT**  I only got a few minutes. I gotta meet Trish for lunch. She doesn't like to be kept waiting.

[SCOTT *standing, arms akimbo.*]

**MANN**  Yeah, I know.

[*Putting on the charm,* MANN *comes around to the side of the desk stage left, leans on it casually, staring up at the 6'1" GEORGE, whose left hand is bandaged.*]

**MANN**  How's the hand?

**SCOTT**  [*Grumbles.*] It's okay.

**MANN**  [*Trying to get* SCOTT *on a subject that he's verbal about.*] The Tigers lost last night.

**SCOTT**  Don't laugh.

**MANN**  I'm not.

**SCOTT**  They blew it in the ninth. Score's tied. Ricciuti singles, he's a clutch hitter. Now they gotta man on first and third. Two out— ninth inning. The next guy strikes out and another loss. They've lost nineteen already. Last night, I dreamt that the Tigers took the Yankees four straight in the World Series.

**MANN**  Keep dreamin'.

**SCOTT**  Watch it, Teeddy. [*Putting the jacket on.*] They gave this to me.

**MANN**   Congratulations. Looks good.

**SCOTT**   I wear it for luck. I'm gonna need all I can get with this team of has-beens outside of Ricciuti. I think I'm goin' to go to Belmont tomorrow. You want to come?

**MANN**   I got the kids for football at six. I'm sure the track is treating you good, as usual.

**SCOTT**   [*Confidently.*] In the end when the sun sets I'll come out ahead. When I win, it's special money for my boys. The way they're growing, they're goin' to need a lot of Belmont money.

[MANN *laughs parentally.*]

**MANN**   How 'bout your own horses, how are they doing?

**SCOTT**   Goddamn it, four horses all the way from Malibu. You gotta beer, Teeddy?

**MANN**   [*Looking at his watch.*] Rehearsal begins in five minutes.

**SCOTT**   [*Friendly command.*] You gotta beer, Teeddy?

[MANN *reluctantly goes to the fridge.* SCOTT *sits at the desk, taps a cigarette loose and tightens it up in his own style.* MANN *arrives, puts the glass on the desk. He holds the open beer bottle. Scott grabs it, pours it and takes a drink.*]

**SCOTT**   Got some scotch?

**MANN**   [*Pleading.*] Please, George.

**SCOTT**   Teeddy!—The scotch! My first of the day.

**MANN**   George, take it easy.

[SCOTT *pours scotch into the beer and takes a drink. Sighs with appreciation.*]

**SCOTT**   Mother's milk. Makes me forget about the critics. I hate 'em all.

**MANN**   The *Times* wants to do a story on you.

**SCOTT**   [*Grunts. Half laugh.*] They misquote you and it turns around and bites you you-know-where. I'm not doing it.

**MANN**   George, it's good publicity.

**SCOTT**    [*Laughs.*] Teeddy, I don't know why I love you, you are such a rascal. Okay, maybe for you—but after the opening.

**MANN**    Thanks, G.C.

**MANN**    [*Seeing that G.C. is mellow and puffing on a cig, Mann tries a different tactic.*] Mike's driving us crazy. He says the stage lights are making a hum.

**SCOTT**    Hum? What are you talking about?

**MANN**    You know, the sound the lights make when they're on.

[MANN *imitates the sound of a low hum.* GEORGE *hums in a high-pitch sound. They hum back and forth. They laugh together.*]

**SCOTT**    That's the way he was with the goddamned dolphins.

[*Imitates dolphin sounds. All the different pitches of a dolphin, "Fa fa fa."* MANN *joins in with the dolphin noises. They laugh and flap their arms, moving around in their version of a dolphin.*]

**SCOTT**    [*Puffing on the cig, thinking, mellow.*] Teeddy, the theater looks bad. It looks like the coliseum in Demille's *Ten Commandments*. Dust flying all over the place. We are all gonna get sick. An actor breathes that crap—he starts coughing, pretty soon the audience too. Then they can't hear us. You've got to get rid of that carpet. It looks like it's from an old Shubert house.

**MANN**    We don't have the money.

**SCOTT**    How much would a new carpet cost?

**MANN**    Ten.

**SCOTT**    Call Jane.

**MANN**    But, George, you're hard up for cash.

**SCOTT**    Don't worry about it, Teeddy. You know those guys that came to see me about doing a commercial for a new car?

**MANN**    Oh yeah, yeah, yeah.

**SCOTT**    They came back. They offered me a million bucks. They want me to do it next week, after we open.

**MANN**  That's great.

**SCOTT**  But the problem is they want me to shave my beard and do a crew cut.

**MANN**  So you look like Patton.

**SCOTT**  Yeah, I already made that movie. [*Gets angry and slams his hand on desk.*] And I'm not doing it again. I let it grow this way for *Vanya*. Those auto salesmen don't understand actors. They're all like Nixon, always trying to pull a fast one.

**MANN**  Okay, take it easy, George. Calm down.

**SCOTT**  Everything counts, in life and in [*Emphasizing the word.*] theater. It's all in the details. Whether your hair is long or short, it's important for your character. Oh hell, Teeddy, you know this better than I do. I'm not shaving my head for a lousy million.

[SCOTT *starts to go.*]

**MANN**  [*Trying to stop his departure.*] I heard Nicole came in on time this morning.

**SCOTT**  He's got to learn how to hold his liquor.

[SCOTT *sits back down. He takes a drink.*]

**MANN**  [*Getting to the subject of the matinees.*] I saw a wonderful play the other night, *Championship Season*.

**SCOTT**  Oh, I like that play. Old Marty Sheen and rolly Polly Durning. They are the best.

**MANN**  And Paul?

**SCOTT**  Sorvino sings well.

[MANN *laughs and gestures flat with his hand.* G.C. *laughs.*]

**SCOTT**  At the matinee I couldn't stand the blue-haired ladies. They talk all the time. Whispering, coughing, [*Starts to get agitated.*] sneezing, unwrapping and munching their candy and clicking their false teeth. I can't take it, Teeddy.

**MANN**  [*Quickly, making it up as he goes along.*] We won't sell 'em any candy.

**SCOTT**   They bring their own. I'm not playing the matinees!

**MANN**   Hey, George don't get so uptight. Have another drink. A small one.

[GEORGE *snorts.*]

**SCOTT**   I'm not drinkin'. I'm not drinkin'. [*Smiles.*] I never drink before lunch.

[SCOTT *starts to leave.*]

**MANN**   But we're all sold out. You gotta play 'em.

**SCOTT**   What do you mean, I gotta play 'em. Play what?!

**MANN**   The matinees.

**SCOTT**   [*Theatrical with a John Gielgud imitation.*] Oh, the matinees, for those blue-haired ladies. The matinees must go on.

**MANN**   That's right, you can make fun of it but it's the bread and butter for the theater. All the other performances pay the expenses. The matinees pay the profit.

**SCOTT**   [*Puts his arm around* MANN.] Sure, go ahead with the matinees...my understudy will do it.

**MANN**   G.C., they bought tickets to see you, not your understudy.

**SCOTT**   I'm not playing for those fucking blue-haired ladies.

**MANN**   We don't get them. They're afraid of the escalator, with their canes and walkers they're afraid they'll fall an-an-annnnd they don't like drama. You gotta play the matinees.

[*Beat. With one eye closed and the other staring* MANN *down* SCOTT *comes right up close to* MANN.]

**SCOTT**   [*With all the contained fury that he is capable of.*] Okay, but if I see one of those fuckin' blue-haired ladies in the audience, I'm walking.
        [SCOTT *turns on his heels, puts on his baseball cap and walks out as though he is the manager of the Tigers.*]
        [*Sings out pleasantly.*] Come watch the run-through this afternoon and tell me what you think. But privately.

[MANN *races back to the house phone, pushes a button.*]

**MANN**   Larry, Larry, Larry—no, no, no, I want to talk to the head treasurer. [*Beat.*] Lawrence, [*Warm and friendly.*] how are you? [*Listening.*] How's the wife? [*Listening.*] Good. And the kids? [*Listening.*] Oh, that's swell. [*Casually as possible.*] By the way, Lawrence, have we sold tickets to any old ladies? [*Beat.*] You know who I'm talking about, the old ladies with the dyed hair. We have? [*Gets uptight.*] You can't sell tickets to blue-haired ladies! [*Impatient.*]. Okay, okay, but don't let them into the theater. And if any them come to the box office, tell them we're all sold out and if that doesn't stop 'em, tell them the show's canceled. And then if they try to come down the escalator, you stand there like Jesus with your arms up and don't let them in, and if you do, you'll be crucified. Mr. Scott will personally nail your hands to the wall and I'll help him. Oh, okay, I know you're Jewish. So was he!

[*Blackout.*]

*Curtain.*

• • •

# Five Story Walkup

compiled and directed by
Daniel Gallant

**Featuring:**
John Guare
Neil LaBute
Quincy Long
Laura Shaine
Daniel Frederick Levin
Clay McLeod Chapman
Daniel Gallant

# John Guare

John Guare was awarded the Gold Medal in Drama by the American Academy of Arts and Letters for his Obie- , New York Drama Critics' Circle- , and Tony Award-winning plays, which include *House of Blue Leaves*, *Six Degrees of Separation*, *Landscape of the Body*, and *A Few Stout Individuals*. His screenplay for Atlantic City received an Oscar nomination. The Public Theater produced his new play, *A Free Man of Color*, in 2009.

# Neil LaBute

Neil LaBute is a writer and director for theatre, television, and film. His latest play, *Reasons to Be Pretty*, was first seen Off-Broadway at the Lucille Lortel Theater. It began a Broadway run in early 2009.

# Quincy Long

Quincy Long's recent productions include *People Be Heard* (Playwrights Horizons), *The Only Child* (South Coast Rep), *The Lively Lad* (New York Stage and Film and the Actors Theatre of Louisville), and *The Joy of Going Somewhere Definite* (the Atlantic Theatre Company and the Mark Taper Forum, optioned by Icon Films). He is currently working on *Loulou*, a musical commissioned by Ginger Cat Productions in Toronto, Canada. He is a graduate of the Yale School of Drama and a member of Ensemble Studio Theatre, New Dramatists, and HB Playwrights Unit. He is originally from Warren, Ohio, and currently lives in New York City.

# Laura Shaine

Laura Shaine is a novelist and journalist, as well as an internationally known playwright. She is widely produced throughout Russia and Eastern Europe.

# Daniel Frederick Levin

Daniel Frederick Levin's musical *To Paint the Earth* (written with composer Jonathan Portera) won the 2004 Richard Rodgers Development Award and was produced in the 2008 New York Musical Theatre Festival. With Portera, Levin also wrote the short musical *The Hungry Lion* and served as a Jonathan Larson Memorial Fellow at the Dramatists Guild. His other plays and musicals include *Campaign* (words and music), the book for *Luna Park* (commissioned by SUNY Cortland, 2008), *Hee-Haw, Going to Belize* (Long Wharf Theatre, NWNH, 2007), *The Waiter* (Makor/Steinhardt Center, 2006), and *The Lake Walk*. He holds an MFA from the NYU Tisch Graduate Musical Theatre Writing Program and a BA from Yale. For more information, visit: www.danielflevin.com.

# Clay McLeod Chapman

Clay McLeod Chapman is the creator of the rigorous storytelling session the Pumpkin Pie Show. He is the author of *rest area*, a collection of short stories, and *miss corpus*, a novel. He teaches writing at the Actors Studio MFA Program at Pace University.

# Daniel Gallant

Daniel Gallant is a theatre producer, playwright, director, and actor. He is also the executive director of the Nuyorican Poets Cafe. Gallant has produced and directed plays, musicals, and other events for the 92nd Street Y and at venues including the DR2 Theatre, Center Stage, the Abingdon Theatre, the Henry Street Settlement, Theater for the New City, and the Cornelia Street Cafe. Contact: gallant.arts@gmail.com.

# Five Story Walkup

## Short Plays and Monologues About the Places We Call Home

by
John Guare
Neil LaBute
Quincy Long
Laura Shaine
Daniel Frederick Levin
Clay McLeod Chapman
Daniel Gallant

**Production conceived and directed by**

Daniel Gallant

# running order

1. *Web Cam Woman* (by Laura Shaine)
2. *A Glorious Evening* (by Daniel Frederick Levin)
3. *Aux / Cops* (by Quincy Long)
4. *birdfeeder* (by Clay McLeod Chapman)
5. *Tripartite* (by Daniel Gallant)
6. *Love at Twenty* (by Neil LaBute)
7. *Blue Monologue* (by John Guare)

Publication final draft: Winter 2008
Send inquiries to:
Daniel Gallant
P.O. Box 503
New York, NY 10159-0503
917-841-4420
gallant.arts@gmail.com

# Web Cam Woman

## by Laura Shaine

[*An attractive* WOMAN *enters—she comes up from the theatre aisle. Establish an imaginary door to her apartment. At the start, she is poised to enter. She speaks to the audience.*]

Hi. Come on, come home with me....Just promise you won't tell. I want to show you something...*private*. Don't let on what you see. Here we are...2B. But you just watch from where you are. That's right—stand here, nicely on the welcome mat, next to the mezuzah—not mine—it was here when I moved in! I didn't want to take it down! Hey, never tear down a prayer. Not that you're *not* welcome, you are! But you can't *go* in my apartment—you can just peek! Now—once I'm inside—this is important— don't ask why—DON'T MOVE! DON'T SPEAK!

Okay! I'm in...

[*She moves fast around the walls of the apartment, back flat to wall.*]

When I talk over here...*they* can't see me. If I flatten myself against the wall, I am out of range. So now what do you see? You see me. And I look...perfectly ordinary...normal...right?

Nice eyes, good trim figure—I work out! Tasteful dye job. Not from a bottle. From a *salon*. And my apartment—2B—it looks perfectly normal, ordinary, too...an ordinary studio, rent stabilized, but stabilized too high, like a patient in ICU with a high fever—ha-ha. An ordinary sofa bed—it's cute, isn't it?—only $899 from Jennifer Convertibles—an ordinary coffee table, ordinary TV...ordinary bowl of mixed nuts!

Except for one thing!

The seven cameras!

[*She establishes the seven fixed locations along the ceiling.*]

Camera one! Camera two! Camera three! Camera four! [*Gestures off.*] Camera five, bathroom! Camera six! Camera seven! They are trained on the center of my... very ordinary, normal apartment. Don't tell!! Promise.

[*She checks her watch.*]

[*She slinks around, delivers following line downstage to audience.*]

Men pay to watch me; this is how I make my living. I am what they call... a Webcam woman. I can't believe my good fortune: I just had to tell someone... who isn't, you know, part of it. *Wow!* They won't expect me for another five minutes—the mikes are not "on" yet... the cameras are always on... but...

This is easier than going to the office. I was an office temp.

[*She slinks around the perimeter of the room, inhales to get less of a silhouette.*]

[*To herself.*] Suck it in, Suck it in. [*To the audience.*] Now, I just stay home and do what I do and it's permanent. And men, the video voyeurs, sign on—I accept MasterCard and PayPal—to watch me do... what I do. The trick is, I have to *forget* they are watching, or it isn't fun for them. I have to be... myself. I can... lie around on my couch, read the paper... *they* do expect me to masturbate, and—well—I do. I think they want me to masturbate *more*... it is amazing how you sense... this electrical "other"—which is, I guess, the "static" of their attention—I can never really forget—oh, yes, the masturbation—isn't it *boring*, waiting for me, maybe 24 hours, to start? And I can't get creative—it has to be just ordinary, normal, little at-home casual diddling, almost unconscious—not peep show stuff.... I don't put on make-up, oh, maybe a little eyeliner, but no fancy panties.... But they never know *when* I am going to do it, so I guess that's the element of suspense in it for them, as I read the *Times*, or vacuum. I wonder—*how great is this for them*? But they never complain. They like that it is... *natural*.

Hey, I am making $10,000 a month! I used to worry about making the rent, the Time Warner bill, the Con-Ed. Now, I can afford slipcovers. It's fabulous. Isn't it? [*She checks her watch.*] Three minutes! I got to tell you something—

[*She flattens herself, lower, we have the impression of a mouse running round the edges of her cage.*]

I had sex once, with a man, for *them*. The man didn't know *they* could see.... He didn't notice all the cameras. But something went wrong; he kind of...shriveled inside me, and...and he excused himself and pulled out...out of me, out of my apartment.

I think of that guy, sometimes.

[*Upright again.*]

There are forty-nine of them. I know, of course, from the charge cards. They live in all the contiguous United States, and now I have one in Honolulu. A lulu in Honolulu.

I am so happy and relieved that I discovered this new way to make a living.

They pay so nicely: never miss. I used to have to get up and catch the D train by 8 a.m. to get to work by 9. Work, work, work—really dull, at the computer all day long.

Now, I sleep in!

[*She dons a beautiful ivory white silken dressing gown.*]

They watch me sleep...

You know, it's funny—it disturbs...my dreams. There must be something to R.E.M. sleep that is...*private*, that doesn't want... to be observed. So my sleep is getting light. Fitful.

I dream I am...being not just watched, but that men are chasing me to the edge of a cliff and I wake—with this yank—like being forklifted back to consciousness—and I can't catch my breath, here in the not-quite-dark—I use a night-light, so they can still see me—and [*She starts to crack a bit.*] I get a little scared sometimes, my heart pounds and pounds. I have them, the orgasms, the paroxysms, so many, some nights but after the first two orgasms they just get...irritating. I know they are getting their money's worth. But I get...no... [*She launches into the Stones classic.*] "Satisfaction...but I try, and I try, and I try... and I try..."

Until I am...well, *dry*, and rubbed raw. *This isn't how it's supposed to be!*

Some of them speak to me—that's extra, but I will allow it. They address me on the speakers. [*She points.*] See those little perforated metal "mouths"—those are their speakers—which I have to turn on in [*Checks watch.*] two minutes! 120 seconds! They can direct my movements. [*She imitates a deep male voice.*] "Arch your back." "Writhe." "Cry out my name!" Confession: I don't like the word "masturbation"—it sounds so . . . turbulent. You know what? I don't want to do it!—I'm not in the mood, even for myself! I just want to be alone! In peace! Or to be with someone real, someone present!

[*She is starting to lose it.*]

I remember . . . belly flesh! Kissing someone's navel . . . Oh, those were the best sleeps, belly to back, arms . . . around my waist. . . . Warm in winter—I felt safe. I am not safe now, am I?

[*She checks her watch.*]

Okay. Mikes on. I can't be absent too long . . .

[*She flips the audio mikes on and slips the silken sash from her robe. She performs two skips, as with a jump rope.*]

I perform little fitness sessions, so they can see me work out a bit.

[*She playfully loops the silken sash around her neck, makes a comic gesture as if garroting herself.*]

But this is what you really want, isn't it?

[*She stares hopelessly out, the sash a noose.*]

This is worth, what, a thousand on MasterCard? PayPal! Only I never get to collect, do I? But . . . God.

[*She closes her eyes.*]

It will be worth it . . .

[*She addresses the cameras.*]

My name, my name was—Eva Marie! My mother named me that! After Eva Marie Saint in *On the Waterfront*!

[*Her eyes pinball, she is connecting to her true self.*]

No, wait. I don't want to kill myself.... Kill Eva Marie Saint?

I want to...to get even! I want to...*thwart* you. And you! And you! And you! [*She gives the fist to each camera. She pulls the rope away from her neck, cracks it like a whip.*] You've ruined it for me—it started with the e-mails—why did I get those messages? "Enlarge your dick!" "Molly Bang Butt!" "My boyfriend has a BIG BANGER and I have a Tiny MOUTH!" I couldn't go into my own in-box and now you are in my own room, my inner sanctum—Oh, EFF YOU—I WON'T PLAY ANYMORE! No more CYBER MOLESTATIONS, if you please.... I want you to pay and pay and pay, and not ever get to see me do what you want me to do! You know what?! [*She makes a mock punch, shadow-boxing the cameras, one by one.*] John! Larry! Mike! Ike! Gordon! Lionel! GEORGE!

You made me fulfill *your* fantasies...now you can suffer mine!

[*Music: "Someone to Watch Over Me" begins...softly. She dances, as if with a partner, dreamily, her arms around herself, She turns her back to the audience, gives a funny, "EFF you" twitch to her hips, looks, smiles defiant over her shoulder.*]

This is it, pay pals!

[*There is the sound of men breathing, from many men. Music: "Someone to Watch Over Me." She is smiling, moving sensuously in her solo dance for that "certain someone." Spotlight on her solitary, ecstatic dance. Isolated spot on her face, beatific, longing.*]

[*She sings.*]

There's a certain someone, I'm longing to see...I know that he... will turn out to be...someone to watch over me!

[*Black out.*]

• • •

# A Glorious Evening

## by Daniel Frederick Levin

[HARRY *is sitting at a table with a flower on it, looking out at the audience. The level of realism for the following is low, particularly for processes that occur. Delivery should be understated, acted with restraint, with only perhaps a hint of emotion at the end.*]

**HARRY**    [*Pause.*] I'm really looking forward to tonight. How are you feeling... are you cold? Good.... It was really beautiful out tonight, wasn't it? Did you notice there was like a sweet smell in the air when you were coming here? And a good sweet smell, not a bad sweet smell that you don't know where it's coming from. A good sweet smell, I don't know, it's probably some early flowers, some mulch thawing out, a little wood, probably some sulfates.

God, you look...

So, my cell phone is off, computer off, Blackberry, don't have one. The TV is sleeping for the night, the radio... the radio, maybe a far-off wisp of a jazz song, if anything. But thank God those are all inventions. Thank God we don't really need any of those things. Thank God all we need is... this.

I made a few, eh-em, improvements. [*Indicating flower.*] There's one of these on the bathtub ledge, for the bath before we... I didn't draw the water yet. I didn't want it to get cold. But I figure that's maybe when we can listen to that jazz, you know? Is there anything better than listening to jazz against running water? And we'll find a station with not that many instruments. Just maybe a saxophone... and a bass... just that. No piano. We don't need piano.

[*Smiles.*]

I love you.

Are you sure you're not cold? Hot? I can open the window more.

[*Realizing something.*]

You know what? I think I forgot to brush my teeth. I'm... do you need anything? OK.

[HARRY *makes tooth-brushing motion, not that realistic.*]

I'm brushing my teeth. I'm brushing my teeth. I'm brushing my teeth. I'm brushing my teeth. I'm brushing my teeth. I'm brushing my teeth. I'm brushing my tongue. I'm spitting. I'm rinsing. I'm back.

Hi.

Did I miss much?

[*Pause.*]

I have plenty of protection. And it's the gentle kind. Everything is taken care of. There's nothing at all to worry about.

[*He breathes.*]

What a glorious night. Temperature is right. Smell is right. Sound is good. Vision is wonderful. Touch will be amazing. Taste will be... pretty good, well worth it. Well worth it. Smell. Sound. Sight. Touch. Taste. Smell. Sound. Sight. Touch. Taste. Smell. Sound...

I need just one sec. Will you be all right for a sec? Excuse me.

[*He pauses. Stands up.*]

I'm using the bathroom, I'm using the bathroom, I'm using the bathroom, I'm using the bathroom, I'm using the bathroom, I'm using...

[*Pause.*]

I'm using the bathroom the other way, I'm using the bathroom, I'm reaching for the switch, I'm using the bathroom, I'm using the bathroom, I'm trying to be quiet, I'm using the bathroom, I'm using the bathroom, I'm using the bathroom, I'm using the bathroom, I'm looking for matches, I'm using the bathroom, I'm using the bathroom, I'm using the bathroom, I'm using the bathroom, I'm finishing up, I'm finishing, I think, I'm ripping off paper... I'm ripping off again, and ripping off again... and again... and again... and I think I'm finished... and I'm finished... and I'm finished, I'm done.

Hi.

Sorry about that. Now I just feel...perfect.

Are you feeling all right? [*Rapid fire.*] Cold hot bored wired up down shy bold deaf blind stifled? Y'sure?

[*Sighs.*]

It's such a beautiful evening. There's this mood...this...well, it's like the jazz...it's...

[*Noticing something.*]

I'm having a little trouble swallowing. I'm having trouble swallowing. I'm having trouble swallowing. It's like choking, but I can breathe. I'm having trouble swallowing. [*Louder.*] I'm having trouble swallowing!

It passed.

[*He breathes for a moment.*]

I was saying, swallow, it's like the jazz, best on an, swallow, old record, swallow again, I'm thinking about swallowing, I'm thinking about swallowing, I'm thinking about swallowing, I feel hot.

Are you OK?

I have a little more saliva. It seems to have passed. It seems to have passed.

[*He sighs again.*]

What a beautiful...I just can't wait. I can't wait for later. I want to first draw that bath. Then I want to go to the bathroom. I want to swallow. I want to be quiet. I want to fantasize. I want to do everything...I want to feel intense, intense pleasure. I'm so excited, you know?

Would you mind leaving? Right now? It's really beautiful out. You'll get to smell that sweet smell. Remember? The mulch?

Now. Go on. Leave. Go on. Get out of here. Get out of here. Get out!

[*Bringing himself under control, and retreating back.*]

Swallow.

Breathe.
Swallow.
Breathe.
I'm imagining.
I'm breathing.
I'm really looking forward to tonight.

• • •

# Aux / Cops

## by Quincy Long

### cast

>SIDNEY DIPOLITO, 20s, wants to be an auxiliary policeman
>POLICE LIEUTENANT, Middle-aged, in charge of police auxiliary
>>unit

### setting

Various apartments and an office.

### time and place

The play takes place in the present time somewhere in one of New York City's outer boroughs.

• • •

### The Lieutenant's Office

**SIDNEY**  So then I pushed her. Pushed her down.

**LIEUTENANT**  Pushed your wife down.

**SIDNEY**  Yeah—I. And I, uh—I slapped her.

**LIEUTENANT**  Slapped your wife.

**SIDNEY**  But I didn't beat on her. I didn't beat her face or mark her up in any way. I didn't do that. I wouldn't do that. I just, what I said, put her down on her behind and slapped her because of the things that she had said about how me and Joey were at the game together, playing around and dah, dee, dah, when I should of been helping out and that. And I couldn't take it, you know. I just couldn't take it no more, because I had did that. I had been to her mom's and seen what there was to do there, and I couldn't do what I'm supposed to without I had some help from some of the rest of her family, who is never showing up when there is work to be done. They are the last ones to be found when there is stuff to be lifted, you know what I'm saying? So, that's what I did, all I did, and it ain't on my record or nothing, but I feel as how this is full disclosure here, that I should amplify on my remarks to your question and answer fully as to if I ever been in trouble with the cops, because I haven't. Not really. Which is why I want to be associated with them.

**LIEUTENANT** Well, I appreciate, Sidney, what you told me here. This is a full and frank disclosure and inasmuch as you was never fully arrested—

**SIDNEY** No, no. Never arrested. It was a warning only.

**LIEUTENANT** Well, then, this, then, what you told me is not sufficient unto itself to keep you off of the auxiliary. Are you reconciled with your wife since the incident? How was the matter resolved?

**SIDNEY** It was resolved in the way that I told her to keep her big fat mouth shut if she didn't want the cops coming to the house. Because I do have a temper. I do have my pride. And I will be pushed only to a certain point and beyond that I am not responsible for the actions that I take. And as far as I understand, that is the reading of the law on the matter. You can only push a guy so far, is that right?

**LIEUTENANT** Well, that sort of thing, interpretations of the laws and so forth, that is something for the courts to decide and for the lawyers to debate and so forth. I mean, who's to say? What I'm getting at here, Sidney, is I'm wondering how you'll be out on the street when, say, some smart woman gets in your face. Some woman with a load on who has some unpleasant things to say about your masculinity even. That kind of thing can and does happen, because soon as you put on the uniform you become a target for filth and abuse from people—people who may have had bad experiences with the police, or think that they have had bad experiences, or people with a bad home life, or low lifes or just, you know, things of every variety. How do you think that you would react in the sort of situation when some floozy says, like, 'Hey, you dickless bastard! Yeah, you! I bet you beat your wife, ya fucking fruity assed asshole! You ain't even a cop. You got no dick. You got no balls. You got nothing and you're going nowhere! You are a big, fat pretend!' Things like that. They know how to go right for the jugular, these people. As if they got a sixth sense for the things that gonna make you blow. How you gonna react to that is my question?

**SIDNEY**    Well, I think I'll, I'm capable of reacting pretty good as far as my emotions and that.

**LIEUTENANT**    Uh-huh.

**SIDNEY**    I mean, I know how to control. My father?

**LIEUTENANT**    Yeah?

**SIDNEY**    My father taught me violence in the basement, the two of us putting on the gloves with each other. I have knocked my father down. Have you knocked your father down, Lieutenant?

**LIEUTENANT**    My father's eighty-two years old, Sidney.

**SIDNEY**    Yeah, but when he was younger, did you, the two of you, ever, like, get into it?

**LIEUTENANT**    My father isn't—my father and I do not enjoy that kind of a relationship. My father's a—he was a baker, Sidney. He had hands that were covered with flour. He was never a police type of individual. He liked to make pies. He liked to make cakes with angels on them, and roses, and swirly swirly. That was his world. You talk about basements. Our basement had an oven.

**SIDNEY**    Yeah?

**LIEUTENANT**    A brick oven that he and his father had built together. My basement was not a place of blood, Sidney. It was a place of wonder.

**SIDNEY**    Wow.

**LIEUTENANT** Just the smells alone that would come from that basement. So, I cannot imagine with my father the kind of things with your father that you're talking about. That's beyond my conception, that kind of stuff with him. Now on the job, I'm a different kettle of fish, but the violence is something that I separate out of the home completely. I never take the violence home because that, in my experience, is what spoils the home and makes it—you got to have a shelter from that, from the kinds of things we see and do here on a normal day to day. You got to have a place where that kind of thing ain't—not only isn't it going on, it isn't even a possibility, which is why we don't have a television.

**SIDNEY** You got no TV?

**LIEUTENANT** What I just say?

**SIDNEY** You said you got no TV.

**LIEUTENANT** And that's what I meant. I mean what I say, Sidney. That is something that you'll come to know about me as we go along here, if we go along. That's a quality that you got to cultivate as a police officer, or even an auxiliary. We who wear the uniform are speaking with one voice, the voice of the law, and that voice don't change from here to there or from one thing to another. It's a hard thing to do, to cultivate, because out there are people who are this way here, and that way there—

**SIDNEY** Yeah. Yeah.

**LIEUTENANT** You know what I'm saying.

**SIDNEY** Oh, I see that all the time. All the time. Mimsey, mimsey with you, and with you I'm, whoa, whoa, a whole some other way. And I hate that, Lieutenant. I hate it. I hate it when people are deceitful in that way, like Danielle, who I was talking about earlier, which is my wife. With her work she is one way and at home she's another way, and with her friends she's like this, and with my friends like that, and it just drives me crazy how she can be so many ways with so many different people. I can't respect that. I say, this is who I am. This is me. This is what I say. This is what I do. Then I go out and I do it. I don't go for none of that other kind of behavior. It's just too confusing.

**LIEUTENANT**   You seem to have a lot of emotion directed towards your wife, Sidney.

**SIDNEY**   Well, she's my wife.

**LIEUTENANT**   Yes, I know. I know that. I'm just wondering about your stability on the street around, say, a domestic incident.

**SIDNEY**   I think my domestic experience will stand me good out there, Lieutenant. I have been through it, like other guys maybe have not, and know what's right and wrong, and won't have any trouble in saying like, "Hey, you sit down over here, and you, you go over there, and let's just think this out like the adults that we are and not get all blown out of proportion, because this is your wife here, and you love her, and she is a sacred and beautiful vessel that nothing like this should be happening that the police are called."

**LIEUTENANT**   That's good. That's good. That's good, Sidney. That's important that you don't be afraid to put it out there, what you feel, as long as it conforms, because that can still the troubled waters in a situation that's, uh—

**SIDNEY**   Inflammatory, yeah.

**LIEUTENANT**   I can find my own words, Sidney.

**SIDNEY**   Sorry.

**LIEUTENANT**   I can finish a sentence, which I wouldn't have made it to Lieutenant otherwise.

**SIDNEY**   I was—I just got excited.

**LIEUTENANT**   You're excitable, Sidney.

**SIDNEY**   I know.

**LIEUTENANT**   An excitable guy.

**SIDNEY**   I'll watch it.

**LIEUTENANT**   But I'll tell you what. You got the necessities of an auxiliary police officer in you. You got the size for it. You got the desire. You got high school. But like all of us, you got your weak points and insufficiencies. It's a balance, Sidney DiPolito. Always a balance. And I have weighed you. You probably didn't know it, but that's what we been doing here. I have weighed you on my personal scales and found that you got more good than bad. More positive than not. You are not a psycho, and you can come along with us if you complete the training. What do you say?

**SIDNEY**  Wow, that is—that's—that's so great. I wasn't sure, you know. I mean, the way you go about it I figured I was being tested in some way, but—I mean, I'm excited. I'm very excited about—

**LIEUTENANT**  We got a training cycle starting up Wednesday night. You free Wednesday nights?

**SIDNEY**  I'm free every night, Lieutenant.

**LIEUTENANT**  You don't want to be telling the girls that.

**SIDNEY**  What girls?

**LIEUTENANT**  What I mean, you don't want to look too available.

**SIDNEY**  Oh. Oh. Oh. I get you. I got you. Yeah. Let me—hm, Wednesday nights. Wednesday nights. Let me think. I got to look in my diary here, Lieutenant, see if I'm free. I got a lot of things on my plate, you know. I got the symphony.

**LIEUTENANT**  Right.

**SIDNEY**  Then I got the ballroom dancing.

**LIEUTENANT**  Ballroom, hah.

**SIDNEY**  And I got, let me see here, oh my gosh, I forgot, Lieutenant. Wednesdays I got the opera.

**LIEUTENANT**  Yeah. Yeah. Yeah, the opera. Jesus, you don't want to be missing that.

**SIDNEY**  [*Sings.*]
*O sole mio*
*You got the BO*

**LIEUTENANT**  Oh my God.

**SIDNEY**   *Toreadora*
        *Don't spit on the floora*

**SIDNEY/LIEUTENANT**   *Use the cuspidora*
        *Whaddya think it's fora*

**LIEUTENANT**   Ho, boy, oh, gosh, okay. That's fun. That's fun. You're gonna be okay, Sidney. That's fun to have around, that stuff, a sense of humor, cause otherwise it can get, it gets, whew.

**SIDNEY**   Yeah.

**LIEUTENANT**   Okay. Okay, then.

**SIDNEY**   Okay. See you in a—see you next Wednesday.

[SIDNEY *exits.*]

• • •

# birdfeeder

## by Clay McLeod Chapman

Wasn't until winter when word finally got around about Michael, a group of hunters discovering his body about three miles into the woods. First day of deer hunting season usually brings back a month's worth of venison stretched along the front hood of every Chevrolet in town—only this year, most trucks came back bare, their empty fenders still caked in a crust of dried blood from last season's kill.

Looked that way, at least. Maybe it was just rust.

Instead of heading to Sally's Tavern, where everyone parks their cars to compare their quarry, seeing who has the citation, who brought back the biggest buck, sneaking their beers out into the parking lot even though they know it's against the law, Sally turning a blind eye to her customers as they buy their beer and duck out the door again—this afternoon, first day of deer hunting season—most men just rushed right over to Sheriff Flaherty's office on their own, as sober as a bunch of newborn babies, leading him and a handful of his officers up Route 2, right where the highway lines up alongside the woods, nothing but miles and miles worth of trees, parking their trucks in the ditch just next to the road and cutting through the forest. Heading right to Michael.

They say it was John Whalthorne who found him. He'd been following this buck for about a half mile, keeping his distance until he knew he had a clear shot—his eyes wandering through the woods by way of the scope attached to his rifle—only to catch some color in his crosshairs, this flash of blue.

Turns out to be Michael's Levi's. The weather had washed the brightness out, months' worth of rain rinsing the dye away—his favorite pair of pants having faded into this phantom hue. This baby, baby blue.

His bones were nothing but wind chimes now, knocking up against each other in the breeze. Birds had begun to take him away, one peck at a time—plucking what pieces of him they could pull free with their beaks, bit by bit. He looked like a birdfeeder up there, hanging from that branch.

Everyone knows the woods is where you go when you want to keep a secret. The deeper into these trees you reach, the darker the secret you want to keep.

Only secrets I've ever kept are of Michael.

He'd lay a leaf against my chest, watching it rise and fall with every breath—the frond mimicking my ribcage, only smaller, as if it were two chests pressed against each other.

His breath always tasted of cigarettes, like dried leaves at the back of his mouth. My father always thought the two of us were sneaking off into the woods to have ourselves a smoke, smelling cigarettes on my breath every time I'd come home—but the funny thing was, I never had a cigarette in all of my life. Only Michael.

We'd make our way to this clearing in the trees, taking the entire day just to walk there—hiking further and further into the forest, until there was nothing around us. Nothing at all. Not the hum of a truck, not the whir of some lawn mower. Not another human being for miles. We'd lay on our backs, slipping out of our T-shirts—feeling what sun could make its way through the trees, these specks of light resting themselves on our chests. That's where I'd kiss him, letting every patch of light lead my lips across his body—as if the sun were saying, *Kiss him there*. And—*Kiss him there*.

Thinking about Michael out there, all winter. Hanging by that branch, the tension in his neck relenting more and more. Thinking about his body breaking down, changing colors. Shifting pigments. Thinking about all those birds swooping down, pecking at his neck. Tugging on his lips as if they were earthworms. Taking away what they could carry back to their babies, dangling his lips over their beaks, feeding his kisses to their family.

You know—it wouldn't have been far off for people to believe Michael had run away, having done it a couple times already. Only difference is, he'd always come back. Whether it was a few hours or a day on the road, Michael would always make his way home. So when it reached a week, his mother started to worry. Like really worry. But by then Michael was already in the woods, slowly disappearing—trying to hide himself inside the stomachs of every animal willing to nibble on him. Thinking—*Nobody would ever look for me in here.* Thinking—*It's safer inside these stomachs.*

The weather and elements had decimated the rest of his clothes, chewing through his T-shirt until it was nothing but scraps of fabric. You couldn't even recognize the Metallica decal ironed along the front. The *E* and the *T* were just about the only letters left. The others had peeled free, flaking off into the air.

I was there when he bought that shirt, wearing it to school the very next day. I remember how firm it felt when it was new, like cardboard, the cotton starting off all stiff, the creases in its sleeves keeping crisp for weeks—before it finally descend into its tenderness. He loved that shirt. He would pull it off and place it under my head, as a pillow— the two of us resting on the ground, looking up at the sky just above us, a few stars hanging over our heads, the trees blocking out the rest, braided by branches, as if I'd put both of my hands right over my face, a latticework of fingers hiding the sky from my eyes.

We'd spend the night out in the woods, telling our parents that we were sleeping over at each other's house. Holding him, I remember listening to the trees warping over our heads, every bending branch making this squealing sound in the dark—until it almost sounded like my arms were bending as well, the weight of Michael in my grip causing my limbs to twist.

*What if someone finds out about us? What do we do then?*

*Don't worry*, he said. *We're safe out here.*

He was wearing those blue jeans the last time I saw him, nearly six months ago now. Pretty much wore those pants every day of his life, anyhow—but I know it was when we were together last, when I last laid eyes on him, that I was the last person to see him alive.

Because there was no note, no cry for help. Just his body breaking down.

People keep asking me why. *Why would he head out into the woods alone and hang himself, waiting out there all winter for someone to find him?* Suddenly I'm an authority on his unhappiness? I'm the expert on what makes him tick? Even Michael's mother's come to me, desperate for some sense of closure, just so she won't have to blame herself for what happened. *You were his best friend, Sean. He would've talked to you about these things. . . . Did he ever mention depression? Did he ever say anything about suicide?*

I knew  he was out there.

When Michael first disappeared, I went out into the woods by myself—going to the only place where I felt safe, where I could be alone. And that's when I saw him, swaying. His head bowed against his chest.

It was better for someone else to find him. Someone other than me.

If I'd been the one take Sheriff Flaherty out into the woods, other questions would get asked. Questions like—*What were you doing out there in the first place? What were you two boys doing so far out in the forest, alone?* Questions like that don't stop themselves from getting asked, even if you provide an answer. In a town as small as this, sometimes—the answer isn't what people are after. Sometimes they want your secrets.

That's what frightened Michael more than anything. That's what sent him out into the woods by himself. Sometimes, saying your lips are sealed isn't enough. The best way to keep a secret is to cinch your throat shut, cutting off the air that cushions your deepest, darkest truths.

Deer hunting season would come in a few months, only for someone to stumble upon him. They'd rush back for Sheriff Flaherty, dragging him through the woods—cutting Michael's body down. Doing it properly.

Until then, I'd know where I could find him. I'd know where he'd be.

I've kept him secret for six months now, never mentioning Michael to anyone—because there are more secrets where that came from. More than I can count.

I keep his eyes, as blue as his jeans. I keep his lips, as thin as earthworms. I keep the taste of his mouth out in those woods.

Nobody knows about him and me out here.

• • •

# Tripartite

## by Daniel Gallant

### cast of characters

> **OSCAR**, in his early thirties
> **RYAN**, in his mid-to-late twenties; Oscar's brother
> **RENEE**, in her mid-twenties

### setting

The outside porch of the suburban home in which Oscar and Ryan grew up; present day.

• • •

[*Lights up on* RYAN *and* OSCAR, *sitting on the porch of their family home.* RYAN *is the younger brother.*]

**OSCAR**    What an odd vacation this is. In a place I never saw as restful.

**RYAN**    Mom's still not home. [*Pause.*] Are you ready for your interview?

**OSCAR**    It happens next week, back up north.

**RYAN**    But have you practiced? Why not practice? Let's pretend this is the interview.

**OSCAR**    Yeah, OK. Work before fun. So here I am, entering the interview.

**RYAN**    Hello, Mr. Edmund. What makes you the right man for this job?

[*Pause.*]

**OSCAR**    My ability to dodge direct questions.

**RYAN**    Mr. Edmund, what is your worst flaw?

**OSCAR**    I like to think of my flaws as strengths in disguise.

**RYAN**    Then what is your greatest strength?

[OSCAR*'s cell phone rings.*]

**OSCAR**  I'm too modest to have any. [*Answers cell phone.*] Hello? [*Pause.*] Hi, Mom. I'm going to repeat everything you say so that your other son, who's sitting next to me, can take it all in—[*To* RYAN.] She doesn't want us borrowing the car tonight—we can't, Mom, 'cause *you* have the car. You're in it right now, calling us. The wonders of technology. So that part's settled. [*To* RYAN.] Jeremy still has a cold, or maybe not a cold, maybe he's fine, we shouldn't worry—[*Into the phone.*] but there's definitely *something* wrong with Jeremy—[*TO* RYAN]—she says I shouldn't interrupt, and I should tell Oscar—[*Into phone.*]—you're talking to Oscar, your other son is Ryan. [*Pause.*] *You* chose the names. [*To* RYAN.] I should tell Ryan that he's welcome to bring whomever he wants to dinner; we have an extra chair because something other than a cold is wrong with Jeremy, who won't be joining us tonight—[*Into phone.*]—how close to finished is this call? I was in the middle of an interview. [*To* RYAN.] She loves us blah blah blah. [*Into phone.*] I did. I will. No car tonight. G'bye. [*Hangs up the phone.*]

**RYAN**  What is your greatest strength?

**OSCAR**  Who are you bringing to dinner?

**RYAN**  I met her on the train.

**OSCAR**  See, that's a really messy precedent to set, because if you start bringing women home who you met on the train, I'm going to have to top you, and I'll do it by bringing home some girl who's an astronaut.

**RYAN**  This one is named Renee. She's into science, human rights, piano.

**OSCAR**  Well, that's quite a pedigree. [*Pause.*] Mom worries me. She doesn't worry you, but I pay close attention, and I've never seen her quite this bad before. Her style of conversation's changed. Her cooking too. She conjugates verbs in a different way.

**RYAN**  You're talking nonsense, Oscar. Do you know what nonsense sounds like? Out of your mouth it's pouring, like concrete. Mom's fine.

**OSCAR**  I could care less if you see it. I could once have cared more, but what good does it do me if you're concerned about your mother's physical condition? I just want to know that she's looked after. Doesn't need to be myself or you that does it. And I also want to know you're with someone.

**RYAN**  I'm what? I'm with what?

**OSCAR**  See, I missed the boat, and then the boat missed me. There's several women out there who I should have married; two of them were green-eyed Capricorns and one's a pastry chef from Scotland. But I stutter-stepped. I hesitated. The result is—I'm alone. Now women wonder why, at my age—

**RYAN**  But you're young!

**OSCAR**  Why I'm alone, and though they flock to me for sex, they never stick around to propagate the species. You should find a tolerable mate while you're still young enough for parenthood and compromised romance. You should seek out a woman with good manners. And just pardon me for saying, but the one you want ain't Thea.

**RYAN**  Thea's gone. Four months back. You sound odd, man. Worse than mom does. Agitated.

**OSCAR**  Do I, Ryan? Agitated? Loud? Do I sound loud? I sound loud 'cause I have to shout for Mom to know I'm present. See, I visit her a minimum of twice a week, and sometimes we talk twice a day, and she's in this decrepit, crumbling home, and sometimes she can't hear me, 'cause her mind's on shit that happened long before the two of us were born, or maybe never—and her pulse is weak.... I holler, and Mom still can't hear me, so I write her my sincerest thoughts on Post-its, which I post around her bed, or I hide in her bathroom and I holler. I can shout and scream and yodel just as loudly as I like, so long as I do it out of her sight. 'Cause she can't hear me.

[*Pause.*]

**RYAN**  Oscar, I'm doing very well. I'm happy with my day job, and my studio apartment. Pretty much, I'm happy.

**OSCAR**   Someone's always happy, and it might as well be you.

[*Pause.*]

**RYAN**   See that girl, across the street?

**OSCAR**   I see some locks of gorgeous auburn hair.

**RYAN**   Renee is underneath them. I asked her to come early.

**OSCAR**   [*Craning his neck to look across the street.*] From the train, huh?
Human rights...piano...

**RYAN**   Find your own.

**OSCAR**   Don't worry, bro. Don't sweat it. I won't poach.

[RENEE *enters through a gate at the back of the yard.*]

**RENEE**   Hello!

**RYAN**   Hello there!

**OSCAR**   You should be more careful, walking into unfamiliar backyards.
There's no telling who you'll find.

**RENEE**   Hi, Ryan. Hello—...oh.

**OSCAR**   No telling who you'll find.

**RENEE**   [*As she recognizes* OSCAR.] Uh-*huh*.

**RYAN**   You know each other. That's OK. That happens.

**RENEE**   [*To* OSCAR.] Can't recall your name.

**OSCAR**   These human rights pianists with good pedigrees live only in
the present. Don't remember much.

**RENEE**   I'm bad with names—not only yours. Street names, pet names,
state capitals and even types of wine...

**RYAN**   That's OK, you can call me anything you want. Our parents mix
our names up all the time—they call him Ryan and me Oscar.

**RENEE**   [*To* OSCAR.] Right, right, *Oscar*. That's the name that fits your
face. Now I remember. Maybe. Some defunct café...Sambuca
and a jazz quartet, on Arbor Day. Was that you?

**OSCAR**   That, plus the aftermath.

**RENEE**   [*To* RYAN, *apologetically.*] For several years, I drank more than I ate. My memories of that time aren't reliable, except in tiny lightning flashes, like haiku. But I recall this house—the mailbox, and the chimney that exploded . . .

[*Pause.*]

**OSCAR**   [*To* RYAN.] You met a woman on the train who lives down the street from us. At least she did, when this was home.

**RYAN**   [*To* RENEE.] I never spent much time around the neighborhood—

**OSCAR**   You still don't. You don't know your block, your address or your staircase.

**RYAN**   Home is where I pay my rent, and not where I was raised. This building has no claim on me. This house has Mom to watch it, and this house does an entirely sufficient job of watching Mom.

**OSCAR**   You left when you could and you only return when it suits you. No surprise, then, that you thought Renee was unclaimed territory.

**RENEE**   Those are not kind words.

**OSCAR**   My brother can handle my abuse.

**RENEE**   But that shit's aimed at me. You called me "territory." Any ambiguities about the reason we broke up are now resolved. Assuming we were ever once an item.

**OSCAR**   We were, and then we dramatically were not. My fault, I'm sure. What can I say? I have a history of backing the wrong horse, especially when that horse is me.

[*Pause.*]

**RENEE**   Ryan, you're cut from different cloth than this degenerate. You two are the most unlikely brothers.

**RYAN**   Yeah, my most winning quality is that I'm not Oscar.

[OSCAR *glares at* RYAN.]

**RENEE**   Some odd thing must have happened in your fetal stages.

**RYAN**   Yeah, I had a hard time in the womb, 'cause *he* kept taunting me from the outside, gloating about birth order.

**RENEE**   Maybe he just wanted back in.

**OSCAR**   Renee, I have to stay I'm stunned by how quickly you took to Ryan. Man, she's taken to you fast. Magnetism's buzzing through the air between your shiny faces, and I'm glad to be a witness.

**RENEE**   What's with Oscar, Ryan?

**OSCAR**   What's with Oscar? Here's a preview of Oscar's impending meltdown: Oscar can't see why you sided with an alternate configuration of his own DNA. Oscar can't see how he failed your litmus test, but the next fetus down the food chain passed.

[*Pause.*]

**RENEE**   Jeez, this is going to be a real long dinner.

**RYAN**   [*To* RENEE.] Did we mention Oscar's diabetic?

**OSCAR**   Maybe that's the reason why the human rights piano player went for Ryan. He does have more insulin.

**RENEE**   Relax.

**OSCAR**   So far that's all.

**RENEE**   Relax. I'm not quite sure which escapades we shared, or why they left you so unhappy. But please soothe yourself. Consider this: perhaps I gravitated towards your bro 'cause he reminded me of you.

[*Long pause.*]

**OSCAR**   Renee, why don't you show yourself inside.

**RENEE**   A drink sounds splendid, thank you.

[*She exits into the house.*]

**RYAN**   I reminded her of you. Yet she forgot your name.

**OSCAR**   Don't puzzle this one out too hard. We kissed, we groped, we did whatever happened, but the sum total was nothing. Nothing of substance or consequence.

**RYAN**   No?

**OSCAR**   Just an empty and impersonal romance. We both were plastered the entire time. But it looks like she's sobered up real nicely since. If you sense possibility, pursue it, and forget the complications I've dropped on your plate.

**RYAN**   That's kind of a tall order for me. Pouncing where you have already pounced.

**OSCAR**   Don't feel intimidated.

**RYAN**   Oh, I don't.

**OSCAR**   I'm sure she won't compare us.

**RYAN**   Don't mind if she does.

**OSCAR**   You just maintain that confidence. Maintain it on the field of battle.

**RYAN**   Don't get all St. Crispin's Day–ish on me now, dude.

[*Pause.*]

**OSCAR**   You know, the best part—what works in your favor—is that she will like you more 'cause she thinks it's taboo. Now go inside and mix a drink for her.

**RYAN**   But—

**OSCAR**   Drinks ahoy.

[OSCAR *gives* RYAN *a shove;* RYAN *heads offstage.*]

[*Lights fade; time passes. Lights rise again on* RENEE *and* OSCAR, *standing on the porch.*]

**RENEE**   Ha. Ha heh ha-ha-ha. I had a dream that you and I went off somewhere expensive and fucked all over everything. But how exciting and harmless to realize—only a dream.

**OSCAR**    I can't duplicate your laugh, but I'd like to try. When you're not around. Where did we go, in your dream odyssey?

**RENEE**    We went to what my subconscious thinks Madagascar looks like. Palms and flocks of loud, flapping endangered critters with marvelous plumage. And an agrarian economy. Plus somehow, a total lack of contraceptives. In a dream world…well, I'll just let that statement hang there.

**OSCAR**    But I won't, because in a dream world, you can dally with two brothers. But that's not the world I inhabit. Flirtation is intended to be brief. But you've been coming back to our house every day. We're only here a week. More to the point, you aren't just showering my brother with attention. Some of the runoff from that shower is meandering my way.

**RENEE**    Don't blame a girl for weighing options.

**OSCAR**    But you've tried me out before.

**RENEE**    I'm beginning to wonder, though, how thoroughly we tangled. See—I would never claim to recall every orgasm I've had, but I've held on to very vivid memories of how my lovers smelled and tasted.

**OSCAR**    Cheese sauce and Arrid Extra Dry, in my case.

**RENEE**    I don't think we've dated, you and I. I don't think we've anything-ed.

**OSCAR**    So you're a historical revisionist. That's a dangerous path for an academic to take.

**RENEE**    No, a revisionist I'm not. But I'm impressionable, even when Sambuca isn't flowing through my veins. If someone says— emphatically—that such and such a thing took place, gives evidence and drops compelling hints, I'll snap the story up. My synapses are wired to accept all well-told tales.

**OSCAR**    Except you don't remember names.

**RENEE**    Uh-uh. 'Cause that would be a waste of mental real estate. Names do not tell you anything about a person. There's a thousand Julies in Toronto; forty-five Renees who drive Toyota hybrids with Virginia plates. But just one Julie is my sister; only one Renee is me. [*Pause.*] I definitely screwed an Oscar and I definitely know your face, but the particulars don't match. *That* Oscar bought me gin but promised scotch. I bet you keep your liquors straight.

**OSCAR**   Your point is so well hidden that I couldn't find it with a bloodhound and a GPS receiver.

**RENEE**   Knowing how susceptible I am to strong assertions made by charismatic men, I automatically mistrust the tales you tell.

**OSCAR**   Nice. Have you *heard* of logic?

**RENEE**   Most men try to talk me into bed. You seem to want me out of sight and sound. So your approach is untraditional.

**OSCAR**   Not an approach, my dear, but a retreat. Cease-fire. My brother's waiting to be conquered.

**RENEE**   Huh. Your brother. Ryan met me in the dining car. He was intrigued, but only lukewarm—up until he heard about our past. Mind you, that's "past" with huge-as-hell quotation marks around it.

**OSCAR**   You and I tried. But it didn't take. That means we shouldn't romp again. I have a noble brother. Romance him, or get the fuck off of our porch.

**RENEE**   You invented a false liaison between us to make Ryan want to win me.

[*Pause.*]

**OSCAR**   OK, suppose I did. See, romance isn't always quite his thing. Sometimes the kid requires a jump start.

**RENEE**   Oscar, I do *not* appreciate the way that you've impugned my honor and obstructed me from jumping into bed with you. [*Pause.*] I don't accept the past fling you invented or the disinterest you've feigned. I was born gorgeous and persistent. I'm accustomed to star treatment.

**OSCAR**    Then you're on the wrong porch.

[*Pause; RENEE catches sight of RYAN, approaching from within the house.*]

**RENEE**    Well, I suppose I ought to wile some time away with Ryan, find out what you're hoping that I'll see in him.

[RYAN *enters.*]

**RENEE**    [*To RYAN.*] Oscar was telling me that you two are the most courteous of brothers. Never fought or quarreled—loyal and respectful, he informed me. I find that sort of amity incredibly attractive.

[RENEE *puts her hand on* RYAN's *arm;* OSCAR—*surprised*—*glowers.*]

**OSCAR**    [*Putting his arm around* RYAN.] We're real close. Close brothers.

**RYAN**    Too close, sometimes. Often. Distance would be a blessing.

[RYAN *pushes away from* OSCAR, *toward* RENEE. RENEE *moves away from* RYAN. OSCAR *walks alongside* RENEE, *as does* RYAN. RENEE *abruptly sits.*]

**RENEE**    Winter passes, and vacations end. Another beverage, barkeep.

[OSCAR *takes* RYAN *aside.*]

**OSCAR**    Look. She's bored. Un-bore her.

**RYAN**    Why? And how? I'm not a dancer and I'm not a clown. And you're the one who's barking up this brunette tree.

**OSCAR**    Me? Her? My efforts and flirtation are on your behalf. I would be thrilled to see you locked in love with Renee—or for that matter, any member of her gorgeous gene pool...

**RYAN**    Why are you so anxious? Why throw me at her?

**OSCAR**    Why? Why romance women? Why bother copulating? Because opportunity spoils quicker than mayonnaise. Because on the flip side of her ennui is the best time that this house and your twin mattress ever saw. Because seduction is my gift, your shortcoming, and therefore my responsibility to teach you.

**RYAN**    My odds of learning how to play that game will increase exponentially if you back off.

**RENEE**   Oscar! Ryan! Boys! A lovely girl is languishing in boredom on your property. Come here!

[*They both rush to her side.*]

**RENEE**   I see... you're much more willing when you're *ordered* into place. Like tiny soldiers. Well, Lance Corporal Oscar, please fetch me a tall glass of your finest.

**OSCAR**   Finest what?

**RENEE**   Whatever. *Anything* that's fine. As long as it's stored deep inside your house. [*She stares at* RYAN *and runs her finger down his leg.*] As long as it will take you... hours to prepare. In fact, drink it yourself.

**OSCAR**   You want to drown my sorrows? You want to unwind my clock?

**RYAN**   A drink would do you good, Oscar. Why don't you raid the liquor cabinet and find something exotic? Make way, world, 'cause my bro's 85 percent too sober.

**OSCAR**   [*Dazed.*] Guess a small sip couldn't hurt...

[OSCAR *exits into the house.*]

[RYAN *tentatively sits near* RENEE.]

**RENEE**   Oscar's frothing at the mouth. I have reminded him how envy feels.

**RYAN**   Um, yeah. But, see, I haven't come to terms yet with your intertwining past. Whatever you and he did interferes with my ability to fall for you completely. If there is a history between you two. So is there a history?

**RENEE**   My dear, if I tell you Oscar lied, your respect for him will plummet. If I tell you we made frequent and outrageous love, you won't care much for me.

**RYAN**   Guess I'm transparent.

**RENEE**   Men have survived worse flaws.

**RYAN**   But I'm afraid for Oscar.

**RENEE**  And he's afraid for you, which is refreshing—in a yin-yang sort of way. Oscar's melancholy and impulsive, and he wouldn't have an inkling how to handle kids. He's hoping that *you*'ll take the family-values route, that you will find a dame and have a child and give the DNA he shares with you a detour to eternity. He'd rather be an uncle than a father. [*She sees that* OSCAR *has reappeared and is watching them.*] He expects that you will bear the gene pool's torch. [*Grabbing* RYAN*'s shirt.*] So how are you with fire?

**RYAN**  I'm not bad. Not all that fucking bad.

[*She pulls him in toward a kiss, but* OSCAR *steps into view.*]

**OSCAR**  Well, there's a hard punch to the gut. Again you choose my brother over me.

**RYAN**  Sorry—but punches were made to be rolled with. You pushed me toward her.

**OSCAR**  Yes—with a heavy heart and insincere encouragement. You could have had the decency to disregard my pep talk. [*Pause.*] When Renee was chasing me, I didn't give a damn. But now Renee digs you, it's a whole new ball game. Good thing that I bet against myself.

**RENEE**  You've gone from mockery to misery in record time.

**RYAN**  Yeah, what'd you find inside the liquor cabinet?

**OSCAR**  Scotch. That's what done me in. A fifth of scotch. A liquid prism of truth. I see you all for who you are.

**RYAN**  There's only two of us.

**OSCAR**  [*Clearly drunk.*] But each of you stands in for many others. For the ancestors who trusted me to keep their name alive. For the bucolic marriages I might have had. For the three children I won't raise. Staring back at me through your four eyes are predecessors who I've failed, descendants who'll be cheated of existence. Pets I'll never own. My shortcomings are timeless.

**RENEE**  There are other women. You'll have other shots at bliss.

**OSCAR**  My aim is poor. My game's a mess. It's five o'clock.

**RENEE**  If five o'clock's already here, vacation will be over soon. And if vacation flew that quickly, middle age ain't far behind. We'll be retired and extinct before we know it. [*Pause.*] So solve your problems, brothers, or the clock will solve them for you.

**OSCAR**  Are you choosing Ryan over me?

**RENEE**  What, Ryan? No. [*Pause.*] I'm married. Did I fail to mention that detail? Here's a note to Oscar: Don't invent a past for someone, 'less you've done a background check.

**OSCAR**  Wow. Double play, Renee. The dreams of two blood relatives extinguished in an instant.

**RYAN**  I can handle disappointment. I'm an artist.

**RENEE**  You're a work in progress. The first few steps out of the chrysalis are the toughest.

**OSCAR**  Why don't you take a few steps toward the door, and then some more steps after those?

**RENEE**  A pleasure, gentlemen. [*She exits.*]

[*Long pause.*]

**RYAN**  And suddenly, I'm cold.

**OSCAR**  I hate the winter.

**RYAN**  It's the only season I associate with home. I mean, this house.

**OSCAR**  I hate the winter. Period. I know three Shakespeare monologues by heart, and one of them's about the winter. "From whose bourn no traveler returns." "The dread of something after death."

**RYAN**  Isn't that the motto for New Jersey?

**OSCAR**  [*Rising.*] Well, it's just past five, and Amtrak waits for no man.

**RYAN**  Think I'll stick around another couple days. [*Pause.*] So kick ass at the interview, lance corporal.

**OSCAR**  Always good to see you.

[OSCAR *smiles and exits;* RYAN *remains seated, picks up his cell and dials.*]

**RYAN**   [*Into cell phone.*] Yes, I'd like a pizza and two beers. Can you write a message on the pizza? [*Pause.*] Because she doesn't eat cake, that's why. So can you write a message? In string cheese, or anchovies, or peppers, whatever condiment you choose. And here's the message—and I want it just this way, precisely, word for word— [*Pause.*] "Thank you, Mom."

[*Lights fade—curtain.*]

• • •

# Love at Twenty

## by Neil LaBute

[*Silence. Darkness.*]

[*Lights up on a* YOUNG WOMAN *standing onstage, looking down at us. A cell phone in one hand. Purse over the other shoulder.*]

**YOUNG WOMAN**   …1-2-3-4-5-6-7-8-9-10-11-12-13-14-15-16-17-18-19 and 20! Ready or not, here I come. [*Smiles.*] God, remember that, from when we were kids and you'd play games, like hide-and-seek or crap like that, and one person would be it, covering their eyes and counting to twenty or however many and then you'd have to go find everybody or run around, that kind of thing? Yeah…that was fun. Really, really fun stuff. I loved doing all that, and being 'it,' too, I never minded that. Uh-uh, I didn't at all, which a lot of kids never wanted to do—especially most of the girls I grew up around—because they'd get scared or shit like that, being alone in the dark or whatever, but not me. Nope, I didn't mind it one bit, being that person…I guess I sort of like being the center of attention. A lot.

[*She laughs and stops a moment, checking her phone.*]

And I never, I mean, at that age, I had no idea how important that number would end up being to me. In my life. Twenty. It really, really is because I'm, like, practically that age now. Going to be, anyway, in a few weeks—December, that's my birthday. Not the whole month, obviously, but during it. On the 20th, which absolutely sucks because it's so close to the holidays that I always get screwed on gifts—"We'll just do it all together, on Christmas, and you'll get extra." My folks tried to sell me on that one when I was little…that I was so extra special that we should just pretend that me and baby Jesus had the same birthday, but all it meant was, like, maybe one or two more gifts than my sister got and not even anything big, 'cause my Easy Bake Oven (for instance) was the major package and my mom and dad'd just toss in a few other little bits—clothes, even!—and that'd be that. That was my birthday, which stinks. Completely. So, yeah, that's me... almost twenty. On the 20th. And what else? I mean, since I said it was such a huge deal...oh, yeah, right. This guy I'm seeing, well, he's my professor, actually, in this one history course—it's my second year at college, so that's cool—he's almost exactly twenty years older than me. Yep. "Twenty years your senior," my mom says, which is so gay because she's only, like, twenty-three years older than me, but she sounds like my grandma or something...she always says shit like that, but especially about him. My boyfriend. Well, I guess he's not actually that, technically, because he's got a wife and all that—no kids, though—and that's a bit of a bummer, but he's getting divorced, he totally is, but they've just got a few things to work out. Legalities and all that crap and I've been very good about waiting for him. We started in together last semester—I'm only taking his "Empire Building from Napoleon to Nixon" because it fits my schedule and it's first thing in the morning, so he can give me a ride (my Honda is a piece of shit when it's cold)—but, yeah, we've been a couple for almost a year now, school year, anyway, and he's promised me that we're always gonna be together. Forever. [Beat.] Well, until today, that is. Like twenty minutes ago...

[She stops and checks her phone again, then her watch.]

Sorry...I'm waiting for a call. See, he just texted me. Dexter did. That's him—'Dex,' I call him—and he sent me this juicy message about how good it was last night and how much he adores being in my mouth and, you know, all that stuff...but actually, I was at Tula's last night, this bar downtown where I work—OK, dance—and I haven't seen him since Tuesday so, umm, that's weird. But the hurtful part of it is, the actual bad part of it is this: it's to his wife. Kimmie. That's her name—which really makes me want to barf whenever I hear him say it—not some other student or lady in town, which I could then understand because he's quite good-looking and sexy and all that for this older guy, but it's meant for his wife, who he is supposed to be leaving, and so that means he's lying to me, right? Lying and sleeping with her and all that shit that he's been telling me, assuring me is just not true. And now I know for, like, a fact...is. Yeah. Dexter's actually screwing me and Kimmie and God knows who else and you know what? That just really doesn't work for me... [*Beat.*] Dex seems to be doing a little "empire building" of his own and I figure that shit has just gotta stop. Right? So—I sent a little message of my own, a few minutes ago... to his wife, Kimmie (seriously, can you believe that name?!). One sentence, twenty little letters that very succinctly—a word I learned from the big man himself—explains our present situation, and how he tastes in my mouth, you know, that sort of deal. On their home phone. Then, and here's the kicker part... I texted Dex and told him what's up. Sent it to him on his way to some faculty meeting and told him what I've done, said that he's got a few minutes to make his choice—skip out and run home... hurry back to their fifth-floor walkup and erase the thing before she gets back (Kimmie works for a dentist—gross!) or stand up and take it like a man, do all the shit he's been promising me for so many months now... it's entirely up to him. Or it'll come down to, you know, like, fate or whatever, if he doesn't get my message and Kimmie wanders on back after going to the grocery store—she's supposed to be like this major cook or something—and then she'll hear it all and confront him or call me, and if she does, if that is the case, then I'll fill her in on what's what. I definitely will if that's what happens, I've already promised myself. [*Beat.*] So, you can imagine my anticipation... right? I mean, your whole life can change, just like that, in twenty minutes... Bam! [*Snapping her fingers.*] Kooky, isn't it?

[*She looks down at her phone again. clicks it on, checks it.*]

I mean, what would you do? Right? Sometimes you've really just got to get in there and get your hands dirty when you believe in something so intensely and this is one of those times.... Dex and I are gonna be so happy, so stupendously fucking happy when all this stuff gets straightened out. I really believe that. Or not. Or he will scurry home like some total pussy and fix things for a minute and then I'll know he's not the man I want or need him to be, and at the tender age of twenty I'm gonna realize that it's a long road ahead to happiness. But, hey, at least I'll know, right? At least I'll head off into the sunset with my eyes wide open and understand a bit about the way this world works... and that's something, isn't it? Yeah. At least I'll have that...

[*Suddenly her phone rings. She looks out at us one last time.*]

Oh, wow. Here we go... 1-2-3-4-5-6-7-8-9-10-11-12-13-14-15-16-17-18-19 and 20! [*Smiles.*] Ready or not, here I come...

[*She lets it ring twice more, then goes to answer it.*]

Hello?

[*Silence. Darkness.*]

• • •

# Blue Monologue

## by John Guare

You have to understand Queens. It was never a borough with its own identity like Brooklyn that people clapped for on quiz shows if you said you came from there. Brooklyn had been a city before it became part of New York, so it always had its own identity. And the Bronx originally had been Jacob Brock's farm, which at least gives it something personal, and Staten Island is out there on the way to the sea, and of course, Manhattan is what people mean when they say New York.

Queens was built in the twenties in that flush of optimism as a bedroom community for people on their way up who worked in Manhattan but wanted to pretend they had the better things in life until the inevitable break came and they could make the official move to the Scarsdales and the Ryes and the Greenwiches of their dreams, the payoff that was the birthright of every American. Queens named its communities Forest Hills, Kew Gardens, Elmhurst, Woodside, Sunnyside, Jackson Heights, Corona, Astoria (after the Astors, of all people). The builders built the apartment houses in mock Tudor or Gothic or colonial and then named them the Chateau, the El Dorado, Linsley Hall, the Alhambra. We lived first in the East Gate, then move to the West Gate, then to Hampton Court. And the lobbies had Chippendale furniture and Aztec fireplaces, and the elevators had Roman numerals on the buttons.

And in the twenties and thirties and forties you'd move there and move out as soon as you could. Your young married days were over, the promotions came. The ads in the magazines were right. Hallelujah. Queens: a comfortable rest stop, a pleasant rung on the ladder of success, a promise we were promised in some secret dream. And isn't Manhattan, each day the skyline growing denser and more crenellated, always looming up there in the distance? The elevated subway, the Flushing line, zooms to it, only fourteen minutes from Grand Central Station. Everything you could want you'd find right there in Queens. But the young marrieds become old marrieds, and the children come, but the promotions, the breaks, don't, and you're still there in your bedroom community, your life over the bridge in Manhattan, and the fourteen-minute ride becomes longer every day. Why didn't I get the breaks? I'm right here in the heart of the action, in the bedroom community of the heart of the action, and I live in the El Dorado Apartments and the main street of Jackson Heights has Tudor-topped buildings with pizza slices for sale beneath them and discount radios and discount drugs and discount records and the Chippendale-paneled elevator in my apartment is all carved up with Love to Fuck that no amount of polishing can ever erase. And why do my dreams, which should be the best part of me, why do my dreams, my wants, constantly humiliate me? Why don't I get the breaks? What happened? I'm hip. I'm hep. I'm a New Yorker. The heart of the action. Just a subway ride to the heart of the action. I want to be part of that skyline. I want to blend into those lights. Hey, dreams, I dreamed you. I'm not something you curb a dog for. New York is where it all is. So why aren't I here?

When I was a kid, I wanted to come from Iowa, from New Mexico, to make the final break and leave, say, the flatness of Nebraska and get on that Greyhound and get off that Greyhound at Port Authority and you wave your cardboard suitcase at the sky: *I'll lick you yet.* How do you run away to your dreams when you're already there? I never wanted to be any place in my life but New York. How do you get there when you're there? Fourteen minutes on the Flushing line is a very long distance. And I guess that's what concerns me more than anything else: humiliation. The cruelty of the smallest moments in our lives, what we have done to others, what others have done to us. I'm not interested so much in how people survive as in how they avoid humiliation. Chekhov says we must never humiliate one another, and I think avoiding humiliation is the core of tragedy and comedy and probably of our lives.

I went to Saint Joan of Arc Grammar School in Jackson Heights, Queens. The nuns would say, If only we could get to Rome, to have His Holiness touch us, just to see Him, capital H, the Vicar of Christ on Earth—Vicar, V.I.C.A.R., Vicar, in true spelling-bee style. Oh, dear God, help me get to Rome, the capital of Italy, and go to that special little country in the heart of the capital—V.A.T.I.C.A.N. C.I.T.Y—and touch the Pope. No sisters ever yearned for Moscow the way those sisters and their pupils yearned for Rome. And in 1965 I finally got to Rome. Sister Carmela! Do you hear me? I got here! It's a new Pope, but they're all the same. Sister Benedict! I'm here! And I looked at the Rome papers, and there on the front page was a picture of the Pope. On Queens Boulevard. I got to Rome on the day a Pope left the Vatican to come to New York for the first time to plead to the United Nations for peace in the world, on October 4, 1965. He passed through Queens, because you have to on the way from Kennedy airport to Manhattan. Like the borough of Queens itself, that's how much effect the Pope's pleas for peace had. The Pope was no loser. Neither was I. We both had big dreams. Lots of possibilities. The Pope was just into more real estate.

My parents wrote me about that day that the Pope came to New York and how thrilled they were, and the letter caught up with me in Cairo because I was hitching from Paris to the Sudan. And I started thinking about my parents and me and why was I in Egypt and what was I doing with my life and what were they doing with theirs, and that's how plays get started. The play I wrote next was autobiographical in the sense that everything in the play happened in one way or another over a period of years, and some of it happened in dreams and some of it could have happened and some of it, luckily, never happened. The play was a blur of many years that pulled together under the umbrella of the Pope's visit.

In 1966 I wrote the first act of this play, and, like some bizarre revenge or disapproval, on the day I finished it my father died. The second act came in a rush after that. But then the steam, the impetus for the play, had gone. I wrote another draft of the second act. Another: a fourth a fifth. A sixth. I was lost on the play until 1969 in London, when one night at the National Theatre I saw Laurence Olivier do *Dance of Death* and the next night, still reeling from it, saw him in Charon's production of *A Flea in Her Ear*. The savage intensity of the first blended into the maniacal intensity of the second, and somewhere in my head *Dance of Death* became the same play as *A Flea in Her Ear*. Why shouldn't Strindberg and Feydeau get married, at least live together, and my play be their child? I think the only playwriting rule is that you have to learn your craft so that you can put on stage plays you would like to see. So I threw away all the second acts of the play, started in again, and, for the first time, understood what I wanted.

Before I was born, just before, my father wrote a song for my mother:

*A stranger's coming to our house.*
*I hope he likes us.*
*I hope he stays.*
*I hope he doesn't go away.*

I liked them, loved them, stayed too long, and didn't go away. The plays I've written are for them.

• • •

# acknowledgments

I would like to thank my publisher, John Cerullo of Applause Books—The Hal Leonard Group, and my agent, June Clark, for their support of this edition and my position with Applause Books.

Furthermore, I'd like thank Rick Pulos, administrative/production coordinator of the Theatre Program at Long Island University, my graduate assistant, Liliana Almendarez, and the administration of LIU—Dean David Cohen, Associate Dean Kevin Lauth, and Assistant Dean Maria Vogelstein.

I'd also like to express my gratitude to all the theatres around the country and their literary managers, as well as all the playwrights whose work I read, enabling me to compile this theatre series. A very, very special thanks to Michael Messina.

I follow in the footsteps of a wonderful project—The Best American Short Plays/The Best Short Plays series published by Applause Books, and I would like to thank all the previous editors of this series: the late Stanley Richards, Ramon Delgado, Howard Stein, Mark Glubke, Glenn Young, and anyone I may have left out who came before these fine editors, who've helped make this series a success since 1937.

A quote from the 1989 edition of The Best Short Plays edited by Ramon Delgado:

> From the beginning of this series the past and present editors have sought to include a balance among three categories of playwrights: (1) established playwrights who continue to practice the art and craft of the short play, (2) emerging playwrights whose record of productions indicate both initial achievements and continuous productivity, and (3) talented new playwrights whose work may not have had much exposure but evidences promise for the future. An effort has also been made to select plays not anthologized elsewhere and, when possible, plays that are making their debut in print.... The value of these considerations is to honor the artistry of the established playwrights, encourage the emerging, acknowledge the promising, and offer a varied selection of new plays in one volume.

As the editor of this series, I plan to keep the tradition moving into the future.

—Barbara Parisi